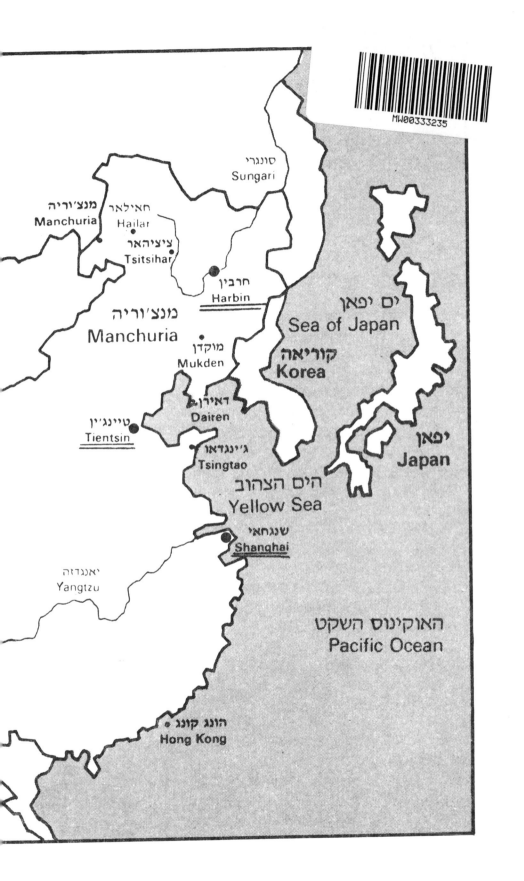

סונגרי
Sungari

מנצ׳וריה
Manchuria

חאילאר
Hailar

ציציהאר
Tsitsihar

חרבין
Harbin

מנצ׳וריה
Manchuria

מוקדן
Mukden

ים יפאן
Sea of Japan

קוריאה
Korea

דאירן
Dairen

טיינג׳ין
Tientsin

ג׳ינגדאו
Tsingtao

היפ הצהוב
Yellow Sea

יפאן
Japan

שנגחאי
Shanghai

יאנגדזה
Yangtzu

האוקינוס השקט
Pacific Ocean

הונג קונג
Hong Kong

MY

JEWISH LIFE IN THE ORIENT 1900-1950

CHINA

MY
JEWISH LIFE IN THE ORIENT 1900-1950
CHINA

Yaacov (Yana) Liberman

JERUSALEM ♦ NEW YORK

Judah L. Magnes Museum, Berkeley, California
Gefen Publishing House Ltd., Jerusalem, New York

Typesetting: Marzel A.S., Jerusalem

Cover Design: Studio Paz, Jerusalem

ISBN 965 229 171 4

Edition 9 8 7 6 5 4 3 2 1

Gefen Publishing House Ltd.
POB 36004
Jerusalem 91360, Israel
972-2-5380247
E-mail: isragefen@netmedia.net.il

The Judah L. Magnes Museum
2911 Russell Street
Berkeley, CA 94705
U.S.A

Printed in Israel

Send for our free catalogue

Library of Congress Cataloging-in-Publication Data
Liberman, Ya'acov, 1923-
    My China : Jewish Life in the Orient, 1900-1950 / Ya'acov (Yana) Liberman.
    p.   cm.
ISBN: 965-229-171-4
1. Jews—China—Shanghai—History—20th century. 2. Jews—China—Harbin—
History—20th century. 3. Liberman, Ya'acov, 1923-   . 4. China--Ethnic relations.
I. Title.
DS135.C5L53   1997
951'.004924--dc21

97-36231
CIP
r97

CONTENTS

PART ONE: HARBIN

Since the beginning of the twentieth century, Jewish history has been marked by anti-Semitism, war and ceaseless bloodshed. In the years of World War One and the Bolshevik era, throughout Europe and in Russia, Jews fled their homes and scattered to the many corners of the world. One of the remotest areas where Jews settled during these years was Eastern China, where they concentrated in three centers – Harbin, Shanghai and Tientsin.

My family was among those Jews who succeeded in escaping a war-torn Russia and subsequently settled in Harbin. My mother and her family fled from Odessa in the Ukraine; my father and his family fled from Samara. They met each other in Harbin and were amongst the first to emigrate to Israel in the early 1930s to join the pioneers in their struggle to establish a Jewish state.

Despite the remoteness of Harbin from the world centers of Zionism, the Zionist message had managed to penetrate into the lives of the members of its Jewish community. Numerous prominent figures have emerged who have played major roles in the fight for freedom in Israel in the early years and who have continued to be active in the political life of Israel until today.

I have the privilege and honor to be the son of Mordechai Olmert. He was a founder of the Betar Youth Movement and leader of the Revisionist Movement in Harbin; my father was instrumental in bringing Zionism into the Far East. Through his work, we see evidence of the success of the Zionist revolution and, especially, the impact of Vladimir (Ze'ev) Jabotinsky, in the lives of so many people.

The story of the Jewish communities of China is a most fascinating yet neglected one. Until now, it has not been properly told. And so, in reading and re-reading *My China*, we note with pleasure how the author transmits the character of these Jewish communities, their flourishing years and the moment of their inevitable collapse.

I cannot think of anyone better suited to write about this remarkable chapter in Jewish history than Ya'acov (Yana) Liberman. Like my father, Liberman was born and raised in China, where, as a youth, he was immersed in the Betar Youth movement, and grew up to become a prominent leader in the Revisionist Party. Like my father, as well, Ya'acov joined the ranks of the Herut Party, and became an important figure in Israeli public life.

A courageous and devoted Jew and Zionist, Liberman gives us a most exciting and moving account of the Jewish presence in China in the first half of this century.

Ehud Olmert
Mayor of Jerusalem

This is the fascinating story of the Jewish community in China – not the ancient community of Kai-feng-fû that disappeared through assimilation at the turn of the century, but the short history of modern-day Jewish settlement in China. Jews from Iraq, India and Russia, who came to China in the late nineteenth and early twentieth centuries, were later joined by the refugees fleeing the rise of Fascism in Eastern and Central Europe before World War Two. Far from the centers of Jewish life in Europe, America and Palestine, this small community developed and thrived under the most difficult of conditions. During the war years under Japanese rule, many Jews were forced to live within the confines of a ghetto. They, nevertheless, were spared the tragic fate of European Jewry under German rule.

During years of adversity, the members of this small distant community were engaged in a flurry of educational, social and political activities. Most of them dreamed of Zion when the land of Israel was under British occupation and they kept their hope alive, even during the war years when hope seemed almost beyond the horizon. The Chinese-Jewish Zionists, primarily followers of Jabotinsky's Revisionists and its Youth Movement, Betar, insisted on the full rights of the Jewish people to their homeland and were prepared to fight for the implementation of their civil rights. With the establishment of Israel, most of them sailed halfway around the world to settle in the land of their forefathers.

The young Ya'acov Liberman was a leader of China's Revisionist Party and of its Betar youth in China up to the day of the Jewish exodus. His memoir ends with his leading the first boatload of "Chinese" Jews to Israel. Written from an intimate first-person perspective, *My China* is an important testament to a once vibrant Jewish community that no longer exists.

Moshe Arens
Former Defense and Foreign Minister of Israel

I was born in Harbin, China, in 1923 to parents who hailed from different corners of Russia and who met in this Manchurian city while escaping the terror that followed in the wake of the Bolshevik Revolution. At a time when thousands of Jews from Russia and Eastern Europe were streaming toward the shores of America, others were trickling through the Manchurian border to the city of Harbin, majestically set in the center of northeast China and bordered by the River Sungari.

China at the time was living out its no-war-no-peace period. Danger lurked everywhere. The Treaty Ports and their concessions had come under foreign control. Although Italian sailors and United States marines had their barracks in Shanghai and Tientsin, and the Germans enjoyed extraterritorial rights in parts of Tsingtao, the French, together with the International Concessions and Settlements, made the greatest incursions on China's sovereignty. The Russian border north of Harbin was a few miles away and of constant concern. The growing territorial ambitions of Japan would become an overt threat to Manchuria's independence and to the Chinese government's peace of mind.

The year 1923 also saw the resurgence of nationalism within the framework of the world Zionist movement. The chief architect of this revival was a young Jew from Odessa, Vladimir (Ze'ev) Jabotinsky, who believed that the key to Jewish national rejuvenation was to be found in a new generation of Jewish youth. In 1923 in Latvia, Jabotinsky founded the Betar movement, originally called Brit Trumpeldor.[1] Much later, its ideology and national philosophy became the guiding force of my own life.

Jabotinsky's Zionism was an integral part of Jewish life in China from the late 1920s until 1951, when the last Jew left the shores of Shanghai. During these years, the Jewish communities of China would experience anti-Semitism, natural devastation and international isolation. Amidst these tragic circumstances, Betar and the Revisionist Party would play a decisive role. Because of my personal involvement with Revisionism and its youth movement, it was only natural that I should become linked to the Jabotinsky movement. That association is clearly reflected in the account that follows.

Although less prominence is given to other forms of Jewish organization that arose at the same time in China, the reader should not assume that such excellent sports organizations as Maccabi (Harbin) or the Jewish Recreation Club (Shanghai) were less popular or successful. On the contrary, these and many other Jewish organizations carried the Jewish banner with dignity and pride.

I give particular emphasis to Jewish life in Harbin and Shanghai because I lived in these cities and partook of their life in every detail. I have only visited Tientsin twice, and very briefly, and my knowledge of Jewish life there comes from articles and stories, as well as from the personal accounts of close friends who eventually moved to Shanghai. Jewish life in Tientsin, it seems, was as full and as well organized as it was in Harbin and Shanghai. The essential difference between the Jewish communities of Harbin, Tientsin and Shanghai was in size and in specific cultural, and physical environment. Therein dwelled the same Jewish

---

1. Jabotinsky named his youth movement, the Brit Trumpeldor (Trumpeldor's Covenant), to commemorate the heroism of Joseph Trumpeldor, killed in the Galilee while defending Tel Haï, an early Jewish settlement in the region. "Betar," the Hebrew acronym for Brit Trumpeldor, was also the name of a fortress in Eretz Israel.

soul, the same Jewish heart and the same Jewish pride that made each of these communities a pearl in the crown of the Jewish diaspora.

It also must be mentioned that while I presently reside in the United States, I am an Israeli subject who (wherever he may have lived or lives) considers Eretz Israel to be his only home. Therefore, the title of this book should not be misunderstood. China is not "mine," nor am I Chinese. As is true of several other countries in the world, nationality in China is derived from blood connection or *jus sanguinis* rather than from territorial relationship or *jus soli*. One cannot acquire Chinese citizenship (or Japanese for that matter) by having been born in either country or by having lived there all one's life. One can only become a Chinese citizen by having been born to a Chinese mother.

On the other hand, we three generations of Jewish émigrés from China never considered it to be our permanent home. In this attitude, we differed significantly from Jews who emigrated to such other countries as the United States, Britain and Australia, where they became permanent citizens with equal responsibilities and benefits.

My China, therefore, refers to a milieu rather than to an acquired second country, to a personal life rather than to an abstract national history. It must be remembered that at no time was there an attempt on our part to cross the illusory border of isolation and to become part of the Chinese colossus. Nor was there any desire on the part of our hosts to change a separationist attitude that suited them just fine. Some readers, strangers to the scene, may find this peculiar. Others with a better understanding of the situation will agree that because we were living in a permanent exile, torn away from Jewish social and spiritual centers, and because of our isolation within a totally strange and different environment, there is more reason to applaud the "pioneers" of the Jewish communities in China who were willing and able to create such a full, rich and productive Jewish existence in a country they never considered their home.

As to China itself, I shall eschew political analysis. I can never forget receiving a book from a chaplain of the U.S. Navy, who spent some six months in Shanghai and became a good friend of many of us in the Jewish community. To my amazement, the title of his book was *China*, and in it he pitifully attempted to describe this vast land and its people. When asked to comment, I found enough generosity in my heart to say: "You can probably attempt writing about China only if you have lived there for a few months or not at all. If, on the other hand, you have spent your entire life in this country, you will realize how little you know about it." And, upon reflection, I still maintain that this is true.

To many people, China is a huge, mysterious land of millions of people, who are totally strange to our modern world, who are absorbed in their own culture and bound by their ancient traditions, who have been viewed as vast millions of human ants pushed to their grey destinies either by foreign devils, as Caucasians were stereotyped, or by tyrants in their own midst. And yet, to those of us who were born in China, the everlasting memories we so zealously cherish are neither of the Chinese people nor of their life-style. "Our" China is an informal history of the way we lived and worked to achieve a full and healthy Jewish life in the Far East. For us this existence outweighed the colossus surrounding us, because our own lives were directed by an inner motion of communal integration. This interaction has neither affected nor was affected by the local population, and its problems. For more than three generations we lived a relatively sheltered, self-centered life within the three Jewish communities, neither integrating nor assimilating with our hosts. In any other context, with any other people, this in itself would have been sufficient cause for anti-Semitism and deep resentment. But not in China; not among the Chinese.

And so it was, until the day we left. And even our departure and the final closing down of our communities was unique. Throughout the centuries, and herein lies the tragedy of the Jewish people, its communal existence has been fraught with devastation, forced evacuation, flight from persecution, mass extermination. The self-liquidation of the Jewish communities of China was as spiritually elevated as its entire existence. The exodus of Jews from China in the years from 1949 to 1951 was well organized, voluntary and festive. All left for destinations of their choice, with the majority reaching the land of their dreams – Israel.

My China, therefore, is a personal account – written against the background of my interaction with two of these communities (Shanghai and Harbin) as that dynamic was affected by the historical and political developments of the time.

I am indebted to many family members, friends and associates for their help and advice, their recollections and suggestions. My very special gratitude and love goes to my wife, Lea, my faithful and devoted life companion, who believed in me, stood by me and encouraged me from beginning to end. Throughout my forty-nine years of marriage, she has been my inspiration and my guiding light.

This book is written in loving memory of my parents, Gisia and Sema Liberman, who in their own right were active and loyal servants of these Jewish communities in China. Loving and caring parents, they were fine human beings and friends as well, and I shall cherish their memory forever. When my father passed away, a total stranger came up to his open grave and said: "There lies a good man." May we all be worthy of such a heritage.

Finally, I dedicate this work to my three children: Tovik, Rina and Leori. May they always share in their parents' pride of belonging to a very unique family of Jewish immigrants from China and may the spark of Jewish unity and love of Israel always light up their hearts and their spirits.

This account is based on personal recollections and notes, augmented by interviews and discussions with dozens of my contemporaries. I was greatly assisted by my vast personal collection of newspaper clippings and journal articles. Much valuable information was derived from the files and *Bulletin* pieces of the Igud Yotzei Sin (The Organization of Expatriates from China in Israel). Due to circumstances, however, I find that I lack complete documentation of names and in a few cases, of Betar sources. Wherever possible, I list the first and last names of my friends and associates. I beg the reader's indulgence for names that are not cited in their full form. Finally, I should like to express my indebtedness to all of my friends who have shared in this adventure and who in a sense are my co-authors. I also should like to thank Dr. Ruth S. Rischin, San Francisco, the editor of this manuscript, and Seymour Fromer and his able staff at the Magnes Museum, Berkeley, for their role in realizing my narrative in book form.

– YL

HARBIN

Chapter 1

THE EMIGRATION TO HARBIN

Between the end of the nineteenth century and 1930, Harbin was slowly transformed from a small unknown Chinese village into a modern city, often called "The Pearl of the Far East." Much credit for this transformation should go to its Russian immigrants, many of whom were the employees of the Sino-Eastern Railway and to others who were desperate exiles from the Bolshevik "paradise" of the recently formed Union of Soviet Socialist Republics. Among them were a significant number of Jews. Whether moderately well-off or penniless, the Russian Jews of Harbin were united in a common desire to create an acceptable environment in which to live, work and worship with as little outside interference as possible.

After the 1917 Revolution, a small but significant number of Jews chose Harbin as their temporary home. Eventually, some of them would spread further and would become instrumental in the development of the Jewish communities of Tientsin and Shanghai.

With great eagerness, the Jewish emigrants to Harbin established businesses – factories, restaurants, import-export offices and shops. Those with less means, as well as the younger generation, including neophyte entrepreneurs, found employment among the affluent members of the community. The more destitute were assisted, first on an individual basis, and then gradually, by organized charitable institutions and societies such as the Home for the Aged and a Public Welfare Kitchen. Eventually, a well-equipped, modern hospital with its own clinic serviced all newcomers, most especially the destitute in need of medical care. All of these charities were run by devoted men and women who gave selflessly of their time, money and talent. A unique bonding of individuals and community soon came about.

My parents contributed significantly to this community solidarity. My father, Semyon Liberman, emigrated to Harbin out of economic necessity. Born in 1893 in Sevastopol, in the Crimea, he grew up in a home in which money was scarce. Immediately upon graduating from high school, he had to help support his three sisters and a brother. When in 1916 he was offered a job as an accountant in Harbin, he moved his siblings to this story-book city in the faraway Orient, where they began a new life.

No two backgrounds could have been more different. My mother, Gisia Zuboreva, was born into wealth in the city of Nikolaevsk on the Amur River, a city of Russia's Far East. Her father was the respected head of an industrial fishing complex that operated its own fleet of barges and ran a canning factory. For many years, until the Communists took over, the small lake by my grandparents' estate, in Grandfather's honor was named Zuborevsky Protok [Zuborev Channel]. In 1918, as the Bolsheviks approached, Grandfather Zuborev escaped empty-handed with his family to Harbin. With him went his wife, his two sons and two daughters. My mother was among the family members who fled. However, her older sister, Sarah, by then a married woman, remained behind.

Once in Harbin, the Zuborevs settled into a small apartment on Birzhevaia Ulitsa [Stock Exchange Str.], where they set up house-keeping.

In 1920, my parents "discovered" each other. Next year – they were married. Although Dad was not ideologically inclined, he joined the General Zionists of Harbin. However, communal activities were more to his liking, and his favorite would be the founding of the Jewish Hospital and Clinic (Mishmeres Holim), of which he was a long-term president.

As my parents, like other newcomers, would discover, schooling in Harbin was provided by a variety of educational facilities. Although the instruction in most primary schools was given in Russian, in two English-language schools and a Talmud-Torah (Jewish school), the Hebrew language was also taught as part of the curriculum. For secondary school education, however, the majority of the Jewish youth in town flocked to the *Kommercheskoe Uchilishche* (the Commercial School), a Russian-language high school of such high standards that its graduates matriculated with ease to the best European and American universities.

The Talmud-Torah occupied a very special place in the life of the Jewish community of Harbin and loving memories of the devoted leaders and teachers of the only Jewish institution in town remain embedded in many a heart. The religious needs of the community were provided by Chief Rabbi Kiseleff, a man of great knowledge and wisdom, patient and tolerant; a man who bore a fathomless love for his people. He had the full support of the Jewish Spiritual Society, which oversaw Jewish life in Harbin. The main synagogue became more than the religious center of the community. Jews flocked to this magnificent structure on holidays, to mark a Bar Mitzvah, to observe memorials and to attend communal meetings of protest and solidarity. Services were enhanced by the presence of our talented Cantor Zlatkin and an excellent boy's choir. Other functionaries in the ritual life of the community were its *shohet*, Reb Litvin, who for many years supervised the ritual slaughter, and our *mohel*, Reb Rolband, who was a master of the ritual of circumcision.

From his emigration to Harbin in the 1920s, up to his brutal arrest and deportation to the Soviet Union in 1945, Dr. Avram Yosefovich Kaufman remained its leader. A gifted organizer, fervent Zionist and an excellent lecturer, orator and writer, he was a charming and brilliant human being as well.

The foundation of Harbin's Jewish community goes back to the early twentieth century, when a few Jewish families from Russia began to establish themselves in the muddy village on the Sungari River. This was a period when Russia, encroaching on Manchurian territory to the north, won the right to build and supervise the Chinese Railway that one day would connect Khabarovsk with Manchuria. Together, the Russians and the Chinese would transform Harbin into the center of northern Manchuria and endow the city with an unmistakable European-Russian character that has remained its hallmark to the present day.[1] To the outside world, China's weakness was the result of internal animosity and dissent. At the very time when the Jews of Harbin were consolidating a Jewish community, China was undergoing constant political changes and bitter fratricidal strife that toppled the Ch'ing dynasty from the throne, allowed warlords to usher in anarchic rule and ultimately made possible the advent of Dr. Sun Yat-sen. Throughout this turmoil, Harbin's tiny Jewish population remained unaffected and continued its tireless efforts to build a vibrant community that one day would number some twelve thousand.

These early Jewish arrivals, however, were not a homogenous group. Although schooling and a house of worship were of primary concern to the early settlers in Harbin, the newcomers came with wide-ranging and extremely diverse ideological affiliations. Indeed, social and philosophical

---

1. See Irene Eber, "Passage through China," in the *Exhibition Album* dedicated to Far Eastern Jewry. (Tel Aviv: Bet-ha-Tfuzoth – The Museum of the Diaspora.)

quarrels were endemic to the Russian Jews. Debate was continuous among Russian Jewry in general. Political tolerance within the community would only come with its maturity. Russian Jewry, politically active during turbulent years in Russia, brought with it all of the sophisticated political "isms" of the day.

In the early years of the twentieth century, Zionism occupied a prominent place among these social philosophies, and consequently, a variety of Zionist parties sprang up in Harbin. The most permanent of these was the General Zionist Organization, or the party of the Algemein Zionists. While Professor Chaim Weizmann was their world leader, Dr. Kaufman, the popular head of the Harbin community, was their local chief. He managed to bring all varieties of Zionists together for practical purposes.

That spirit of rapprochement and consolidation, however, eluded the Bundists, whose politics were an amalgam of Judaism and Socialism. A continuous source of dissent and divisiveness during the formative years of the Harbin Jewish community, the Bundists in their opposition to Zionism were remote from world Jewry's goals of political rejuvenation and Jewish solidarity. Gradually, Zionism prevailed, the Harbin Bund disintegrated and the unity of the three Jewish communities was assured.

Elsewhere in China during the first two decades of the century, attempts to create Jewish centers arose wherever Jewish immigrants lived and worked. These were organized by Jews fleeing Russia, who either stopped short of, or passed by the great city of Harbin. Communities were established in Mukden, Tzitzigar, Chiefu, Tsingtao and Dairen. Short-lived, in many instances these were remarkable communities, in that no matter how small their membership (at times they numbered no more than a dozen people), they coalesced out of an intense desire for communal belonging. In a tiny community in Manchuria, for example, this effort resulted in the actual purchase of land and the building of a synagogue and a small school!

Towering above them all, however, and outlasting them by several decades was the Jewish community of Harbin. Its vitality was not due simply to the large numbers of Jews who flocked to this city, but rather to the unrelenting devotion of those early pioneers and their loyal followers, who molded a group of refugees into a proud and creative Jewish community.

Chapter 2

1923-1929. "MY HARBIN"

When did my impressions of Harbin actually begin to form? My first recollection of the city goes back to the year 1928, when my family anxiously awaited the arrival of my Aunt Sarah from the Soviet Union.

Although many Jews living in Harbin had escaped from Russia immediately after the Bolshevik Revolution, only in the 1920s, and after hair-raising border crossings, did most refugees settle in this Manchurian city. Until Stalinism made attempted flight futile and suicidal, refugees continued to pour into Harbin.

Among them was my aunt, a resident of Vladivostok. My parents were anxious to see Aunt Sarah and Uncle Mulia emigrate to Harbin much earlier. Uncle Mulia, the manager of the Russian branch of Lurie & Co, a large international trading firm, felt that he could not abandon the home office without salvaging whatever he could. Soon thereafter, Mulia was arrested by the state security organ, the GPU. After weeks of agony and despair, Sarah learned that her husband had been thrown into a local prison. Arriving one morning at the prison gates and bearing her usual dry food, socks, a warm sweater and a change of underwear, she was informed that Mulia was not in his cell. Running from one official to another, she finally had a bundle of old clothing thrust into her arms. When Sarah asked what had become of her husband, the official replied:

"He was eaten by dogs." Hours later, friends found my aunt lying unconscious in the snow by the prison yard fence. After her hazardous journey by foot, rowboat and horse-driven cart, Sarah Feinberg finally managed to cross the Manchurian border. Like many others, she had been accompanied by *provodniaki*, special guides who made their strange livelihood guiding desperate refugees past barricades and across borders toward China. Aunt Sarah stayed with us for many years following her escape, but she never recovered completely from her deep misery and depression.

Not all Russian émigrés suffered Aunt Sarah's fate. The majority who settled in Harbin were unscarred physically or mentally, and adjusted easily and enthusiastically to life on Chinese soil. Nevertheless, these new arrivals in China, Jews and Gentiles alike, bore the status of refugees and were called White Russians to distinguish them from citizens of the Soviet Union, who lived in relative isolation. Socialization between Jews and Gentiles was minimal and, consequently, they were perceived as two exclusive ethnic entities. Gentiles became categorized as White Russians, whereas the Jews preferred to be known as stateless Russian Jews or simply as Jews from Russia. Nevertheless, the two separate communities of Russian and Jewish immigrants made joint and commendable use of the various existing facilities in town and patronized Russian cultural institutions. Both groups enjoyed Russian theater, ballet and occasional performances by local and visiting opera ensembles. They also mixed socially in various clubs, commercial societies and sports organizations, and occasional friendships were forged in school. Of course, there was no lack of competition and a healthy rivalry that sometimes erupted into unpleasant confrontations and intense animosity.

Both groups read Russian-language newspapers and journals, frequented libraries and public concerts, lectures and discussions. All derived their news and information from the two leading dailies in town:

Zaria (The Dawn) and *Rupor (The Mouthpiece)*, as well as from the weekly *Rubezh (The Frontier)*. In addition to Jews and Gentiles, the so-called Russian refugee population comprised a third group, a gang of Russian anti-Semites, led by the notorious Konstantin Rodzaevsky. They were represented by the daily newspaper, *Nash Put (Our Way)*, that used ethnic provocation and personal blackmail to spice up its pages. In addition to these publications, the Jewish community had its own Russian-language biweekly, *Evreskaia Zhizn (Jewish Life)*, published by the Zionist organization and edited by the head of the community, Dr. Kaufman. In the 1930s, a second Zionist biweekly came to life and became a popular mouthpiece of Betar and the Revisionist Party.

I spent my boyhood years in this environment. It was not unusual for a well-to-do middle-class family to hire a nanny for its offspring. I was introduced to my first *niania* at the age of five. A heavyset, meticulously dressed woman in her late fifties, she always wore starched dresses that buttoned down the front, trimmed with white lace collars. Once, after a particularly heavy rain storm, on our daily walk through town, *niania* attempted to take me by the hand so that I would not splatter myself in the filthy puddles along the pavement. That kind of coddling was not for me, and, pulling her toward a large pool of water, I jumped into it with both feet, splashing her from head to toe. The next day my mother was busy interviewing a succession of *nianias* for her mischievous son.

As I approached my eighth year, it no longer became necessary for my parents to surround me with overseers, whose constant turnover gave me the reputation of being a difficult child. Not that I became tamer – I was merely becoming more mature and therefore too old to be accompanied by prune-faced, starched matrons. My father then decided it was time personally to take charge of my upbringing. Since Dad was busy in the office during most of the day, this turn of events should have been welcome to me, were it not for my mother's constant lectures regarding my abominable behavior. Nevertheless, I cannot complain about the severity of the parental punishment to which I was subjected. Only once was I whipped by my father; but then I crawled under my bed and was spared a real beating.

One day when I had been grounded and wanted my freedom, I composed a short poem in Russian, an apology and a promise to change my ways. My father was so pleased at my ability to handle rhymes that he immediately agreed to pardon me and even offered to take mother and me to the movies. As it happened, we went to the première of an early talkie, *The Merry Widow*, starring Jeannette MacDonald and Nelson Eddy. After that first literary success, I composed rhymes quite often and not only for the purpose of countering an occasional reprieve. In fact, I became quite skilled at versifying and soon it became an effortless endeavor. Even today I occasionally enjoy versifying, and find a power in poetry that can seldom be emulated by prose.

As I passed from boyhood into adolescence, I became more at ease in my mother's presence and was more relaxed in her company. Although I longed to become closer to my father, he was away most of the day. Of medium height, my father was heavy around the waist, and well on the way to losing his hair. What was left of it, he carefully parted on the side with a barely noticeable parting that soon disappeared as he balded. He wore heavy-rimmed eyeglasses, without which he could neither read nor see clearly. From early photos, I knew that Father had worn a mustache in his late teens and was a very handsome and popular bachelor. What never failed to impress me was the respect with which he was always treated by his peers. Throughout my life, I was repeatedly aware of the general opinion formed by all who knew him: "What a wonderful man Sema Liberman is!" As manager of an international trading company, owned by the well-known Kabalkin family, father held an important job. Thanks to his wit, charm and talent for telling jokes and anecdotes, he was often the center of attention at the many parties in town. Dad was always in awe of his bride and considered himself fortunate to have successfully captured the heart of a very beautiful woman, many years his junior, who had been so popular among the eligible bachelors of the community.

When it came to me, Dad did not enjoy the role of disciplinarian; that was more my mother's job. He would often come home eager to hear of his son's latest accomplishments. Instead, more likely than not, he would be greeted by mother's complaints about my inadequacies, mischief-making and other "crimes" of pre-puberty. Much as I became accustomed to my mother's anger at my misdemeanors, I could never ignore my father's displeasure with me, whether deserved or incited by my mother's remonstrations. But Dad loved Mother so blindly that, in his mind, she could never be wrong, and I more than once felt the injustice of that bias. I thought the world of my father and there was nothing more important to me than to please him and make him proud of me. In time, our relationship matured into friendship, and there was no end to the happiness I felt in having achieved this bond with my Dad.

Gradually, as I became more independent, I began to explore my city, and became more attuned to its spirit and atmosphere. Since most of us lived in Pristan, the lower part of town, we walked to work and everywhere else. During the 1920s, and even later, for that matter, no one in Harbin owned a car. The most popular way to get around town was by *izvoshchik* – a cabby with a carriage, much like those that one can still see today in New York City's Central Park. For rare trips to Novyi Gorod, the New City, and the elevated part of town, we used public buses. Some of my friends were the proud owners of bicycles, but these were costly and even to walk my bike on the city streets would provoke the envy of my peers.

To really feel the pulse of the city of Harbin, you must locate its heart. And only when you find the source of the heartbeat will you understand and appreciate the city itself. Kitaiskaia Ulitsa (Chinese Street), the main street of Harbin, is its heart and its soul. Wherever you go, you are bound either to pass or cross this street that mirrors the life and the mood of the city and often reflects its major events. There are longer and wider streets in the world. The Champs Elysées in Paris, Piccadilly in London and Fifth

Avenue in New York are rich in historical associations and each city has a unique urban character. But to a boy like me, no street could compare to Chinese Street, which combined a main thoroughfare, a shopping mall, a promenade, a restaurant row and a parade ground.

When the Russians relinquished their rights to the railway, one could register that transfer in the diminishing crowds and the slower, sadder pace of the passers-by. When the famous and beloved Dr. Kazenbeck passed away, one could sense the mood of the city on Chinese Street where throngs of citizens, eyes filled with tears, walked behind the catafalque of the revered doctor. And with the birth of the puppet state of Manchukuo in 1931, one could read the resentment, the cynicism and the anger in every passing face. In fact, it was on Chinese Street that one could best discern the character of the future Soviet "conquerors," when as an aftermath of the Nagasaki and Hiroshima atomic explosions, the Red Army marched into Manchuria. It was on this street that Soviet soldiers would drive right into the display windows of shops and boutiques and plunder their merchandise.

To the Jewish population, Chinese Street had its own significance. As one peered from the Sungari shore toward the city, one could note that Chinese Street branched into dozens of smaller streets, one of which was the Kommercheskaya Ulitsa (Street of Commerce). Occupying a large part of this street stood the Hall of Commerce, housing one of the largest Russian-language schools, a theatre, a library, a spacious playground and a restaurant. Next to this complex lay a large open field with a wooden hut, serving as a space for track and field events during the summer months and as a skating rink in winter. Farther down the street lived hundreds of foreigners, among them many members of the Jewish community.

Among the non-Jewish shops on Chinese Street were many corner kiosks that sold *booza*, a Caucasian soft drink, and *baklava*, a Greek pastry, gastronomic delights that were ever so popular among our youth. Scores of other shops on Chinese Street belonged to Jewish merchants who traded in women's clothing, furs, jewels, shoes and hats. The Victoria

Café, owned by the Bresler family, and the Café Mars, owned by the Zukermans, were among the best in town. Farther down the street one could catch the enticing aroma of a first-class delicatessen that sold red and black caviar straight from the barrel at a few pennies a pound!

Another delicatessen around the corner on Artillery Street belonged to a friend of my father, Owsiej Lias, whose son became one of my closest and dearest friends. Lias sold milk products and pickled vegetables, the taste of which was equalled by none. Many of my younger contemporaries would stop by for a glass of *kefir*, fermented goat's milk, which is no doubt the mother of all yogurts.

Amidst all these shops and restaurants, and majestically towering above all of them, loomed Churin's department store, the largest in town, where one might shop to one's heart's content or rendezvous. Next to Churin stood the architectural pride of the city, the Hotel Moderne, which housed the largest auditorium (used for theater, movies and concerts), a ballroom, restaurants and shops. The hotel was owned and managed by a prominent member of the Jewish community, Joseph Kaspe, whose personal tragedy had a deep and lasting effect on every Jew in town.

I passed from childhood into boyhood during the years of Japanese domination. Except for emergencies requiring Japanese security and political control, the permissiveness and tolerance on the part of the Japanese administrators led to chaos and anarchy. This atmosphere encouraged Japanese underworld figures to surface, to plunder, to torment and to exploit the population without fear of retribution. In Harbin this element found a willing and anxious ally in the person of Konstantin Rodzaevsky and his bandits and hooligans. One of his top lieutenants was a criminal named Martinoff, who, with his gang, was responsible for kidnappings, targeted at the Jews, that terrorized the city of Harbin. None more stunned our community than did the kidnapping and murder of Michael Koffman,[1] a founder of Harbin's largest bakery, Meyron Meizin, and the young musician, Simon Kaspe.

A brilliant pianist, Simon Kaspe had come from France, where he was a citizen, to Harbin to visit his parents and to give several piano recitals. After his abduction, the French Consul interfered and insisted that the ransom demanded of his father be delayed, so that the French government might have an opportunity to intervene with the Harbin authorities. Soon after, Joseph Kaspe received a second note from the kidnappers. Enclosed in this one were Simon's ear lobes! Almost immediately thereafter, the kidnappers, afraid of being caught by the authorities who, due to the Consular intervention were now hot on the case, began running from one hideout to the other, brutalizing and eventually shooting their victim.

At Simon's funeral, in keeping with Jewish tradition, Joseph Kaspe insisted on seeing his son for the last time. When his wish was granted by members of the Jewish Burial Society, the Hevra Kadisha, poor Joseph let out an inhuman scream. In the coffin lay a mangled corpse with an unrecognizable face – half was swollen and half was in a state of decay from frost and gangrene. Joseph Kaspe was brought back home to the Hotel Moderne a broken man. That day, he did not only lose his son – he lost his sanity as well.

The murderers were caught, tried and sentenced. However, due to the intervention of the Japanese gendarmerie, which had willingly capitulated to Rodzaevsky's pleas that an anti-Communist agenda had been the only premise for the plot, they were released.

Dr. Kaufman, whose courageous protests against the Kaspe affair were met with insults and provocations on the editorial pages of Rodzaevsky's *Our Way*, could scarcely imagine that some thirteen years later, he, too,

---

1. Mr. Koffman's younger son, Boris, became my close friend in Shanghai, as did George Terk. Boris died of a virus infection in his late teens. I was blessed with George's friendship for many years. He died of a heart attack in Los Angeles.

would suffer a tragic fate. Like Kaspe's, his victimization would leave its imprint on the Harbin Jewish community in its last phase.

It was a black day for all residents of the city, when in 1945 some two dozen leaders of every existing community were invited to the Hotel Moderne by the Soviet authorities, who had walked into Manchuria a few days before General MacArthur accepted the Japanese surrender on the deck of the *Missouri*, in the Bay of Tokyo. None of the gathered dignitaries, including Abram Yosefovich Kaufman and several other members of the executive committee of the Harbin Spiritual Association, returned home that night.[1] The group included Moses Zimin, Israel Orloff and Alexander Raskin, all of whom were transported secretly across the border and eventually incarcerated in the GULAG, with but a few survivors. Dr. Kaufman was among them. He was met at Israel's Lod airport by his loving family and hundreds of grateful immigrants from Harbin, whose cause he so gallantly championed and for whose preservation he had sacrificed so much.

In the 1920s, however, the Hotel Moderne was a showpiece of Chinese Street. Harbin itself was a thriving, pulsating city, wherein both young and old found a safe haven and a productive, exciting and interesting life. Here, in the vastness called China, remote from other Jewish and Zionist organizations and leaders, a proud and honorable generation of young men and women emerged that one day would be a precious Jewish resource in our struggle for statehood and the rejuvenation of our people.

---

1. Many others were arrested and transported to prison camps in the Soviet Union. Two of my Betar colleagues, Yosef Halperin (the talented poet) and Misha Kachanovsky (head of the Betar Tel Haï Fund), were among them. Yosef died in a camp somewhere in the Soviet Union, while Misha was rescued, thanks to the efforts of his family and the State of Israel. He lived a healthy and productive life, until his early sixties, when he was stricken by a heart attack.

Chapter 3

1929. BETAR AND REVISIONISM TAKE HOLD

In the 1920s and 1930s world attention was focused on the new Europe, on the emergence of Fascism in Germany and Italy, on the specter of international Communism and on Japan's aggressive policy in Manchuria and South China.

Anti-Semitism in Europe was rampant. Almost ten million Jews were living in Europe, and each passing day was bringing them closer to the abyss. As early as 1923 in Latvia, Ze'ev Jabotinsky, with the able assistance of Aron Propes, had organized the Brit Trumpeldor, the Jewish national youth movement that came to be called simply, Betar.

Whether in Europe or in Palestine, or even in faraway China, young Jews were enraged by the injustices inflicted on their people, and by their passive acceptance. Suddenly, with heads held high, proud and resolute, Jewish youth everywhere began to speak of Jewish Statehood, self-defense, honor and justice, of equality and independence!

In Harbin the young Jewish community was no different. Here, too, young people decided to organize. They, too, vowed to learn the art of self-defense, and they, too, aspired to steep themselves in the historical past of their people. Defensive sports, athletics and team games were zealously pursued. One group of Jewish students, under the capable leadership of Genna Mordohovitch (Zvi Meroni), organized themselves under the name of Ha-shomer-ha-tzair. According to Mordohovitch, the exact date of inception was May 18, 1929. Ha-shomer-ha-tzair is a name actually taken from a leftist Zionist youth organization that existed at the time in Palestine and Europe and that was beginning to have an impact on Jewish youth in pre-revolutionary Russia. It took several years for members of Harbin's Ha-shomer-ha-tzair to realize that ideologically speaking they had very little in common with an organization that had been founded to promote Socialism among young Zionists everywhere.

The true architects and founders of this first branch of Jabotinsky's Youth Movement in Harbin included: Leva Piastunovitch, Mordechai (Motia) Olmert, Nissan Lifshitz, Paul Pinsky, Reva Levin, Abrasha Ifland and Lela Kotovitch, who constituted the first executive council of the newly formed organization. However, they were not alone in their efforts.

By a happy coincidence, Alexander Yakovlevich Gurvitch had recently arrived in Harbin. Russian-born and German educated, Gurvitch spoke both German and Russian fluently. In Europe he had been an active member of Jabotinsky's Revisionist Party and was privileged to meet and work with the great leader before leaving for China in 1929.

Alexander Yakovlevich helped to establish Betar and to disband the Ha-shomer-ha-tzair organization. He ably conveyed Jabotinsky's ideas and teachings to the nationalistically minded youths of Harbin, and together with them he succeeded in raising the banners of Betar and the Revisionist Party in the city of Harbin. Gurvitch became the first president of the Revisionist movement in China. In future years he would serve as the *netziv* (leader) of Betar in China and would forever be revered as one of its founders.

Thus, a new chapter was opened in the history of the Jewish community in China – a history in which many of us played out our various parts and which helped mold our lives from beginning to end. As we glance back with nostalgia and pride to those days, we recall how young girls and boys willingly forsook entertainment, luxury and a carefree existence for daily self-discipline.

It is not unusual for nationalistic organizations to subscribe to lofty ideals and barely achievable goals. But the rank and file membership of these organizations is made up of average youngsters who join the nationalistic ranks because it is "in style," because they liked its activities or simply because of the attraction of the opposite sex. When, however, someone proved himself or herself by actually showing a readiness to sacrifice everything for the sake of the ultimate goal, that someone became a hero overnight. Songs would be sung about their deeds. Books and plays would be written about their achievements.

In our Betar in China there were scores of such heroes who formed the movement, led it, showed the way to others and were a living example of devotion and sacrifice. The pioneers who helped to create the Harbin Betar, and in later years the Betar branches in Tientsin and Shanghai, were all, without exception, true Zionists – dreamers of a Jewish homeland and patriots of a national rejuvenation. Jabotinsky provided the framework and eloquently spelled out for them their own feelings and beliefs. This generation of Betar leaders, living far away from centers of Zionism and Revisionism, nurtured themselves on Jabotinsky's feuilletons and latest articles. Soon, they converted words and dreams into action and reality.

Not all agree on what constituted Betar's most significant contribution to organized Jewish life in China. Some will argue that it was the security Betar provided with its brave stand against hooliganism and anti-Semitic violence. Others will claim that Betar's education, physical training and social activities contributed to the healthy upbringing of Jewish youth. Many would agree that Betar's colorful parades on the streets of Harbin, Shanghai and Tienstin, as well as its members' achievements in athletic competitions and team tournaments, contributed greatly to the prestige and honor of all Jews in China. However, there is no doubt whatsoever that Betar's most significant contribution to Zionism was the early *aliyah*, emigration to Eretz Israel of Harbin's pioneers from the ranks of Betar. They all voluntarily had given up the comforts of living at home with their families for a life on barren soil to which they were welcomed skeptically by the Mapai-controlled Yishuv of Palestine.[1] They all arrived bearing certificates reluctantly handed to them by the Jewish Agency officers, only because there was no one else interested in filling the minimal quota allotted to the faraway communities in China.

These courageous young men and women served as shining examples of sacrifice and patriotism, which they all continued to display so gallantly throughout their productive lives in Eretz Israel. Whether as pioneers in Plugot-Avoda,[2] as underground heroes during the days of struggle or as members of the Knesset (Israel's Parliament) after the birth of statehood, all but one continued a close association with the Jabotinsky Movement.

Not only did two members of this group of "Chinese" pioneers become members of Israel's legislative body, but Ehud Olmert, one of its sons, born in Israel, became a prominent parliamentarian and served as Minister of Health in Itzhak Shamir's government. Today he is mayor of Jerusalem!

Ehud's father, Mordechai, was one of the pillars of Betar in Harbin. He had traveled a long and difficult road before reaching the halls of Israel's Knesset. In his early career, he had studied farming and agriculture in Denmark. After many years of pioneering work at Nahlat Jabotinsky, he became the moving spirit behind Herut's Department of Settlements and key villages.[3]

Another member (actually the first) of the Knesset from China was a young man from Harbin, Eliahu (Ilyusha) Lankin. Books have been written about the remarkable contributions of Ilyusha to the Irgun

---

1. Mapai, or Miphleget Poalei Eretz Yisrael, is the name of the Israel Workers' Party which controlled the Jewish Agency.
2. The Plugot Avoda was the name of the working brigades of the Betar in Palestine.
3. Nahlat Jabotinsky was the first permanent settlement of Betar in Eretz Israel. It was established in the days of the British Mandate and situated on the outskirts of Benyamina. Herut, or Tnuat Ha-Herut, was the political party founded by Menachem Begin and his underground colleagues after the establishment of the State of Israel. Eventually it replaced the Revisionist Party in Israel and embraced all members of the Jabotinsky Movement.

Tzevai Leumi (the National Military Organization). A prominent member of the Irgun executive council, Lankin spent years in detention and returned heading a large contingent of Irgun volunteers on board the famous *Altalena*,[1] the ship that carried armaments and ammunition to Israel in 1948. Many years later Lankin served a four-year tenure as Israeli Ambassador to South Africa, before returning to Jerusalem and resuming the practice of law.

In this context, Robert Bitker, too, must not be forgotten. The only *netziv* or leader of Betar in Shanghai who left for Palestine as an immigrant prior to the rebirth of the Jewish State, Bitker was appointed by Jabotinsky to head the Irgun underground. His appointment was made immediately after its painful split into the Lechi, under Abraham Stern, and the Irgun, under the command of Jabotinsky.[2]

Unfamiliar with Palestine, not yet fluent in Hebrew and relatively inexperienced, he lacked the capacities required to lead this underground movement. It soon became necessary to replace him and to smuggle him out of the country right under the noses of British Intelligence. Bitker then resumed command of the Shanghai Betar for a brief period before leaving to join his family in the United States. The Irgun command was passed to David Raziel.

Others, perhaps less prominent, also made important contributions. Some became well-known writers, educators, business owners and entrepreneurs. Their names and their contributions toward Jewish Statehood will never be forgotten. They have added both pride and glory to the name: a Betari from China![3]

---

1. On the *Altalena*, see Chapter 15.
2. "Lechi" is an acronym for Lochamei Herut Israel, Fighters for the Freedom of Israel. The main split with the Irgun was caused by Stern's insistence that the war with Britain must go on even during the world war against Fascism. After World War Two ended, the Irgun and the Lechi often cooperated but never combined.
3. The Betarim who reached Palestine during the early thirties include: Misha Abugoff, Daniel Berkovich, Robert Bitker, Nikka Germant, "Fish" Gershevich, Abrasha Ifland, Israel Kabalkin, Lela Kotovitch, Yasha Krasnoff, Nema Kroll, Sania Kroll, Eliahu Lankin, Ya'acov Lankin, Morechai Lesk, Erik Levin, Reva Levin, Nissan Lifshitz, Reva Lifshitz, Moshe Michelovsky,

Several of our pioneers have died. Among them are two of the very first, Abrasha Ifland and the beloved leader of Harbin's Betar, Mordechai (Momchik) Lesk. Most, however, are still alive and continue to contribute to the growth and security of the Jewish State.

Finally, Abram Milichiker was deprived by fate of joining the ranks of achievers in Eretz Israel. One of the few leaders of the Harbin Betar who rose from its ranks, Abram, in his quiet, persistent, dedicated way, was an example to all around him. Betar and its ideology became the very essence of his beautiful young life. In his dedication, in his capacity for friendship, Abram had no equal. A model Betari, up to the day of his premature death, Milichiker remained the perfect embodiment of Jabotinsky's dream of a new generation of Jewish youth.

As Betar grew in strength and reputation, its larger circle included loyal friends of the organization who were prominent in the Jewish community, among them Joseph Berkovitch and Leo Tomchinsky. With the development of the youth movement, its political arm, the Revisionist Party expanded its varied activities. Soon, with the financial assistance of Friends of Betar, the movement began to publish a biweekly magazine called *Ha-degel (The Flag)*. The regular publication of Jabotinsky's latest articles and feuilletons guaranteed its success and a wide readership. Many local writers, led by Shura Gershkovich, the driving force of this publication, became steady contributors. Among them were Alexander Gurvitch, Sema Klein, David Udovich, Leo Nadel, Michael Ionis, Yana Moiseev and Rasha and Yosef Halperin.

As a boy, I was unaware of the historic implications of their work. On the other hand, my activities now drew me to the young people's

---

Zvi Mordohovitch, Sarah Morohovskaya, Mara Morguleff, Israel Nadel, Mordechai Olmert, Gena Raisky, Lelia Ravikovitch, Mulik Rolband, Senia Rosen, Israel Solovei, Peter Steinberg, Grisha Vernikoff and Bella Woogman. Some names may have been inadvertently omitted.

community center and recreational center. Here I met many youngsters my age and developed friendships that lasted a lifetime. By coincidence, the Betar summer facilities were located next door to the recreation area called the *ploshchadka* (literally, little market square.) The two properties were separated by a long fence with many a crack between the boards, which made it extremely easy to peer from one into the other. The *ploshchadka* space encompassed a large playground, a garden, a small shell-shaped outdoor stage, a room for crafts activities and a roofed shelter, while the Betar area held a small building, two dressing rooms, another roofed covering used for boxing and physical exercises, a large glassed-in hall (used as a dressing room for skaters in winter), a large track and volleyball and basketball courts. On the Betar side of the fence, in large letters, a sign read: "*Vzdorovom tele, zdorovyi dukh*" ("A healthy spirit in a healthy body"). Little did I know how much time in the future I would be spending on this side of the fence.

In the meantime, my interests were completely monopolized by the community center, its boyhood challenges and my newfound friends.

Chapter 4

1932. THE YEAR OF THE FLOOD

The year 1932 began frigidly if uneventfully. Sub-zero winters produced seasonal delights: in the afternoon, ice-skating in rinks, sledding down snowy river banks and traversing the frozen Sungari River, by means of the *tolkai-tolkai*[1] (push-push, in pidgin Russian); at supper time, fortifying our bodies with Siberian dumplings called *pel'meny*; and then after dark, nourishing our souls with an evening at the theater. Each is worthy of comment, as each, in its own right, was memorable.

Delicious in any season, *pel'meny* are best in winter, stored in snow and then dumped into boiling chicken soup. The best *pel'meny* in Harbin used to be served at the "Stop Signal" restaurant on the other side of the Sungari River. To get there, one had to navigate the river on a *tolkai-tolkai*, a contraption that looks like a chair, or sleigh. In fact, it is operated by a driver who pumps a spear-like stick between his legs that hits the ice below and creates a motion that can generate a frightening velocity. The passenger sits bundled up in the chair and dreams all the while of the boiling soup and *pel'meny* that await him. Thus would my friends and I escape from the dreary world of classes and teachers.

---

1. Tolkai-tolkai should be pronounced "tol-KAI" with a diphthong effect on the last syllable.

In spite of the freezing weather, our houses were warm, protected by cotton-insulated double windows. From October to March, wall stoves, heated with wood and coal, burned day and night. Winter days and nights lured us out-of-doors to the public skating rinks, where bands would play in the evenings, and pairs and singles would perform figure and race skating to the delight of those who came to learn or simply to watch.

As I grew older, I often wondered what the Chinese population was doing while we continued to enjoy life in this city. That question continued to perplex me for many years. Hardly any Chinese youngsters shared our activities, and the grown-ups seemed to have moved out of sight in order to leave us, their guests, in total privacy.

In reality, of course, this Chinese invisibility was but an illusion based on lack of insight and observation. The Chinese outnumbered the foreigners more than a hundred to one. We lived among the Chinese masses in splendid isolation and our paths would cross only when our own needs depended on their assistance as shopkeepers, street peddlers, brokers, salesmen, cooks, drivers or *amahs* (Chinese or Japanese live-in maids). We were also very much aware of the Harbin handymen, whom we needed, and of the beggars, who needed us.

For the Jewish community as a whole, the year 1932 also began well. The city's Jewish women were the first to learn the Chinese language and to use it vociferously during their daily games of mahjong. The game was played with ivory-colored cubes, measuring three-by-five centimeters, with various Chinese lettering drawn on the inner, white portion. These ivory pieces were assembled on a foot-long wooden container. When a lady would throw in her matching cards, she would shout out in Chinese, "Pong, Kong or Chow!" Once the right combination was collected on the container, the winning lady would turn the cube holder outward, displaying her winning set and exclaim, "mahjong!" Between the shuffling of the ivory pieces and the ladies' excited screams of different

Chinese words, the noise level in the house would become deafening. In fact, it was rumored that on more than one occasion, robberies took place in homes or apartments during mahjong games, and not a single player noticed the rude intrusion.

But in all fairness it must be noted that mahjong was not the only preoccupation of the Jewish ladies, whether in Harbin, Tientsin or Shanghai. In the early 1930s charity funds were collected by the various ladies' committees of the community. In addition to undertaking philanthropy for the needy, the hungry and the sick, the Harbin Jewish women also helped solicit funds for the Talmud-Torah, the Israeli Fund Collection boxes and the Hevra Kadisha (Burial Society). Betar had its own annual Hanukah evening, a splendid communal event that financed a variety of Betar activities. Before long, women of the Jewish communities of Tientsin and Shanghai also took over the collection of funds from the men, with gratifying results. All in all, the Jewish communities of the Far East became exemplary in the development of their philanthropic agencies and in the yearly expressions of individual generosity.

In 1932 I became nine years old. I also began to experience the first pangs of peer pressure. As a result, I began to rebel against the sissified clothing mother selected for me. Her preferences were for heavy wool knicker suits that buttoned below the knee, and long, knitted socks that covered the calf. Boys of my age preferred to wear long full slacks in winter and short-shorts during the summer months. We also liked turtleneck sweaters during the cold season and solid-colored open shirts in summer. At times, we were able to convince our parents to dress us as WE liked best. However, at parties or on holidays it was simply futile to argue.

Because of the cold winters and very hot summers, I was forced to wear fur-lined hats with ear-muffs from December to March, and cork hats, much like those worn by officers of the Light Brigade, in summer as protection from sunstroke. Since hats were mandatory, I was often taken by my father to Gurvitch's haberdashery. Strange as it may seem, these visits had their peculiar rewards. A kindly old man, Mr. Gurvitch was famous for his strange way of stuttering in a loud bass with long gulps for air between vowels. With the cruelty of youngsters my age, I found this amusing and often turned my hat-buying agony into a pleasant and entertaining experience at Mr. Gurvitch's expense. However, as soon as I was old enough to protest against this ridiculous attire, I joined many of my friends by discarding the headgear in both the winter and summer months.

Most of my friends, of many different backgrounds, attended summer camp at the *ploshchadka*. During these months, I first met some of the girls and boys with whom I was destined to share many wonderful years of friendship. Boris Koffman and Ura Terk were a part of our group. Others included Teddy Kaufman (son of Dr. Kaufman, who is currently the president of Igud Yotzei Sin in Tel Aviv);[1] Joe Wainer, who later became my close friend and roommate in school; Ura Horosh, whose stage career I helped to launch; Mira Treyman (my first girlfriend); and countless others. I became active at the *ploshchadka* together with my two cousins, Bertha Oppenheim and Boris Zuboreff, with whom I always enjoyed a very special camaraderie.

In those carefree summer days, we engaged in sports, arts and crafts, singing and folk dancing. We all, except for Ura Horosh, managed to rid ourselves of our governesses! To supervise his every step, Ura's mother, however, had insisted on keeping his old German governess, Frau Pauline. The whole town came to recognize Frau Pauline in search of her elusive charge as she would shout *"Urikum, geh nach haus!"* ["Urik, go home!"]

---

1. The Igud Yotzei Sin, the Association of Immigrants from China, was created by a small group of former community activists in China. It has a very large membership, with branches today in New York, Los Angeles, San Francisco and Sydney, Australia. It publishes a bi-monthly magazine in Russian, English and Hebrew. Teddy Kaufman has been its president for well over twelve years. Igud's main purpose is to provide financial assistance to the needy.

Among the many games we played, there was one that eventually helped me make the baseball team in high school. It was called *lapta*, from the Russian word *lopata*, or shovel, and it consisted of fielding and batting. The game required no bases, and those in the field ran a straight line at a distance of thirty to fifty meters from the batsman. Positioned next to the batsman, the pitcher would throw the ball gently into the air, about two meters high, the batsman would then smack it and run for dear life! The only way to get the batsman out was for the fielding team to catch the ball in mid-air or to pitch the retrieved ball at the runner and hit him (hopefully below the neck) before he returned to the baseline from which he ran. A cheap sport, it could be played with any ball the size of a baseball, and any bat, even a heavy tree branch. Nevertheless, it was considered a rough game and was usually played only by boys. During my *lapta* phase, I discovered that I could run faster than my peers, a capacity that I began to develop, until one day I was crowned "champion sprinter of Harbin." But this was to come much later in life... However, even in my boyhood, I became interested in athletics and on more than one occasion I would peer into the cracks of the wooden wall to see what was taking place on the Betar side of the fence.

By now, Betar in Harbin had acquired a reputation that far exceeded its basic goals and purposes of educating Jewish youth to become nationally-minded Zionists and future pioneers of an independent Jewish State. Betar became a guardian of Jewish honor, a security force and a symbol of Jewish conscience and pride. Betar's glory in Harbin peaked when tragedy befell the entire population of Harbin.

It came almost without warning. The papers wrote of the dangerous rise in the water level of the Sungari River, and the authorities mobilized a small force of volunteers to prevent possible flooding. But no one knew, nor could anyone imagine, the extent of the impending devastation but a few days away. A small group of Betarim, under the command of Lelia

Ravikovitch, mobilized to ward off disaster, and gathering at the Sungari shore by the city side, immediately joined hands with local volunteers to fill sandbags and to barricade the river banks. As the river banks began to overflow, water seeped through the sandbags, ran over the barricades, and from under the sewage lines, until water had flooded Pristan, the lower part of the city.

The Betar volunteers at once increased to a force of more than fifty young men and women, ready to do whatever was required to save lives, help people and to ease the suffering all around. The major task of the Betar volunteers was to rescue the old and transport them from flooded houses to secure buildings, whether the synagogue, the welfare kitchen hall, the school or the hospital. Its next assignment was to assure those in need that they would not remain without drinking water or food. Knee-deep in water or in requisitioned rowboats, Betarim rushed from one victim to the other, delivering bottled water and fresh bread to as many persons as possible. They worked in shifts, day and night, relieving each other only when total exhaustion warranted a short reprieve.

Eventually, the waters began to recede. The rowboats began to disappear, and the streets began to fill up with cleaning teams and curious bystanders. Finally, the first rays of sunshine began to brighten the depressed spirits of both the rescuers and the rescued. Soon the water receded, and we saw the full force of the devastation and death that the flood mercilessly had left behind. Carcasses and corpses had to be removed by hand. The remaining refuse was slowly swallowed by the city sewers. And soon enough, the flood was over.

Over – but not forgotten. It now remained only a bad memory, a horrible dream – indeed, a nightmare! But linked eternally to these memories of doom and destruction was Harbin's gratitude for the humanitarian efforts of the young Jewish boys and girls who had risked their safety in order to help the entire population in time of danger and need.

Of course, some managed to escape from Pristan to higher ground while the water was slowly creeping into the city. My family was among those fortunate few. On the third day of the flood I found myself temporarily living in Novyi Gorod. At the time, I did not appreciate my good fortune. On the contrary, I deeply resented the move that deprived me of the fun, friends and action on the flooded streets of the city. To be sure, I was too young to understand the glorious rescue operation of Betar and not old enough to have taken any part in it.

The summer of 1932 would mark a turning point in my personal life as well. I remember vividly the afternoon when my father returned from town with mail from the post office, since there had been no home deliveries during the flood. A letter had come from Aunt Nuta and Uncle Yasha Veinerman in Shanghai, inviting me to stay with them during the coming school year. Knowing nothing of my parents' plan to send me to an English school in Shanghai, I was shocked. While we had talked about such a possibility, nothing had been resolved, and I had hoped that the plan would fail.

It is difficult for a nine year old to be torn away from a happy home environment and friends all at the same time. And this for me was Harbin! I often disagreed with my countrymen who missed Harbin during the years of the Bamboo Curtain and who often yearned to revisit the city of their childhood or birth. I did not. For me, a landscape stimulates no nostalgia whatsoever. If you have seen one Buddhist temple, you've seen a thousand! There is nothing exciting about dead cities – only living cities vibrant with one's own family and friends have meaning.

And here, suddenly, at the age of nine, I was faced with having to give up all of this, granted, for the sake of education. The question of residence and supervision suddenly was resolved. By September, I made my rounds of sad farewells and prepared myself for the journey. After a long and monotonous sea voyage, my mother delivered me to the Veinermans in the great city of Shanghai. I arrived dejected and heartbroken and angry as could be! Strangely, neither my mother nor my father understood my own trepidation at moving from home. I loved my parents dearly, but I could never understand their desire to part with me nine months a year from my ninth year to my seventeenth, when I graduated from high school, just in order to give me a good "foreign education." All the more incomprehensible seemed their decision, since graduates of the Harbin Commercial School became doctors, lawyers, engineers and educators. They matriculated to colleges and universities in Europe and the United States, and none of them had any problems with the English they had learned in Harbin. Nevertheless, because I knew my parents meant well, I have remained forever grateful to them.

Chapter 5

FIRST IMPRESSIONS OF SHANGHAI

To reach Shanghai from Harbin in 1932 required a week's journey by rail and by ship. At the Harbin railway station, my mother and I boarded a first-class sleeper of the Chinese Manchurian Railway Company. Two days and one night later we arrived at Port Arthur-Dairen. I especially enjoyed our short stops where I would run out onto the station platform to rubber stamp the name of the town through which we were passing onto a page of my small travel diary. Leaping aboard the train just pulling out of the station and observing the panic-stricken expression on my mother's face became a regular part of the excitement. Oh, the evil ways of youth! I also liked our regular visits to the dining cars under the supervision of Wagon Lits, where delicious food was served on tables set with starched tablecloths, napkins and flowers.

Dairen protrudes into the Yellow Sea, northwest of Shanghai. While the vast inland territory has been the prey of the gangsters and thieves who have been allowed to roam freely with very little intervention from the Chinese authorities, the sea lane, leading to Tsingtao and Shanghai, has been very well guarded and consequently it has been open to heavy commercial traffic.

Boarding a Shanghai-bound ship at Dairen, we embarked on a rolling sea voyage of another four and a half days. As our little Japanese vessel,

the *Dairen Maru*, approached the narrow waterway of the Soochow Creek
leading to the Whangpoo wharf, my feelings of apprehension gave way to
anticipation and excitement. Disembarking, I clasped my mother's hand,
looked around me and formed my very first impression of Shanghai:
Everything seemed SO big, SO uncontrollable and SO dirty!

Once I settled in at the home of my aunt and uncle and registered at
the Public and Thomas Hanbury School, I began to pay more attention to
my physical and social surroundings. The Veinermans' apartment was
located on the second floor of a house on Seymour at the corner of
Bubbling Well Road. My bedroom window afforded me a generous view of
both streets in this central part of the international settlement.

Mother soon left, and I was now a charge of Aunt Nuta and Uncle
Yasha, the dearest and kindest people on earth. I was also fortunate to be
with the Veinermans at a time when their four sons were still at home.
Shura, the youngest son, was to become a good friend until his death in
New York of cancer.

My transportation, like that of thousands of others, was confined to
the private rickshaw that would take me to school, to visits to my friends
and to shops and movies. The difference between a private rickshaw and
a public one is in its appearance. The public rickshaws were to be found
on every corner of town; their appearance was shabby and that of its
puller, or the rickshaw-man, was even worse. By comparison, the private
rickshaws worked only by appointment; their seats were soft and clean,
and the wooden and brass parts, shiny. The rickshaw-man himself was
dressed neatly and his feet were covered with rubber shoes or new
sandals. He strutted proudly, as he negotiated his vehicle between the
masses of people, trams and buses crowding the streets of Shanghai.

Occasionally, I observed the fate of the common rickshaw-man
through my window. Often, the bearded Indian Sikhs of the British
municipal force would chase after these poor rickshaw-peddlers to rip off
their rickshaw licenses from the backs of the seats. They did this as
punishment for illegal parking or any form of aggressive solicitation of
business. To renew these licenses was often an impossible burden for

these poor, hard-working beasts of burden. However, compared to the thousands of street beggars of Shanghai, the rickshaw-men were considered a privileged class.

Aside from a few thousand Chinese businessmen and several dozen millionaires, Shanghai swarmed with starving, sick and homeless beggars – men, women and children, driven to eating bark from trees. Dead children or babies lay on the pavement, their bodies rotting with lice and gangrene. If you were an early riser, you could very well have witnessed a scene in which street cleaners would pile corpses on cart wheels; or you might pass by a newspaper-covered "corpse" that twitched as it was about to be dumped by sanitary workers into a cart with the dead!

Filth was omnipresent, cholera rampant and dysentery a part of everyday life. Nonetheless, foreigners and wealthy Chinese citizens established ghettos of luxury and prosperity within the limited areas of both the French concession and the international settlement. Here were situated the foreign residential area, the main streets such as Bubbling Well Road or Avenue Joffre, commercial offices and banks, night clubs, restaurants and theatres. Yet even here, one happened upon peddlers and beggars struggling to survive.

Due to the presence of the many French, Italian, British and Japanese soldiers and sailors – as well as United States Marines – bars and bordellos were abundant, and prostitutes and pimps plied their trade on the busy streets of Shanghai. Indeed, European Shanghai was an exciting, bustling blend of modern Paris and ancient Rome, mixed into a giant pothole of mystic, dangerous and colossal China, with all its traditions, cultures, poverty and wealth.

For most foreigners this was the only Shanghai they knew, and they loved being there every precious moment. But Shanghai's urban sores were not the result of the concessions alone. After all, it must not be forgotten that while the legality of concessions derived from the military power of the conquerors, the hospitality of the local population toward its guests was a direct result of China's goodwill and tolerance.

♣   ♣   ♣

Such was the other side of China that I came to know during my three years of schooling in Shanghai. And with each year, new scenes unfolded, as I observed the contradictions of my surroundings, and the determined continuity of life in what I already began to call "my China."

At the start of the school year in the British School in Shanghai, I feared that I might not endure so strange a regime, in which students were caned for misdemeanors. Nor did I take to the dull British humor of my peers and the unemotional, rather cold British temperament. Fortunately, I mastered my moodiness and was able to look on the bright side of my new circumstances that certainly were made cheerier by the presence in Shanghai of my two Harbin friends, Boris Koffman and Ura (George) Terk. Another boost to my spirits was the expectation that in summer I would walk once again the streets of my beloved Harbin and enjoy the warmth and friendship of my family and many friends.

During the years from 1932 to 1935, the Shanghai Jewish community numbered some 10,000 Jews, including the 500 or more of the original Sephardi community, who had been the first to establish Jewish life in this great city. By 1932, a parallel Ashkenazi Jewish community was already well established.

The Jewish Hospital and Clinic, over which ruled a team of devoted men and women, faithfully served the settlers until the final exodus of Jews from Shanghai. The Jewish needy were taken care of by the Shelter House, directed largely by volunteers, who not only gave of their time but also contributed money in order to keep this important organization alive and productive. Communal burial needs were supplied by the Hevra Kadisha, or Jewish Burial Society, which saw to it that the cemetery was well kept, burials properly conducted and memorial stones placed on the graves of those whose families lacked the necessary funds for those essential services. Religious affairs were supervised by the beloved rabbi of the community, Rabbi Ashkenazi, a wise and saintly man who hailed from a Lubavicher family, and who was revered by all who came in touch with him. The Rabbi's wife participated enthusiastically in the many social and charitable functions organized by the local Jewish women. The Ashkenazis had two daughters. The youngest, Esther, became a very dear friend and a prominent member of "our crowd."

The Jewish Recreation Club, the sports center of the Jewish community, not only catered to the physical development of its many members, but it formed Jewish soccer teams, and sponsored boxing matches, ping-pong games and various other athletic events as well. Many of the JRC teams competed successfully and proudly in Shanghai's international sports events.

During the season of inter-port games that usually were held at the soccer stadium or at the race course, the Jewish Recreation Club would muster its soccer talent into one team, called "Palestine." When this team of Jewish patriots and athletes met its main rival, the Sokol Club, which played under the name of "Russia" and that at times showed itself to be anti-Semitic, the excitement in town would rise to a dangerous pitch. Members of the Jewish community, including elderly men and women, were often seen during these contests jumping in the air from happiness at every goal scored by the "Palestine" team. Very often the Jewish sportsmen led by their indestructible goalie, Molly Ditritch, and by the famous Greenberg brothers, would emerge victorious. This would be a day of rejoicing, a Jewish holiday of sorts.

Modeling themselves on the Harbin community, Shanghai's Jewish women began to play a prominent part in the life and activities of the Shanghai Jewish community. In addition to assisting the many existing Jewish organizations, they established a Shanghai branch of the Women's International Zionist Organization. Jewish women were active everywhere but their greatest achievement was in the area of solicitation of funds, collection of raffle prizes and the sale of tickets to various functions which promoted Jewish charity of one kind or another.

Zionism did not occupy as prominent a place among Shanghai Jewry as it would in the years immediately following World War Two.

Nevertheless, as news of severe injustices inflicted upon our people in Germany reached China, the Shanghai community responded. Leading all efforts on behalf of a decimated world Jewry were the two organizations that carried the nationalistic banner of Ze'ev Jabotinsky: the Revisionists and the Betar youth. However, even in those years, the General Zionists succeeded in creating a branch under the name of "Kadima." They, too, promoted the idea of a Jewish homeland and supported emigration to Eretz Yisrael.

While the Revisionists and the Kadima members organized occasional meetings and lectures, it was the youth of Betar who continued to initiate vigorous psychological and physical training programs for their peers who would go as pioneers to Eretz Yisrael.

Since I considered myself a transfer student, I felt little desire to become involved in the life and activities of the Shanghai Jewish community. My home was Harbin and this was where my involvement in Jewish life would begin. However, I could hardly ignore the occasional impulse to participate in some of the events of the existing Jewish organizations. Of these, I especially enjoyed cheering on the many Jewish teams that competed for medals and honors. I also liked attending performances of Jewish plays in the Shanghai Jewish Club, a fulcrum of Jewish life in the city, which I occasionally visited with my aunt and uncle or with their sons.

During one visit to the Shanghai Jewish Club, I stopped to watch a parade of uniformed youngsters dressed in blue skirts or pants, topped with brown shirts with blue-cornered collars and blue ties. Behind them marched younger children wearing similar shirts, short pants and scout kerchiefs of different colors. The very air seemed to be charged with electricity, when these neat rows of Jewish youngsters marched by the applauding spectators at the Jewish Club. The parade was led by a tall, healthy looking young man carrying a blue-and-white silk flag, accompanied by two pretty girls in their late teens. Immediately behind the flag-bearer, marched a group of buglers and drummers giving the beat to the whole parade.

It was then, for the first time, that I saw Shanghai Betarim and felt a magnetic attraction to their ranks. It was not the bugles and drums nor the precise gait of the marchers that drew me to them, nor the flag waving proudly in the breeze nor the determined glances of its bearers. Certainly my feelings were not aroused by the ideology or the goals of this organization, of which I was as yet totally ignorant, and yet I felt the keenest desire to be a part of the lives of each and every one of these wonderful youngsters, whose very presence made me feel that I could take on the world. The faces, the uniforms, the flag, the beat of the drums and the sound of the bugles, together with the sense that all of this was Jewish – yes, mine – imbued me with pride, of which I had not yet been aware. I decided to join Betar on my return to Harbin in the summer of 1933.

One of the most prominent and significant achievements of the Shanghai Betar was the creation of the Jewish Troop within the popular Shanghai Volunteer Corps. On the initiative of Betar leaders and backed by all senior members of the organization, the Shanghai Volunteer Corps command was persuaded to create a Jewish unit and to allow it to bear the emblem of the Magen David (the six-pointed Jewish star) as its insignia. In addition to the Betar members, other Jewish young men joined the Troop. Its professional leader was Captain Noel Jacobs, a British Jew and war veteran, a born leader, a gentleman and a friend, who soon became a highly respected and dearly loved commander of the Jewish Troop.

As in Harbin, the overall titular leadership of Jewish life and its spokespersons was the executive committee of the Shanghai Ashkenazi Jewish community. Among them were the respected businessman, Boris Topaz, its long-term president, and Grisha Shifrin, a generous donor to Jewish causes, well known for his generous nature and deep involvement in Jewish organizational life.

♣   ♣   ♣

By the time I had adapted to Shanghai life with all its mystique, excitement, filth, wealth and poverty, it was almost time for my six-day journey back to my family and friends.

School is the last thing on anyone's mind just weeks prior to summer vacation, especially the discipline-ridden school I attended. Here, even the nicest of people became influenced by British rigidity. Take for example Alex Terk, brother of my very best friend (George), who was older than us by some five years and who became school monitor. One day, as he was driving George and me home from school, he stopped the car abruptly in reaction to some profanity I uttered and asked me to get out of the car. George followed me into the street, and we somehow managed to negotiate our way home, albeit with a significant delay. As a result, Alex was scolded by his parents, while we emerged as martyrs. After that, I learned to curb my tongue.

Just before the summer holidays, I signed up to participate in our school's sports day festival, where lemonade, cookies and pastries were served to all participants and guests. The main event (in which I did not participate) was cricket, a typical British game, elegant, uneventful and monstrously boring, in which all players are dressed in laundered white attire and matching hats. The principle of the game is rather simple: The batsman hits a heavy ball (double the size of a baseball) with the flat end of a bat and runs between wickets that have been placed some thirty yards apart. He continues to bat until he is tagged out, at which time a new batsman comes in. When three batsmen are out, the fielding team goes to bat.

I, however, was assigned to a soccer team, my favorite team sport. Toward evening the unexpected happened: I ran in the 100-yard dash – and won! This was quite a feat for a ten-year-old boy, and I became quite popular among my peers for the next couple of days. For the second time, I realized my potential as a sprinter and my success gave me both confidence and a newfound ambition to participate in many more track and field events in both Shanghai and Harbin. With this modest achievement, I left to spend my summer vacation in "my" Harbin.

Chapter 6

DEFENDING JEWISH HONOR

Traveling to my beloved city by train was totally new to me and, as we approached the outskirts, I could not restrain my anticipation. Upon espying my parents and many friends who had gathered at the railway station platform, I jumped off the still-moving train – right into my parents' arms. Oh, what a moment of true happiness!

Somehow, the city streets seemed to be narrower and its many buildings appeared to be smaller. In actual fact, Harbin itself had not changed. I had. I was now a year older and, thanks to my British education and cosmopolitan way of life, I was more mature and experienced. Compared to Shanghai, Harbin was a small town, but it would offer all the pleasures and comforts, all of the entertainment and excitement a ten year old could possibly want.

A city may well remain unchanged physically or technically, while its inner soul may undergo a transformation. This spiritual change, induced by political circumstance, was quite evident to me on my first return to Harbin in 1933. After two years of rule under the Japanese military regime, the puppets of Manchukuo, including the so-called Emperor Pu-Yi, had stiffened their control of Harbin's administration and made life less bearable for the Chinese population as a whole. Foreigners were minimally affected for the while, and life in the Jewish community proceeded tranquilly.

While my interests primarily were tied up with the life of Jewish Harbin, a concern for the Chinese population as a whole began to vie for my attention. I began to realize that our hosts, in actual fact, were prisoners in their own home. They were ruled by Japanese conquerors, and the puppet state of Manchukuo was a fiction created to conceal brutal and naked aggression. The Manchukuo flag with its yellow background, a color we all knew stood for cowardice and deceit, even struck me as an unintended irony.

I began to pay more attention to the Chinese people, especially to those who came in contact with the Jewish population, and with my family and me. I began to distinguish three basic types in Harbin Chinese society: the laborer, the merchant and the *compradore* (a native agent and go-between). The laborer worked on the streets and on buildings; the merchants peddled their wares to offices and homes; and the *compradores* were the people without whom it was impossible for us as foreigners to transact any serious business. At the age of ten I did not realize that there were two other strata at the extreme poles of society: the eternal beggar and the arrogant millionaire! But these two categories were more in evidence in Shanghai than in Harbin, and by 1951 they were totally eliminated as a class.

Having lived among the Chinese people in Harbin and Shanghai, it became quite evident to me at an early age that the Chinese are an exceptionally talented people. Most Chinese citizens in Harbin spoke Russian, even if at best sometimes, a pidgin Russian. In Shanghai the Chinese learned to speak English and many even adopted a very British accent in the process! With the penetration of the Japanese into Manchuria, Chinese citizens were the first to learn how to speak, read and write Japanese, despite the dissimilarity of the two languages.

As a result of their linguistic facility, in my opinion, the Chinese have had a deleterious influence on some foreign children. Pidgin Russian or English is spoken by maids and *amahs*, and often a foreign employer communicates with them in the same way. Consequently, many children of foreigners speak only pidgin Russian or English during their formative years.

In summer, I continued to attend recreational camp with my friends from last year. Only now my friends included members of the opposite sex as well, and I discovered an impulse to show off whenever I found myself in their company. This was especially true when the girls were as pretty as Kira Kuprianovich, Nadia Ginzburg, Lucy Bogdanovskaya, Mira Treyman and even my own cousin Bertha. Of course my antics were acknowledged by a stare, or a shove that in turn prompted me to retaliate by pulling their long, pretty hair.

One morning, walking toward the playground and turning from Chinese Street into Commercial Street, I heard terrible screams interspersed with thud-like sounds and the crushing of bones. Turning my head toward the small police hut guarding the city's jail, I saw a Japanese gendarme mercilessly beating a Chinese prisoner who was on his knees, begging for mercy. Stifling an impulse to vomit, I began to run in the direction of our playgrounds. For days this scene remained before my eyes, and I was frustrated by an avalanche of questions forming in my mind, questions to which I had no answers.

That day I had a man-to-man talk with my father, the first of many that would follow and that I remember with both nostalgia and love. Dad explained to me the injustice of conquest and the occupation of lands. He told me of the legal system and the importance of being able to determine right from wrong. We did not know what crime, if any, the flogged man had committed, but if he was guilty of any wrongdoing, he was entitled to a just punishment. There is no question but that the Japanese sadist was abusing the law and under normal circumstances would have been severely punished. Dad concluded his remarks with the words, "Son, you must live a life of honesty and decency and always preserve your good name. Riches, luxuries and fortunes come and go. Your name and your reputation stay with you forever. You cannot buy a good reputation – you work on it, you build it, you create it. And once it is established, it is there to stay to your dying day." Certainly, my father lived by that credo until the last day of his life.

Soon we were all enjoying a summer routine dominated by the daily schedule of the *ploshchadka*. By now I had discovered that I had no ear for music. Moreover, my voice carries! In other words, when I sing, I not only sing off-key, but I also do so boldly and loudly. A very popular music teacher in Harbin, Dora Elkin, taught us choir singing during the summer, and in order to keep the others from becoming totally confused, she requested that I refrain from participating in her singing group.

Instead, during chorus practice, I roamed freely about the area and regularly visited the neighboring grounds occupied by Betar. The sports activities soon attracted my attention. By now I had become acquainted with some of the Betarim of my own age. In time, I developed a lasting friendship with Boris Tzvibel, Boris Goltzman and Leva (Levchik) Olshevsky. Leva became one of my closest friends, and we spent many years of our lives together in Shanghai and Israel.[1] Boris Tzvibel, for example, became an outstanding athlete and soccer player. He was my strong rival in the 100-meter dash in the years ahead, but the fact that I usually beat him to the finish did not stand in the way of our very warm friendship.[2]

Leva brought me the application for membership in Betar, an affiliation that would change my life. After a short discussion, I signed all

---

1. Boris Goltzman settled in the Soviet Union, where he died. Leva (Arie) Olshevsky became an important executive of Israel's major airline company, "El Al." Shortly after his fiftieth birthday, he was stricken by internal hemorrhaging and suffered a fatal heart attack. Hundreds of people, including many émigrés from China and all of his friends, attended his funeral.
2. Boris Tzvibel, now retired, lives in Australia with his family.

the necessary forms. However, due to my Shanghai schooling during the winter months, I did not pass the entrance exams, and so I did not become a "real" Betari until 1935, when I was twelve years old.

At the summer camp I was also introduced to a boy from Tientsin who had just lost his father and had come to live in Harbin with his mother and younger brother. The boy's name was Joe Wainer, and my entire youth became interwoven with his, so that even today I think of Joe as a close relative rather than just a friend.

Joe Wainer was the antithesis of what is often considered to be a "typical" Jew. Wiry and thin, he had a long face, punctuated with a wide mouth, a small, well-shaped nose and bluish-green eyes. His head was crowned with straight, unruly blond hair which would constantly fall over his short forehead. Joe gave the impression of being a carefree, timid youngster who did not reveal at this age his competitive nature. However, from the day we met, it was obvious that Joe was a born sportsman, qualities that he steadily nurtured until he excelled in both tennis and badminton. Mild-mannered, Joe was persistent, and on occasion, quite stubborn.

Engrossed in my new friendship, I did not immediately notice the abnormally tense mood about me. Someone seemed to be in serious trouble. The reader will recall my account of how in 1931 the young pianist son of the Hotel Moderne's Joseph Kaspe was kidnapped and held for an enormous ransom. My friends and I wanted to do something about this tragedy, but what?

Our group decided to meet at my house on Artillery Street. One of the girls initiated us into spiritualism, the new craze among youngsters in our town. We sat around a table that displayed an alphabet and numerals (one to ten) painted in a large circle, while our medium dangled a borrowed wedding ring suspended by a hair above the letters and numerals. The rest of us lightly held hands and watched the ring move toward one letter, then another, forming words and sentences. The spirits were called out by the medium from our collective suggestions and usually belonged to some famous personalities of the past.

As a result of this ingenious contact with the spirits of the outer world, we learned the "exact" whereabouts of the Kaspe kidnappers' hideout: the swinging ring pointed to letters and figures which we tallied and then read as being that of the railway station, some five hundred miles north of Harbin! Without hesitation, we called Dr. Kaufman with the news. He listened calmly, took down the name of the station we gave him and told us to leave the matter in his hands now and to promise henceforth to withdraw from the case. It turned out that no such village or station existed and that by the time we had given our sensational details to Mr. Kaufman, poor Simon Kaspe already had been slain.

Although the kidnappers were led by Martinoff and his White Russian bandits, the anger and fury of the Jews of Harbin was not limited to them alone. It was equally directed against the Japanese authorities who not only protected these criminals, but who actually allowed them to function openly within the framework of the White Russian émigré community. The vast majority of the White Russians had nothing to do with these acts of banditry and murder. They were decent, honorable citizens who completely rejected this criminal element in their midst. Open support and inspiration of this abominable stratum of society came from a Fascist organization led by Konstantin Rodzaevsky, the editor of the anti-Semitic daily paper, *Nash Put (Our Way)*. And it became "their way" to come out with articles blaming Jews for all of the ills of the universe and to spread false accusations against prominent members of the Jewish community of Harbin. Since they declared themselves to be anti-Communists and supporters of the Japanese "New Order in Asia," they too were embraced by the protective hand of the military regime.

Given the permissiveness of the Japanese and the arrogant boldness of the White Russian anti-Semites, the Jews of Harbin were faced with a dilemma. While to react was dangerous, to be timid was clearly self-destructive. The ongoing debate would never have been resolved, had it not been for Betar youth. Guided by the principle of right versus might, and by the logic of preserving security and honor through boldness and self defense, they took matters into their own hands.

Thus it came about that for every attack on Jewish property, Betarim would seek out and find the perpetrators and punish them severely. One day, while I was still enjoying my summer vacation in Harbin, a young group of former Cossacks from a nearby station came to visit their friends, Rodzaevsky and Company. Together, they had decided to beat up Jews. The victim they found most appropriate for their pleasure was a Jew either too young or too old to defend himself. Betarim understood Rodzaevsky's mode of operation. And so, we sent out several youngsters in different directions in town, each followed by a group of older boys in ambush. It did not take long before one of the youngsters was attacked by a dozen of the visiting and local hooligans. Within moments, Betarim pounced on the attackers and a classical street fight ensued. As a result, two of the Rodzaevsky group were hospitalized, and one was seen the next day walking down Chinese Street, his head wrapped in a thick bandage. Afterward, incidents of physical violence against Jews and their property subsided remarkably. Some members of the community disapproved of the methods that we had used, but they all admired the results.

It is not a coincidence that during the following years, the Yishuv (the Jewish community in Palestine) was embroiled in a similar debate of *havlaga* (non-resistance) versus *haganah* (retaliation). I wonder if the Jewish State would ever have been established had the ideology of *havlaga* prevailed.

Chapter 7

1934: BETARIADA I (TIENTSIN)

During my second year of school in Shanghai, it became a matter of grave importance to Boris Koffman, George and me that we not miss any current issues of *Vogue* magazine to which Boris's sister subscribed. We discovered that the magazine carried tantalizing blown-up photos of beautiful women, often clad in skimpy negligées. Other than seeking out that vicarious thrill, we tended to be well-behaved boys, whose main interest in life was still soccer.

My classes went well, except for workshop. I simply was not good at carving inkwells out of blocks of wood. As a result, I was often rewarded with "coconuts," *viz.*, knocks on the head by my teacher! Needless to say, I did not like either the class or the teacher.

Summer arrived before I knew it, and once again I was on my way to Harbin. Back home, I devoted myself to serious training under the guidance of Betar's burly sports instructor, Verner Ivanovich. In between workouts, I noticed other athletes exercising and practicing, and soon I began to realize how important it was for a sportsman to be in top condition. During these sessions, I ran into a stranger who was learning the art of boxing from Herman Zelig, our new trainer from Germany. According to Zelig, the future pugilist, a White Russian by the name of Andrei was destined to win international fame. As it turned out, Andrei

Shilaeff did become a lightweight champion of the Far East, but he died in the boxing ring in the United States, before he had a chance to seriously launch his career in America.

As my summer vacation was nearing its end, a selected few of Harbin Betar's very best sportsmen were preparing themselves for exciting days ahead. At the Betar headquarters in China a program deserving of special mention and praise was in the making. For the first time ever, Betarim from different cities would gather to compete in a Betariada, or a multi-athletics meet.

As a geographical compromise between Harbin and Shanghai, the event was to be held in Tientsin. The requisite funds were collected by the sports committees of the three branches of Betar. Many participants helped to pay their own expenses out of their own pockets. It was indeed a bold and difficult endeavor. When fifty Betar sportsmen paraded with their flags at the opening ceremony in the city stadium, we sensed that a truly important event was under way, one that soon helped Betar in China to win for itself a place of recognition and respect.

Sports and physical fitness are the prerequisites of a healthy society. Zionists soon realized the importance of cultivating able-bodied women and men, who would one day stand at the forefront of the Jewish struggle for independence. As early as 1903, the first seeds of this new concept were sown by the educational codes of the Zionist Organization. Indeed, the Sixth Zionist Congress in Basel had announced the organization of the first Union of Jewish Gymnasts. Shortly thereafter, the Jewish sports organizations, Maccabi and Ha-poel,[1] began to create branches wherever sufficient numbers of Jewish youth warranted such groups. Finally, by 1932, in Tel Aviv, the first-ever Maccabiah took place, attracting Jewish athletes from many parts of the world. Although some athletes in China's Betar might have competed quite honorably with the very best in that

---

1. Actually Maccabi, a world union of Jewish athletic organizations, preceded the Zionist groups. Its first branches, founded in the 1890s, were located in Berlin, Constantinople, Bucharest and St. Petersburg. It, in effect, can be viewed as a precursor of Ha-poel, the Israeli Workers' sports organization, founded in 1924.

Maccabiah, they were too far removed from the Jewish centers of the world to be included in this historic event.

On the other hand, it is amazing to note that in 1934, the first sports meet between three different branches of Betar took place in the farthest corner of the Jewish diaspora. The first-ever Betariada was not held in Palestine or Latvia, Czechoslovakia or Hungary, not even in Poland, where there were tens of thousands of well-organized Betarim of all ages. Rather, that historic event took place in Tientsin, China, and included the Betar branches of Harbin, Tientsin and Shanghai.[1]

Although there were but a small number of participants from each city, the games and the track events stimulated great interest throughout the foreign population of Tientsin. Some of the events even challenged the records set by the previously held All-Manchurian Olympic Games. Notable among them were the records set by one Betari from Harbin, Danka Berkovitch, who covered the 400 meters in 52.2 seconds, and a Betari from Tientsin, Lelia Roisberg, who set a record of 6.35 meters in the broad jump.[2]

Besides their impressive showing in competitions for individual athletes, Betarim displayed both discipline and talent in such team competitions as ping-pong, volleyball and basketball. Immediately following the closing parade, Betarim organized into combined squads and challenged the top teams of Tientsin. The results were beyond all expectation. Betarim not only excelled in ping-pong, boxing and volleyball, but in selected light athletic events they also managed to defeat the Chinese champion team of Hobei Province with a score of 154 to 150. The results of this Betariada gave additional impetus to plans for participation in the next Maccabiah toward the end of the thirties.

However, these plans did not materialize – and not because Betarim of China were not ready to take their place among the Jewish youth of the

---

1. The second Betariada took place in Shanghai in 1947, and the third and final competition (organized by me as *netziv* Betar in Israel) in 1959.
2. Berkovitch later became a very successful agent of the Subaru automobile company in Israel.

world. Rather, events in the catastrophe of world Jewry unfolded with such speed that normal sports activities had to give way to more important and immediate considerations. Indeed, in those years the voice of Ze'ev Jabotinsky resounded, admonishing the Jews of the world, "Let us now engage in a new national sport – Aliyah bet." And so he called for an "illegal" immigration to Eretz Israel.[1]

The Betariada demonstrated more than athletic prowess. It demonstrated a collective pride in mounting a prestigious event that would enhance the overall reputation of Betar within the Jewish communities of China. The host branch in Tientsin gained impressively. The Betariada stimulated young people to pay more attention to sports, and with this additional interest, the standards and achievements of many Betarim began to reach international levels. Eventually, Betar in Shanghai and Tientsin excelled in team sports, while Betar in Harbin became known for achievements in light-athletics and track. It did not take long for Betar teams in all three cities to achieve admirable results and to gain a highly respectful place among all existing sports organizations in China.

While my own academic schedule, split as it was between Harbin and Shanghai, together with my relatively young age, deprived me of the opportunity of participating in this historical achievement of the Chinese Betar, nevertheless I eagerly followed the daily events of the Betariada as reported in Shanghai's Jewish press. And of course, I was as surprised as were all of the participants themselves, when the unassuming contingent of the Tientsin Betar had accumulated the largest number of points and emerged the winner!

The winter of 1934-1935 was to be my last year at the British school. Next year I would mark my Bar Mitzvah, a year of maturity and manhood,

---

1. "Aliyah bet" literally means "the other or the second immigration."

when my parents were making arrangements for me to spend that whole year of study at home, in Harbin.

Meanwhile, my Shanghai routine continued and my friendships matured and intensified. Although we were as disobedient as many boys of my age, we did manage to achieve a record of sorts: Not one of us was ever whipped by Headmaster Crow! Now, in the final months of school, I was anxious to maintain my record.

On weekends, we would gather in the morning for soccer goal-kicking in Boris Koffman's big yard, eat lunch and then go either to the race course or to the canidrome to watch our favorite soccer team. After the game, we would visit the YMCA cafeteria, located opposite the race course on Nanking Road, to devour chocolate cakes and ice cream sodas. We also had permission to visit one of the many luxurious movie theaters in Shanghai, where the latest Hollywood films premièred. Often, we would join the vast multitudes on the main streets of Shanghai and walk for hours on end, gawking at shops and restaurants that attested to the vast differences between the ancient and the modern, the West and the East. One could behold a small butcher displaying bits and pieces of liver and kidney, all solidly covered with a blanket of flies, cheek-by-jowl with a majestically constructed Wings-On Department Store offering anything from needles to grand pianos and electric trains! Prostitutes clinging to their sailors would amble down one side of the street, while parents with their children would enter well-known family restaurants on the other.

By the time I returned to Harbin, those scenes of Shanghai would often come to mind. And I began to contrast our Chinese hosts in Harbin with those in Shanghai. Gradually, I became aware of significant differences, not only in the Chinese population itself but also between its Western and Eastern conquerors. Finally, I could not help being struck by differences between Chinese and Japanese culture, society and classes.

Fate would assign me to a twenty-year stint in Tokyo and Taipei many years after the period covered by this book. The following chapter unabashedly draws upon this additional experience and benefits from the wisdom and maturity accumulated with age and through time.

Chapter 8

OUR CHINESE HOSTS

It is not my purpose to devote much space to an in-depth, comparative study of the attitudes and characteristics of the Chinese people. However, given the Jewish subculture of China and the impact of conquest on the Chinese, these become legitimate concerns.

China is a multinational country comprising many ethnic groups. Its native population speaks what have been called mutually unintelligible dialects that can be heard in the coastal belt of southern China from Shanghai to Canton. In reality, however, this linguistic diversification can be broken down into territorial subdivisions. As a result, several dozen mutually incomprehensible dialects can be heard in China. In later years, an effort at linguistic integration was made by the Communists in Peking and the Nationalists in Taipei, who declared the Mandarin dialect to be the official language of the nation.

If the Chinese people have been unable to master the existing dialects of their country, their reluctance perhaps can be ascribed to a lack of practical motivation, for linguistically, the Chinese are an extremely adept people. They also are hard-working, clever and patient. Without excessive pressure at home or in school, Chinese students have demonstrated outstanding scholastic achievement. In Japan, conversely, peer pressure and school discipline have engendered unbearable suffering and incidents of suicide.

Despite these differences, Chinese students seem to have a greater facility than do the Japanese for high scholastic achievement, especially in the linguistic area. Even today, when the Japanese have become a nation of tourists, they experience difficulty with foreign languages. The Chinese, however, have displayed a remarkable gift for picking up languages. In Harbin, for example, most Chinese citizens who associate with foreigners speak Russian; in Tientsin and Shanghai they speak English, in the French Concession they converse in French; and in Hongkew many have become fluent in Japanese.

Both the Chinese and the Japanese are extremely industrious peoples. Both have made tremendous strides in manufacturing, agriculture and corporate business. However, they have taken different approaches in their pursuit of these achievements. The Chinese are individualists, and much of their success should be attributed to personal ambition and determination. The Japanese, on the other hand, are better disciplined, and their successes stem from their ability to achieve a remarkable degree of collective effort and corporate loyalty.

Within China itself, one readily notices marked differences between the Chinese of Harbin and those of Shanghai. The Chinese in the North seem milder in character, less ambitious and obviously slower in the pursuit of life than their fellow citizens in the South. On the other hand, there are significantly fewer paupers and beggars in Harbin than in Shanghai. However, Shanghai has exceeded Harbin in the number of its millionaires and moderately wealthy merchants. In particular, the multitude of unfortunate beggars in Shanghai, alas, has become more of a nuisance than a subject of pity, although from time to time, lively humorous scenes have relieved the aggressive solicitation of alms. Such moments were prevalent immediately following the action in the Pacific Theater, when a nine-year-old child reportedly ran up to an American sailor or marine and complained in sing-song: "Help please! No mama, no papa, no whisky soda!" This was always worth a laugh and a coin or two. Harbin's beggars, by contrast, were modest and did not touch alcohol. But they were often challenged in their trade by some Russian beggars who were driven to the streets by the bottle.

Foreigners might attribute Shanghai's beggar population to the greed and envy that has been stimulated by the abundance of every imaginable luxury in the city. To me, there is a much more prosaic explanation. Let us not forget that until the early 1940s, Shanghai was very much under the control of the French and the British. Regrettably, neither administration made effective efforts to combat disease and poverty, thus alleviating the hardships of the starving native population. The Japanese, on the other hand, exercised complete control over Harbin as they did over all of Manchuria. They had an inborn sense of cleanliness and hygiene, offset by an acquired brutality and an ethos that sanctioned the unrestrained use of force, that kept Harbin's beggars under control.

The local populations of Harbin and Shanghai differ not only in patterns of destitution. The Chinese businessmen south of Harbin have been sophisticated in international trade, and as a result the commercial class in Shanghai and Tientsin has been more exposed to the ways of Western businessmen than have their compatriots in Harbin.

For almost twenty years, my father worked as manager for the Anglo-Chinese Trading Company in Harbin. Owned by the Kabalkin family, the firm had its own factory for oil. In addition, it exported soy beans and imported various commodities for the domestic market. After visiting Shanghai, I began to notice that all of the employees working in my father's office were foreigners, with the exception of the boy who served tea and ran errands. On further examination, I discovered that this phenomenon was less an exception than a rule throughout the foreign establishments in the city.

Even in banks under foreign flags, hardly a Chinese employee was to be found. On rare occasions, Chinese businessmen worked as *compradores* bringing buyers and sellers together and pocketing an agreed commission for the effort.

In Tientsin and Shanghai, the native population enjoyed a much larger share of the international business and participated more intimately within the many foreign enterprises there than they did in Harbin. In fact, Chinese businessmen were in pivotal positions in many banks, offices and export-import establishments. Many Chinese dealers in antiques, jewelry, carpets and furs were to be found in these cities as well. This involvement almost doubled when the Japanese took over the concessions and some of the business establishments belonging to the "enemy nationals." Evidently the Japanese placed more trust in transacting business with co-Orientals; or they simply found the local population easier to control.

In many ways, life in all of the large cities of China was almost identical. Foreigners enjoyed both their freedom and their exclusive situation. Little in the way of commercial and social contact existed between foreigners and the Chinese.

We foreigners in China tended to take the Chinese population for granted. We would often cross or walk down boulevards such as Chinese Street in Harbin or Bubbling Well Road in Shanghai without seeing or taking note of a single Chinese. The streets were crowded with people, but more likely than not, foreigners primarily would notice other foreigners in these crowds. This was the general malady of the so-called "white" population of China and, to our discredit, we, the Jews of the Far East, were no less afflicted by it than others.

♣ ♣ ♣

The quality of food in different cities where we lived also became a topic of lively discussion. We would argue mercilessly which city provided the best food or the most diversified cuisine. Our disputes focussed on different Chinese dishes and restaurants ranging from Harbin's *harchevka* (coolie kitchen) to Shanghai's renowned "Sun-Ya" restaurant with its unbeatable sweet-and-sour pork, fried pigeons and monkey brains! Even today at our reunions in one Chinese restaurant or another, we continue an argument that has been ongoing now for more than fifty years!

It was really quite difficult to determine which Chinese dish was better and whether better Chinese food was served in Harbin, Tientsin or Shanghai. In fact, those who have recently lived in or visited Hong Kong or Taipei say that the cuisine there excels any of the restaurants in Mainland China.

However, when the conversation turns to Russian food in China, Harbin remains in a class of its own! There is no doubt that one could get excellent food and visit exquisite Russian restaurants in both Tientsin and Shanghai, but Harbin qualified as the very best. The town was famous for its *bubliki* (bagels), *pel'meny* (dumplings), pheasant and *kurapatki* (baby chicks). As a real treat in winter, youngsters would buy *tanhula* (tiny red apples glazed with sugar and frozen by the sub-zero weather of Harbin). These *tanhulas* were carried by native salesmen, with ten or twelve of them pierced *shashlik*-like on a stick which, in turn, was stuck into a *shaco* container attached to a long stick, carried over the shoulder of the salesmen who walked around the streets proudly shouting: "*tanhula!*"

During the summer months, the very same entrepreneurs would offer ice cream cones on every corner of the city. In 1936 you could buy a large cone for a penny, and its creamy texture and taste would have been a source of envy to any American ice cream company today.

Delicacies, such as red and black caviar, both seedy and pressed, were also readily available and sold by weight from huge aluminum buckets. It was normal for the head of a family, after a day's work at the office, to buy a bit of this and a bit of that and bring it home for dinner. This, of course, could only be done when guests were not expected. In China, and especially in the big cities, entertainment at home meant home cooking! When one had guests for dinner, the Chinese cook would go out of his way to show off his extraordinary culinary skills. In the art of decorating dishes or serving plates of food, no one has yet outclassed the Chinese chef who could simulate a whole fish with a fisherman catching it from atop a rock out of a variety of vegetables!

To be sure, Shanghai and Tientsin excel in the art of regional cuisine, but somehow, the food of Harbin always seemed memorable to me. Even in Harbin, however, there were many who deigned to taste such delicacies, among them members of the Jewish community who observed dietary laws. But it can be said with certainty and gratification that in all these years, no Jew went hungry in China. The Jewish communities and their institutions made certain that this would not happen.

My personal recollection of cultural differences between the two cities in China leads me to thoughts about the two empires, British and Japanese, which played havoc with China's pride, honor and dignity.

The Japanese were a brutal and arrogant conqueror of China. At the slightest provocation, and often without any, they would inflict painful punishments on the local citizenry. Some citizens received a degrading slap on the face, while others were sentenced to imprisonment, and capital punishment. The British were not a benevolent occupation power either. Condescending to the natives whom they viewed as a subordinate and inferior species, the British attempted to keep the "locals" in their place by treating them as second-rate citizens. However, it must be noted that in China the British did not resort to the same brutal force as they did in Palestine, only five years later. The Chinese despised both occupants of their soil and were anxious to see the day when they would become, once again, masters of their own fate and possessors of their own land.

By the spring of 1935, I was preparing to leave Shanghai, perhaps for the last time. My parents decided to keep me in Harbin during the year of my Bar Mitzvah. They planned to provide me with a home tutor, in addition to Reb Slutzker, who was to teach me to read Hebrew and to chant the portion of the Torah for which I would be responsible during the Bar Mitzvah ceremony.

As difficult as it was to part with my friends, I was extremely happy to be returning home to Harbin. My high expectations were realized. The year from 1935 to 1936 was the last one in which I would enjoy a life of freedom from cares and responsibilities – a year of happy and adventurous living. It was also a good year for the Jewish community of Harbin, as it continued to advance in its progress toward attaining the highest possible standards of communal existence, spiritually, culturally and educationally. It, indeed, would be a year to remember.

Chapter 9

1936. BACK TO HARBIN

Soon after my arrival from Shanghai, I became a full-fledged member of Betar and acquired its smart brown uniform, its scout rope and its menorah or seven-branched candlestick emblem that is worn on one's shirt or on the left lapel of one's suit. Together with my friends, I spent much time on the sports grounds, where my athletic abilities came to the attention of Moshe (Mosia) Halperin, chairman of Betar's sports committee, and Werner Tukiyanin, Betar's coach.

Mosia was the backbone of all athletic developments in the organization. Tall and handsome with a Clark Gable mustache, short curly hair, a pleasantly sly smile and a powerful voice (he usually doubled as the sergeant major on all important public parades), throughout my years of maturity in Harbin, he became not only my mentor and friend but my coach and role model as well.[1]

On weekends, my parents would accompany me to the Sungari River, which we would row across, and enjoy a full day on the Sungari's sandy beaches, swim in Harbin's unique pools and eat *piroshki* (Russian pies) and ice cream at the "Stop Signal" restaurant. Only later would I discover

---

1. Today, after a career in the Israeli Ministry of Finance, Mosia Halperin is enjoying his retirement in Jerusalem, where he and his wife reside.

that Harbin's pools were as unique as the city itself. In fact, they were not swimming pools at all, but rather little wooden constructions with smooth floors and wire sides that permitted the Sungari waters to float in and out freely, depending on the direction of the wind. The side roof covered a narrow walkway around the pool, with small dressing rooms on one side. The men's and women's pools were set side by side and swimming often was in the nude.

In the evening we would usually get together with friends, either in one of our apartments or on a designated street corner for games, gossip or long walks, occasionally stopping at a kiosk for *baklava* and a glass of *booza* (a beverage made from a fermented yeast base).

Once a week, we attended Betar meetings led by Abrasha Milichiker, a young man in his late twenties. He conducted the meetings skillfully, often inviting guest speakers to address us on different subjects of current interest. At times, the elder Betarim would also speak or participate in the ensuing discussion. Usually, such meetings were preceded by a short drill and concluded with the singing of the Betar and national anthems.

The walls of the Betar Club displayed both our biweekly *Ha-degel* (*The Flag*) and our weekly "wall newspaper." Many talented journalists of today received their early training with these publications.[1] Often, the Betar would parade with other local organizations. Hundreds of Jews would gather along the sidewalks of Chinese Street and wildly cheer the smartly marching rows of Betarim led by national banners and their own marching band.

As winter approached, the center of activity would move to the two existing skating rinks in the city. One was located in the Apothecary Street Stadium and the other on Commercial Street, at the site of our summer sports grounds. The cold winter kept the ice hard, and the Chinese staff smoothed it by watering it each day. If you were looking for someone in Harbin in winter, you could easily find him or her at one of

1. Today Boris Mirkin is the editor of the *Bulletin*, a monthly publication of émigrés from China. Mirkin is also the secretary of the Igud Yotsei Sin, whose office is located in Tel Aviv.

these rinks. Young and old gravitated to them for romance, sports, fun and fresh air. No one came just to skate. At the Apothecary Street skating rink, a glassed-in wooden hut had been built for the orchestra. The band was composed of White Russian musicians whose repertoire was limited to waltzes and polkas. At the Commercial Street rink, the music was provided by a blaring loudspeaker wired to a gramophone. Some skaters performed their dance routines with brilliance and grace, while others preferred to be pushed on sled-chairs by the Chinese staff. However, when a pretty girl was discovered in one of these chairs, there were enough volunteers among the skaters to deprive the staff of their job!

In skating, as was true of other sporting activities, our Jewish athletes participated successfully. Many won cups and medals for short-distance races and marathons. Above all else, skating entertained and benefited all. And when the cold wind of Harbin's winter would chill right through you on the skating rink, you could skate indoors for shelter. Indoors there was an array of small stoves to warm your body, while the expert hands of the Chinese personnel massaged your frozen feet back to life! For some of us, skating became a daily winter routine, while for others it was a weekly one, but few rejected its pleasures.

At times I would finish my homework early and stroll to the playground of my younger days. Since it was located in the same compound as the Commercial School, every forty-five minutes during class break, the place would stream with students: boys in black trousers, matching shirts with gold buttons and a gold-buckled belt; girls in green dresses with delicately laced white blouses. I loved to watch the girls giggle and flirt on the benches. But even more than that, I enjoyed following the big boys as they played the popular local outdoor game called "*nagruzhaiu osla*" ("loading the donkey"). In this game, literally, a player bends over while the others jump over his back as they place a light object (belt, hat, handkerchief, etc.) on the "donkey's" back. The "loading" continues, until the jumper upsets the "donkey's" accumulated load. When this happens, the "loaded donkey" is released, while the clumsy jumper becomes "it." And so on.

Perhaps our most memorable winter experience was again connected with the Sungari River. Often my friends would play hooky from classes and meet me on the playground. Together we would proceed to the frozen Sungari and cross it by means of the *tolkai-tolkai*, the unique Sungari sled-chairs. Once on the other side, the goal was always the "Stop Signal" restaurant and our favorite dish – *pel'meny*.

In 1936 Harbin's cultural life seemed to be peaking, with theaters performing Russian and Jewish plays and featuring many artists who had made their reputations in Europe and Russia. 1936 also was a boom year for the Harbin Jewish community as a whole. The 1935 Hanukah Ball and the 1936 Purim Ball were the best in Harbin's Jewish history. Made possible by a combined effort of the Jewish community, the Hanukah Ball became popular for its amateur thespian presentations, and these, in turn, helped to make the evening a financial success. The Purim Ball became a traditional Betar event. Much preparation went into it, and it featured the dazzling performance of the Betar gymnasts who thrilled the audience with daring and beautiful pyramids.

Business was good, and therefore not only the wealthy few, but even the middle-class members of the community, showed exemplary generosity and a charitable frame of mind. This generosity spread to both the Shanghai and Tientsin Jewish communities, culminating in a one-hundred-thousand dollar contribution to Israel's underground organization (the Irgun), in the spring of 1948.

After Purim, my family completed the preparations for my Bar Mitzvah. Some say that one's Bar Mitzvah marks his entry into the Jewish family as an equal, conscientious member. I disagree. Many boys pass their thirteenth birthdays, chant their prayers flawlessly and remain as remote from Judaism as from the Jewish people as a whole.

I am convinced that every young person steps across the threshold of Judaism, mentally and emotionally, only after he or she has been called a "*zhidovskaya morda*" ("an ugly Jew"). If this is true, then most of my compatriots and contemporaries became conscious Jews BEFORE they reached their thirteenth birthday. I know I did.

Harbin's main synagogue dominates Artillery Street and the architecture of the immediate area. Built early in the century, this serene, imposing edifice was an exquisite example of the synagogue architecture of the Far East. Here, Jews would assemble during the season of the High Holy Days to be treated to the unforgettable voice of its Cantor and the high voices of its boys' choir. Regular prayer meetings or memorial services would also be held in the main synagogue, often with Betar and (at a later time) Maccabi guards of honor standing with their respective banners on the *bimah* (the synagogue dais where the reading desk is placed). Since Harbin (as well as Tientsin and Shanghai) Jewry abided by Orthodox ritual, the women were seated in the balcony, while the men prayed on the main floor. Children would wander in and out constantly, but would spend most of their time in the adjacent garden next to the main entrance of the synagogue on Artillery Street.

In later years, with the growth of the community, it became necessary to build another synagogue, farther down Artillery Street and almost across from the Deshëvaia Stolovaia (the Welfare Dining-room) and the Betar Club. Eventually, the new synagogue shared in hosting special events and had little difficulty in filling up all its available seats during the High Holy Days.

My Bar Mitzvah was celebrated in the old synagogue. My many relatives and friends, together with members of both the summer camp and Betar, well filled the synagogue. Among those present were Dr. Kaufman, his wife and younger son Teddy, as well as Abrasha Milichiker, the leader of Betar.[1] I ascended the *bimah* in my Betar uniform,

---

1. Leaders of the Harbin Betar included: Leva Piastunovitch (1929-1933); Alexander Gurvitch

prompting Milichiker to comment in his address that followed the official prayers: "May you always wear this uniform with pride and honor on all of the important occasions of your life." In my response I solemnly promised "to wear my Betar uniform on every significant occasion of my life, including my wedding." As it turned out, I kept this promise and, as leader of the Shanghai Betar, was married in my full Betar uniform some twelve years later!

Shortly after my Bar Mitzvah, I began to show interest in the Russian theater and, whenever possible, I would see any play showing in town. At times I went with my parents, occasionally with my friends and often (during daytime performances) I would even go by myself. The theater gradually stimulated me to read plays as well as novels. This was the period of my life when I began to develop an interest in books and devoured works on Zionism, Jewish history by Dubnow and Jabotinsky's *Samson and Delilah, The Five, A Word About the Brigade* and many of his memorable feuilletons and articles.

The world was changing before my eyes. Only now did I become aware of our people's struggle for the mere right to exist. The passivity of the Jews in the world seemed to me both infuriating and suicidal. Hitler's aggressiveness toward the Jews of Germany cried out for revenge rather than tolerance and appeasement.

The decision of the British Peel Commission to limit Jewish immigration to Palestine was, to my mind, an obvious act of treason and deceit. Jabotinsky's call for action, illegal immigration, resistance and revolt was the only voice of sanity, the only voice I wanted to hear. It was at this time, in addition to my realization of belonging, that I began to feel

---

(1933-1934); I. Molchanovsky (1934); Mordechai Lesk (1935); Abram Milichiker (1936-1937); and Sema Klein (1938-1945).

the urge to do something about my feelings. This in turn triggered a whole chain of reactions. Above all else, it was a death knell to individualism!

From here on, I would consider many of my actions less egoistically and more collectively, from the broader aspect of their merit for my organization, my people or my cause. Even in the 100-meter dash, I no longer cared about personal achievement alone – rather, I wanted to win for Betar and for the Jewish community.

In Harbin we were not blind to the unfolding tragedy of European Jewry and, with each passing day, I sensed that the Jewish people stood alone. 1936 marked the creation of the modern Jewish refugee on a scale hitherto unknown. It was still possible, even easy, for Jews to escape from the clutches of Nazism. But it was already difficult to find a willing host, a pair of open arms – an invitation to a safe haven!

Throughout the tragic period leading to the Holocaust, and many years afterward, Europe's politicians sought solutions of zero-inconvenience. For example, the plan for settling Madagascar with Jews from Germany was stubbornly promoted by many capitals of Europe. Even President Roosevelt became engrossed with the plan in its initial stages before he was convinced of its disgraceful motive and political futility.

On the other hand, not a single country offered Jews temporary refuge, and no one was prepared to begin serious discussions toward implementing the basic clauses of the Balfour Declaration, that had been universally accepted by the League of Nations. Only two-and-a-half years later, President Roosevelt himself became infamous as he turned away boatloads of refugees from Nazi Germany who were destined to die in the ovens of Treblinka, Auschwitz and Dachau.

Although no details were available, the threatening clouds that were lowering over European Jewry were clearly visible from as far away as Harbin, Tientsin and Shanghai. The only weapon at our disposal was an internationally declared boycott of German goods. This may not have solved any problems, but it made us feel a part of our people, in tune with their suffering, their prayers and their hopes.

As we listened to the public lectures of Abram Kaufman, to those of visiting Zionists and of our own senior members of the Betar organization, events became ever closer and clearer. And the best eye-openers, presenting prognosis and in-depth analysis of the situation, were to be found in *Ha-degel* and the timely and explosive articles of Ze'ev Jabotinsky. It is from him that we first heard the prophetic call urging Jews to "liquidate the *galut* (the diaspora) before it liquidates you." Of course, reverberations of the "official Zionist leadership's" denunciation of Jabotinsky also reached us. But it became clear to me who was right and who was wrong, and from those days onward, Jabotinsky became my mentor, and his political philosophy became mine. And so it was with hundreds of other members of Betar in Harbin, Tientsin and Shanghai.

The summer of 1936 arrived. After studying all available possibilities, my parents, and Joe Wainer's mother, decided to send us to the Pyongyang School in Korea, not far from the Chinese border.[1] A Protestant missionary school with exceptionally high standards, it catered primarily to the missionary families living in Korea's gold-mining territory.

Once again I was devastated by my parents' decision and even the fact that my friend Joe would be joining me did not help improve my state of mind. Now, it was not only a matter of being separated from my family, it was also a matter of being miles away from Betar and its social and cultural activities.

My one consolation was that Pyongyang was only fifteen hours away from Harbin by train, and so I would be able to return home during both winter and summer vacations. Thus, two Jewish boys became freshmen

---

1. Pyongyang today is the capital of North Korea.

at a Protestant missionary school in Korea. It is strange to realize that when you are old, your life is decided by destiny, but that when you're young, it is charted by your parents. At least mine was.

Otherwise, I would not have been standing on the platform of the Harbin Railway Station, once again bidding farewell to my family and friends.

Chapter 10

THE AMERICAN SCHOOL AT PYONGYANG

Sunk in thought, Joe and I peered desperately through the window of our sleeping car. My father's parting words as he embraced me emotionally on a Harbin station platform still rung in my ears: *"Bud' chelovekom, synochka!"* ("Be a man, my son!"). Tears welled up in my eyes as the train taking Joe and me to a new school, a new environment, a new life, sped along. Little did I know that for the next few years, until our final graduation, we would be destined to live as strangers among strangers.

As we approached the border town of Antung, I realized how expansive and open were the adjoining farmlands of Korea and China. There was no natural border in sight – no rivers, no lakes, no mountains. We passed one continuous stretch of land, now under the firm domination of the Japanese occupation forces. Nevertheless, rigid control operated on both sides of the border. Police traveled incognito, while customs inspectors checked the documents and baggage of every passenger on the train. On one side, the officials wore Chinese (Manchukuo) uniforms, while on the other, but one hundred meters away, they were dressed in uniforms with Korean insignias. Of course everyone knew from whom each took his orders. Yet, not a single Japanese official could be seen for miles.

Conquered by one and the same nation, the two peoples separated by this border at the Antung crossing were vastly different. The Koreans, who had experienced many years of occupational influence, displayed that domination in their arrogance, rudeness and aggressiveness. By contrast, the officials on the Chinese side were usually mild-mannered and kinder. My initial observation was later reinforced tragically, when we learned of the various Japanese prisons and dungeons of torture during the Pacific War, that had been operated primarily by Korean experts.

After a short night's sleep, we reached Pyongyang. From the station, we traveled to the outskirts of the city where the American School is located just on the other side of the railway tracks. Set off from the compound by a short wooden fence, it consisted of seven complexes that included dormitories, classrooms, chapel, auditorium, dining room, kitchen and large fields for all sorts of sports activities such as tennis, soccer, track and even ice hockey.

To me, the place looked as if it were at the edge of nowhere. In fact, most of the teachers lived in homes on the outskirts of the campus, while the only Korean teacher, Mr. Sam Wang, lived in the city with his family.

The educational standards at the Pyongyang School were slightly higher than were those of American public schools at that time. The academic curriculum, comprising literature, history, math, biology and foreign languages, was supplemented by an offering of electives, including typing, sewing and art. I was convinced at the time, and remain convinced even today, that the educational level of the Commercial School in Harbin was significantly higher than that of my new school in Korea. While we were studying basic geometry, my Harbin peers were immersed in physics. On the other hand, the Pyongyang School was rich in extracurricular activities – something for which Russian schools had neither the time nor the interest.[1]

Through its diversified sports program that offered basketball, soccer and other team sports, as well as individual competitive athletics, I won

---

1. This observation concerns only the Russian schools in Harbin.

the respect of my peers. Joe was especially good at both tennis and badminton. These skills helped us to mix with the other students, all of whom shared an intimately common background, since they came from the same missions representing a similar way of life, goals and ambitions. While Joe and I were treated well, it became clear to both of us that our acceptance was superficial and that however much we might be a part of team sports, we would forever remain strangers. Frankly, I shared their sentiment and accepted our estrangement in good grace.

During my years in Pyongyang, I often played volleyball, basketball and soccer for the school and ran the 100-meter dash with no serious opposition. As seniors, Joe and I represented our school in tennis doubles.

In my senior year, as well, two other opportunities came my way that enabled me to enhance my popularity among students and teachers alike. The first came on the day of the final exams in public speaking. For each topic, a participant had to draw lots placed in a glass container. Once unfolding the paper lot and reading the designated subject, a student had to step up to the podium immediately and address an auditorium that was filled to capacity with students and teachers. As luck would have it, my totally uninspiring subject was, "The Theme of My Speech." Approaching the podium, I thought of an idea and, in excited tones, immediately proceeded to tell my audience of the daydreams and nightmares that had preceded this test. Once gaining their complete attention and interest, I described the agony of the moment of appearing before my peers, "only to realize that the speech I was about to make lacked a subject!" This "speech without a subject" won me the first prize and the highest grade for the exam. It also earned me a few additional admirers.

Another opportunity for personal recognition came during my performance of *The Valiant* in a senior class presentation. The very next day, the principal of the school called me to his office and very earnestly suggested that I take up acting as a life career.

Each of the above successes assured me of a following among the younger students of the school. Yet after four long years of study, play, laughter and heartache, we were about to part, just as we had met – as total strangers!

It is difficult to determine what causes estrangement among young people. Is it rooted in different social frameworks, or does it derive from irreconcilable ethnic backgrounds and religious beliefs? I am convinced that for my non-Jewish acquaintances, religion was an alienating factor. On my part, I sensed a lack of common interests that make friendships barren of content and true meaning. Without a doubt, there are exceptions to this generalization, exceptions that are both rare and precious. Lucky are those who experience them.

During our sophomore year, we were joined by another boy from Harbin, whom neither Joe nor I previously knew. If I am not mistaken, he was of Russo-Tartar origin and, like the majority of the students and teachers, he belonged to the Protestant church. Although we never succeeded in developing a very close friendship, both of us found more in common with this newcomer than we did with other students. No doubt, the fact that he spoke Russian as we did, had something to do with it – but only to a degree. George Rogoff made an effort to demonstrate to us that he was a man of experience, which he was more than willing to share with us both. And so it came about that George convinced us one evening to make a daring escape from the dormitory into town to discover firsthand the mysteries of night life in the city. Under George's tutelage I made my first visit to the honky-tonk district of Pyongyang, where bars and brothels plying alcohol and sex seemed to blend into one establishment.

If anything was to be learned from this experience, it was the simple fact that a brothel is not the best place for a boy to part with his virginity. Outwardly clean, with portraits of girls hanging on the walls of the entrance hall, these houses would welcome the client with a hot cup of green tea and a wet face-towel. He, in this case I, then was invited to select a girl from the pictures on the wall, to pay his fee and proceed upstairs to an assigned room. Tiny, it was furnished with only a bed on which sat the lady of your choice – except that she did not even remotely resemble the picture you had selected.

Within minutes I found myself on the street sharing my experience with my brothel-mates. They told me that there were cheaper though much filthier places of prostitution in all of the cities of China. But at least I had the good fortune and better sense to avoid them.

Perhaps the most interesting episode of our days of boarding school in Korea dates back to 1938, when we were still sophomores and had just returned from the winter holidays at home in Harbin. The New Year season in Harbin had always been especially festive. Parties, plays, *tolkai-tolkai* rides and the skating rink on Commercial Street – all had to fit into our daily itinerary. Now, homesick for our family, friends and the frivolities of a holiday that had just ended, Joe and I were blue, and we wallowed unconscionably in self-pity.

One day during a break in our classes, a teacher came up to Joe and told him that he would like to talk to us both after school hours. He suggested that we meet in our dorm at four o'clock in the afternoon. What was this all about, we wondered? Long before the appointed hour of our meeting, we were both sitting on our cots in our small dorm. The cots took up the length of two adjacent walls; Joe's faced our joint closet and a drawer cabinet. Mine was opposite the window wall and a small writing desk. There was little else in the room and yet there was hardly place enough for the two of us to move around freely. But larger dormitories accommodated four and even six students – so we did not complain as we enjoyed our privacy.

A mild knock on the door jolted us from our idleness and puzzlement, and we admitted our visitor. A smiling Mr. Luke greeted us cheerfully. Neatly dressed in beige socks, a dark brown sport shirt and a warm beige angora sweater, he wore Hush Puppies, which were a novelty then in our part of the world. Despite his tall thin figure and pale complexion, Mr. Luke nevertheless cut a handsome figure. Seating himself on Joe's bed, he gestured to us to join him on either side. After an awkward pause, Mr. Luke stood up, turned toward both of us and said softly, "Why don't we kneel in prayer?" With those words, he went down on his knees, covering his face with both hands. Since kneeling is not part of the Jewish ritual, my discomfort turned into panic, as Joe followed our visitor's genuflections. In a moment, I stepped forward and gently cupped Joe's elbow as I helped him back toward the bed. We were sitting on our respective beds now, as Mr. Luke offered a short prayer in which he asked for forgiveness of our sin and for the Almighty's help to open our eyes to Jesus.

Sitting down again on Joe's bed, Mr. Luke asked us if we did not really want to become "a part of everything and everybody." He told us that in accepting Jesus, we would no longer feel estranged. He also mentioned "the beauty of life in Jesus," who would care for us in this world and the world to come.

I knew that Joe preferred that I speak on behalf of us both, so I timidly attempted to postpone the decision. I told our uninvited guest that the matters he raised were so serious that we must have time to think about them and to discuss them between ourselves. I stated that we would meet with him once again – in due time. To my surprise, Mr. Luke accepted my suggestion without an argument and said that he would look forward to that next meeting. With these words, he left as abruptly as he had entered and with the same confidence and self-assurance.

Joe seemed even more concerned than I, and turned to me for comfort. Suddenly, an idea struck me, and I immediately tested it on my friend: "Let's write a long letter home and complain bitterly that we are being subjected to intolerable pressures to convert and that, therefore, our further stay here is completely out of the question!" Joe looked at me as if I were losing my mind, so I continued to brainstorm: "Your mother and my parents," I told him, "will certainly not stand in our way of resisting conversion and, therefore, they are bound to insist on our immediate return to Harbin. The idea of returning back to our families, friends, ice skating and parties stimulated Joe's imagination as well. He added, however, "but, we must make it clear that we simply cannot bear to stay here any longer and are waiting for permission and tickets to leave."

Once dispatching our SOS, we found it easier to endure our life at Pyongyang. Instead of sharing in the post-vacation blues of other students, we now enthusiastically anticipated a sudden encore to our just completed holiday! We did not have to wait long. Four days later a telegram addressed to both of us arrived. It was brief, but to the point: "Yana's [my Russian nickname] mother arriving tomorrow seven a.m. Please meet her." The telegram was signed by Sima Wainer (Joe's mother) and my parents.

The next morning, the temperature had fallen to several degrees below zero. Unless you were in perpetual motion, your feet would freeze and thus cause excruciating pain when they began to thaw out at home. The station was almost deserted, as the seven a.m. express from Harbin and Antung ground to a halt under the glass-roofed steel canopy that covered the entire platform.

Joe espied my mother before I did and gestured for me to follow him toward the middle carriage some forty meters away from the main gate. Petite but beautiful, mother was always elegantly attired. Now she was bundled in a mink coat with a matching fur hat and boots lined with strips of mink, framing the middle laces. She carried only a small suitcase in one hand and a matching vanity case in the other. Within moments I was filling mother in on everything we had written about the "conversion incident," as it became known among the three of us for many years to come. In my briefing, I crudely emphasized our determination to go back home at once.

Mother suggested that as soon as she unpacked, she would ride to school together with us and immediately meet with Mr. Reiner, the principal. The twenty-minute ride back to school took us through the center of the city where stores were just beginning to open their doors and streets were slowly swelling with pedestrians. Gradually, we climbed the steep road to our campus, nestled between snow-covered mountains and several frozen lakes. By the time the taxi stopped at the entrance to the main building where the principal's office was located, Mr. Reiner, braving the weather, coatless and hatless, had stepped onto the porch. He greeted mother and hurriedly escorted her in, gesturing to Joe and me to go to our classroom.

Although it seemed like an eternity, it was actually not more than an hour before mother and Mr. Reiner appeared in our class smiling and chatting most amicably. Right then and there, I knew that we were not going back to Harbin with mother! On our principal's suggestion, we were given the rest of the day off from classes "to show Mrs. Liberman the school grounds and your rooms and to keep her company until she leaves tonight."

The moment we were alone with her, Joe asked my mother: "What did he tell you?" Mother went into a detailed recital of her meeting with Mr. Reiner. Neither the principal nor the official faculty knew anything about Mr. Luke's visit to our room, she said. Mr. Luke had had no business to do so and would be strictly reprimanded. We were both very welcome to stay on and there was to be no pressure whatsoever on the subject of conversion.

The day ended with a sumptuous dinner at mother's hotel, after which we all went back to the station so that mother would catch the late evening train on its way from Seoul to Antung and Harbin. It was nice to see mother again, but extremely depressing to return to the school compound. With this episode, our attempt to return home for an unscheduled vacation concluded. In fact, we remained behind until the day of our graduation. Indeed, we both felt that survival, from now on, would not be unbearable.

It must be said that the episode did nothing to affect our final years of schooling adversely. On the contrary, as we were about to graduate in the summer of 1940, we took with us pleasant memories, leaving behind our own good wishes to all. Although we were the only two Jewish boys in a school of missionary teachers and students, we were, at all times, treated with tolerance, respect and benign acceptance. Perhaps this experience helped to strengthen my own Jewishness and enhance my ethnic pride and love of my people.

Aside from all of these events, our school life progressed normally. But twice a year, toward June and December, life became full of expectation, as we eagerly counted the days and hours until our return to Harbin.

Vacations were long – a month in winter and three months in summer! – enough time to pursue my two favorite endeavors – the stage and the stadium. These would figure importantly in the final chapter of my memorable youth in Harbin!

Chapter 11

1936-1939. SAFE IN HARBIN

The summer of 1936, the first of my vacations from the Pyongyang School in Korea, I spent back home in Harbin. Remote as we were from Berlin and the site of the World Olympic Games, we all, nonetheless, felt the fateful repercussions of that summer.

Our conversations seemed to be incessant about the sudden transformation ongoing in Germany, as the German government tried to fabricate an atmosphere of tranquillity and tolerance toward the world at large, including Jews. All anti-Semitic discrimination signs were removed from the streets, youths appeared in Alpine climbing gear rather than in Nazi uniforms and belligerent slogans and threatening marches gave way to sports events, choirs and picnics. The only instances of intolerance and hatred appeared in the press description of Hitler's reaction when Jesse Owens, the Black American track star, walked away with medals for the 100-meter dash, broad jump and 4x100 meter relay! But the very best part of the Olympics, for all of us in faraway China, was to see newsreels showing the daring Black athlete who refused to shake Hitler's outstretched hand during the awarding of medals.

Jewry found solace in such fêtes, not realizing the horrors that lay in store. As the clouds of doom were about to descend on Europe, we were living in a milieu in which it was not only possible to continue our former way of life, but also to improve the standard of living from one year to another. Despite our relative comfort and security, it was necessary for our community leadership in general to maintain relations with the occupying power.

Thus it came about that the local Jewish community leadership decided to make a show of its strength and solidarity, illustrating to the outside world the organizational power and the representative strength of Far Eastern Jewry. This ethos motivated the founding of the National Council of Far Eastern Jews that organized three conferences in 1937, 1938 and 1939 respectively.

The 1937 Conference, held in the main auditorium of the Harbin Commercial Club, proved especially festive. The stage was decorated with the flags of Japan and Manchukuo, and the Jewish blue-and-white banner. All the representatives of Far Eastern Jewry, the Japanese Military Command and the local government were seated at a long table across the stage. In addition to Rabbi Kiseleff and Dr. Kaufman, Professor Katzuji, the Hebrew-speaking Japanese expert on Jewish affairs, joined an array of distinguished personalities.

Among the topics of the day as proposed by the Japanese authorities was that of Jewish support of and gratitude to the Imperial Forces of Japan. It was left for Dr. Kaufman, our internationally renowned orator, to address this subject in his main speech that evening. Kaufman spoke for two hours and when Professor Katzuji was asked to comment on the speech, he remarked: "Dr. Kaufman spoke so much, so well, and yet ... managed to say – nothing!" Since avoiding an impression that the Jewish community supported Japan's aggression was precisely the goal of the speaker, it proved once again Dr. Kaufman's talent and courage.

In the summer of 1938, after my close brush with an attempt to convert me to Protestantism, the joys of my long city vacation seemed boundless. Russian light opera and theater and the repertory theater of the Commercial Club provided endless summer evenings of delight. The *ploshchadka*, during a spell of rain, was also entering its eighth year of operation.

One day, I convinced my friend, Ura Horosh, to steal into the rehearsal hall, where the famous actor-director Tomsky was rehearsing his troupe in Gorky's three-act drama, *The Mother*, the title role of which was played by Davidova. Both Ura and I loved the theater. We enjoyed the smell, the antique odor of the old costumes rescued from the Russian Revolution of 1917, the silent excitement of row upon row of empty seats, the flood-lit stage with its freshly painted set! Yes, indeed, we were truly theater bugs.

After spending hours at the rehearsal, we decided to approach Davidova in hopes that we could then brag about it to all our friends and playmates. Meekly, we approached the stage. Ura looked at me for guidance. I introduced us as her ardent fans. She thanked us and asked what she could do for us. Ura asked if we might bring our friends from the *ploshchadka* to her performance. As if speaking another's words, I blurted out, "We would like to stage our own plays. We need your help. Would you direct us?"

So the Young Dramatic Troupe was born. Within days we had enough members to embark on our first season. Since producing plays requires not only actors but also stagehands, people in charge of costumes, lighting, curtains, etc., there were plenty of jobs to go around. Mme Davidova was not only a superb actress, she was a patient director, a talented instructor and a wonderful human being. Under her coaching, we spent months preparing each new play in our repertoire.

The Commercial Club, which housed the playground, the school and the theater, gave us permission to rehearse and to use its stage for our performances. We soon became a recognized, functioning organization within the cultural life of the community.

During the four years of its existence, the Young Dramatic Troupe staged *The Gypsies* by Russia's greatest nineteenth-century poet, Alexander Pushkin; *Les Romantiques* [*The Romantics*] by the incomparable French playwright, Edmond Rostand; *The Bear* and *The Proposal* by the most beloved of all Russian playwrights, Anton Chekhov; and *Hear, Oh Israel!* by the Russian émigré author, Osip Dymov, who later became famous in New York for his play, *The Bronx Express*. The permanent members of our organization included: Etia Trotskaya, Nadie Ginzburg (Bladevitch), Ura Horosh, Lucy Bogdanovskaya, Nana Nemirovsky, Grisha Smushkovitch, Boris Zuboreff and myself. Of course there were many others whose names, regretfully, I cannot recall. Lucy Bogdanovskaya (now Halperin) appeared several times with Tomsky in his professional theater in Sydney, Australia.

After our first performance, the entire troupe celebrated at a banquet. The toastmaster was my friend Teddy, son of our community leader and Mrs. Adelle Kaufman. With much hesitation and reluctance, Teddy agreed to make the first speech of his life (perhaps excluding the obligatory one at his Bar Mitzvah).[1]

At the conclusion of the war, all members of the Young Dramatic Troupe went to Israel, Australia and the United States of America. Ura Horosh, in his desperate effort to pursue his career on the stage, decided to live in the Soviet Union, where he became a well-known director of stage and of State television dramatic productions. He was one of the very few who went to Russia from China, making a name for himself, while building up his career in an endeavor he loved so very much. Ura, alas, died of cancer at a relatively young age. Weeks before his death, he composed a poem in Russian, in which he parts lovingly with his boon companions.

---

1. Today, Teddy is the spokesman for all of the Jewish immigrants from China.

The next production of the Young Dramatic Troupe was mounted in the winter of 1939, when I again returned for my New Year vacation. Everyone had been working hard on the two short Chekhov plays and I was to be given special coaching by Davidova when I arrived home. The performances went well and received favorable comment in the local press. It was in one of those plays that Ura was given a part of a very old man. His portrayal was so brilliant that there was no doubt in anyone's mind that he was destined for a sensational career on the stage.

That winter I also participated in Betar activities, attending with great interest some open meetings of the senior Betarim at which current affairs and political matters were analyzed and discussed.

Isolated in Korea as I was from Jewish life, I was but superficially aware of the deteriorating situation of European Jewry. Several months after *Kristallnacht* in Germany, Jews everywhere in the world registered the shock.[1] China's Jews were no exception. Meetings were held, protests were openly voiced, so that once again, crisis and alarm brought Jews together. Very little, however, could be done in China or from China, except to embrace and protect every Jewish man, woman or child with the painfully outstretched hands of the Jewish communities of the Far East. Miraculously refugees began to arrive first by twos or by fours, then in groups and finally in boatloads. They landed mainly on the shores of Shanghai, with a few reaching Tientsin and even Harbin!

Not all came by sea. Several hundred refugees fleeing Hitler managed to reach Manchuria via the Chinese Eastern Railway. Some continued southward, while a few remained behind. I recall the tearful scenes of Jews meeting Jews by the Harbin Railway, with food, drink, a word of encouragement and an embrace. For those remaining in Harbin, life was kind: They were absorbed into the community, given jobs and befriended. Among them were the athlete, Helga Stein, the dear friend of my parents,

---

1. *Kristallnacht*, the night of the broken glass, took place 9 November 1938. The Nazis broke storefront windows and destroyed property belonging to Jews throughout Germany and Austria.

Ernest Cohn, and two famous doctors, Helborn and Velli, who became important assets to the Jewish hospital, Mishmeres Holim.

In the meantime, the community life of Jewish Harbin vitally strengthened its internal bonds. At last the second floor of the Jewish Hospital could be completed, a five-year dream of my father, who was its initiator and long-term president.

The revival of the Maccabi Sports Organization also contributed to our cohesion. Although inspired by Dr. Kaufman, Maccabi had been led by Sima Leimanstein, president of its executive council that included many prominent members of the community. Young men and women, who did not share Betar's ideology, and yet were eager to participate in Jewish sports activities, flocked to the Maccabi, which shared its sports grounds with Betar during the summer.

Despite my loyalty to Betar, I had many friends in Maccabi and often attended their various functions and tournaments. Although they were still a relatively new element in the Harbin sports scene, Maccabi soon established its reputation because of a few outstanding athletes in their midst. How pleasing it was to see Nina Moiseeva and Leza Taller carry the Maccabi flag during the opening parade. Leza subsequently won the shot-put, javelin and discus events, establishing new records for Harbin. I was soon to find out that Leza came to Maccabi from Betar, where he had begun his brilliant athletic career. Regretfully, after the war in the Pacific Theater, he, too, decided to live in the Soviet Union. Nina, on the other hand, left for the United States, where, I understand, she won a large state lottery.

During the late 1930s, several prominent Jewish families moved to Tientsin and Shanghai, where the Japanese influence was nonexistent and foreigners, under the illusion of protection from the international concessions and settlements, seemed to live happily and calmly.

In Harbin itself, Jews were not too concerned with the political flirtation between the Axis powers and Japan. The population was comfortable and safe, life was full of promise and the community as a whole was respected, and strong. From all appearances – China remained a safe haven for its well-entrenched Jewish communities.

In Europe and the United States of America, however, Jewish leaders despaired of all hope of reversing the process of annihilation under way throughout Europe. Efforts were made to rescue the Jews of Germany and Austria. Jabotinsky sounded the alarm for the very existence of Jewry of Poland, Hungary, Romania and Bulgaria. He called for world pressure on Britain, to convince the leaders of Great Britain to open the gates of Palestine to the Jewish masses fleeing Hitler. All appeals fell on a mute, indifferent world.

No restrictions were lifted. The shores of America remained closed to the few vessels carrying those able to escape from Germany, while the British, in violation of the terms of the Palestine Mandate, refused to admit Jewish refugees from Europe to a Palestine that had been legally designated a Jewish national home.

The fact that the perpetrators of this crime of omission did not subsequently sit on the benches of the accused at the World Crimes Tribunal at Nuremberg, does not relieve them of the enormous responsibility they bear before the Jewish people specifically and the civilized world as a whole. This, then, was the general atmosphere in Europe surrounding the question of Jewish survival.

The only ray of hope shone from the Far East!

Thanks to the heroic efforts of Japanese Consul General Sempo Sugihara in Kovno, Lithuania, who issued transit visas through Japan to every Jew who asked for them, thousands of refugees from Germany, Austria and Poland were able to escape the Holocaust and to survive in Shanghai.

As early as 1938, Nazi intentions to destroy the Jewish population in Europe were as clear as their overall plan to dominate that continent. Despite Chamberlain's efforts to achieve "peace in our time," the desperate plight of Jewry in both Germany and what used to be Austria became hideously clear in the orations and actions of the Nazi rulers of Germany.

With the death of General Pilsudski in Poland, a dormant but ever-present anti-Semitism became a direct threat to the survival of Poland's four million Jews. It became evident to all leaders in Europe, as well as to the Roosevelt administration, that unless Jews were resettled immediately, their fate would be sealed. Public opinion in the United States stimulated Roosevelt to create the appearance of doing something about the situation. So it came about that with his prodding, an international conference was called at the French resort of Evian-les-Bains in 1938. Only a few countries sent representatives to this conference that was to be chaired by Lord Winterton, "a notorious opponent of Zionism and a friend of the Arabs," in the opinion of Arthur Ruppin, head of the Jewish Agency representatives to this conference. The Evian conference clearly determined that unless the Jews of Germany were immediately resettled, they would all perish. Despite this realization, not a single state was willing to open its gates to humanitarian rescue. In the United States both the President and the Congress supported the existing emigration quotas at all costs, while in Britain immigration to Palestine was restricted not by law but by decree, not by legislation, but by an act of administrative policy. "Could the British government be persuaded to liberalize the policy that had become so severe since the outbreak of the Arab rebellion in 1936?" asked one writer. "The prospects were not good."[1]

Wave after wave of our brethren began their miraculous escape to the hospitable shores of China. During this turbulent period, I left for my final year of studies in Korea.

---

1. R. Sanders, *Shores of Refuge* (New York: Henry Holt, 1988), p. 439.

Chapter 12

1940. TRAGEDY AND TRIUMPH

Days before my departure from Harbin in September 1939, England and France declared war on the Axis powers. Vyacheslav Molotov, in the name of the "high morality" of Communism, signed a non-aggression pact with Ribbentrop, while the United States and Japan were as yet at peace.

Suddenly, in the spring of 1940, the *"drôle de guerre"* ("the phony war") became a war of "blitzkriegs," and France discovered that it lacked the stamina for serious combat. But after Chamberlain folded his umbrella of appeasement and Churchill became Prime Minister of England, the world had an opportunity to marvel at British bravery and self-sacrifice and to forgive its blatant opportunism and moral shortcomings.

Jews mollified their attitudes to Britain as well. Even the Hebrew underground, the Irgun, declared a temporary truce and instructed its soldiers in Palestine to join British forces and to fight as one against the enemy. As a direct result of this decision, Irgun's commander at the time, David Raziel, was killed performing an extremely dangerous mission in Iraq. And only after the establishment of the Jewish state were his remains brought to Israel for a reburial, attended by thousands of grateful citizens.

By May 1940, the time of the Dunkirk debâcle, I already had received a diploma and was crossing the Antung border for the last time.[1] In the summer of 1940, it was still possible to communicate with the outside world from any one of the three Jewish centers in China. We in Harbin followed enthusiastically the travels of Vladimir (Ze'ev) Jabotinsky, who was now in the United States promoting the idea of a Jewish army that would participate under its own colors in the war against Fascism.

During the summer months of 1940, Jabotinsky visited the Betar summer camp on the outskirts of New York City. Before a welcoming parade, prepared by the leadership, Jabotinsky requested a few minutes of rest – a most unusual request for this tireless man, who throughout his entire life dedicated to Zionism and the Jewish people, had known no rest.

Among those who accompanied Jabotinsky to the camp were two persons familiar to all of us in China. The first was Arosha Hanin, who had gone to the United States from Harbin many years earlier to become *netziv* of the American Betar; the second was Alexander Yakovlevitch Gurvitch, the "father" of Betar in Harbin, who had been managing his family business in New York. Neither of them could possibly have known that within minutes they would witness the greatest loss that Betar would suffer when Jabotinsky died of a sudden heart attack while resting on a cot at a Betar summer camp.

We all grieved at the loss of our beloved leader. Betarim sat *shiva*[2] in their clubs, homes, jails and in concentration camps in every city where Jews were residing at the time. Separated from their families, starved and exploited, in Germany, Austria and Poland, Betarim joined the rest of the Movement in saying Kaddish, the prayer for the dead, for the Bar Kochba of our times.[3]

In Harbin, the news of Jabotinsky's death came in the early afternoon. By evening, all Betarim aged seventeen and over were in uniform going

1. Antung, a city of Liaoning Province, is located on the border of China and North Korea.
2. According to this Jewish custom, mourners sit on the floor or on a pillow from sunrise to sunset for seven days after the burial of the dead.
3. Bar Kochba, leader of the Jewish rebellion against the Romans in 132 C.E., at Betar, Palestine.

out in pairs, to all places of entertainment where members of the Jewish community could possibly be found, to inform their fellow Jews of Jabotinsky's death. Boris Tzvibel was assigned together with me to the yacht club area on the city side of the harbor. Many years later, I recall reminiscing with Boris in Sydney about our experiences that night and how very proud we were about our Jewish community of Harbin.

On the thirtieth day after Jabotinsky's passing, he was honored in a memorial service in the old synagogue. Congregants filled the building to capacity, spilling out into the garden and part of Artillery Street. Betar's honor-guard presented colors on the elevated platform as our Cantor Zlatkin chanted the memorial prayer. Toward the end of the services, an unknown, short, neatly-dressed young man walked up to the podium to speak. He was Ya'acov Gotlieb, a Betari from Poland who was presently living in Dairen and who volunteered to give the eulogy. Ya'acov was an accomplished Yiddish orator and his speech created such a deep impression on all present that it became the subject of conversation long after the ceremony.

After these emotional days, once again life began to settle into a routine. For me, the remainder of the summer would be devoted to training for the city championship and to rehearsing for the main part in *The Black Monk*, chosen by our Young Dramatic Troupe for its summer presentation. By July, Ura, Nadia, several others and I were preparing for opening night. Remarkably, my most vivid memories of those days were not our efforts to make this play a great success, nor the acclamations that followed our first performance. Suprisingly, I recall the variety of novel reactions that Nadia stirred within me, as I most of all watched her and acted my part as her lover. Nadia was in her junior year at the Commercial High School. More often than not she wore a green uniform with a white laced blouse, long stockings and brown leather shoes. Her short brown hair was parted in the middle, her eyes were huge black pools and the upper part of her cheek bore a tiny birthmark that added to the overall beauty of her face. Whenever we were together, I experienced a strange discomfort. I felt an undeniable desire to be as close to her as I would dare.

When we got to the kissing scene in the play, I was certain that I was in love.

Nadia was the daughter of a beautiful woman in Harbin, and a father who had died of cholera when she was only five years of age. Her mother remarried and became the wife of a prominent Jewish lawyer who adopted Nadia and loved her as his very own. However, neither Nadia nor her mother ever converted to Judaism and, consequently, the Ginzburg family did not become a part of the Jewish community in Harbin.

During this period of my first real infatuation with a person of the opposite sex, I became obsessed with dressing up, combing my hair and spending more time by the mirror than I would have dreamed of only a few weeks earlier. I hoped that my ears protruded less obviously, but it seemed to me that my nose came to occupy more of my face than I would have preferred. My hair was unruly at the back but combed easily on the sides, and gentle waves created a well-groomed appearance. I was reasonably tall and slim, and from my participation in sports, my legs were strong and well-muscled.

Several girls my age paid more than passing attention to me, older ones, too, embarrassed me with compliments and obvious hints. However, Nadia belonged to neither category. Alas, soon after the last curtain call on the final evening of our performance, we said our good-byes, little suspecting that we would meet again during my visit to Australia, some thirty-five years later!

In August, the sports association of Harbin announced the date for its annual championship. Winners for each event in all categories were presented with wide, silk ribbons, gold-plated medals and diplomas. But the biggest prize in these tournaments was prestige! And the greatest prestige went to the organization that came up with winners in the most coveted event – the men's and women's 100-meter dash.

Triumph had not eluded Betar, for our sprinter Iza Kondakova had won the women's championship in 1939, and in 1940 she competed again with more confidence. For me to win seemed almost impossible, since my competitor was Vasili Protasoff, the former champion, from the White Russian Sports Organization. His supporters included "the musketeers," the Rodzaevsky Fascist youth, and all the slime of the town who were prepared to make sure that no more Jews emerged as champions. Neither Protasoff nor his immediate sports organization had much to do with this anti-Semitic approach to sports, but neither were they in a position to control the anti-Jewish element of the city.

Werner Ivanovich Tukiyanin had been training the top stars of Harbin's Betar for as many years as I can remember. A theoretician, and no longer an athlete, he knew every muscle of the body and how to train an athlete to achieve maximum results in the long and short distance runs, the broad and high jumps, the javelin, discus and shot-put. It was an honor to be selected by him for guidance and training, one tempered by strenuous exercise and a daily spartan regime.

During my final summer weeks in Harbin, I was coached by Werner, as was Iza Kondakova, the established champion sprinter of Harbin. The Russians outnumbered the Jews in Harbin by three to one, and were extremely proud of their predominance in sports. They were not prepared to jeopardize their standing more than they had to. Once giving up all hope of recapturing the title in the women's division, they were not about to risk losing their hold on the championship in the men's category, especially not to a Jew!

Since my reputation and 11.3-second record presented a serious challenge to Protasoff, I was often approached on the street by various unknowns who threatened to break my legs if I appeared at the championship competitions, to be held at the Apothecary Street stadium that coming Sunday. Ignoring the threats, I shared my natural anxiety with my coach Tukiyanin and my friend, the chairman of Betar's sports committee, Mosia Halperin. My two buddies, Boris Tzvibel and Boris Goltzman, were also aware of the entire matter right from the first threat, and refused to let me walk alone on the streets until the competition was over.

On Saturday evening, as I was preparing my spike shoes and my sports uniform with its huge *menorah* emblem across the chest, I was interrupted by a sound of broken glass. Only moments later did I notice that next to my shattered window lay a heavy stone on the floor with a note glued to it. The note read: "Do not run tomorrow – or else..." As I was about to dispose of the note and the stone, my mother rushed into the room screaming, "Oh God!"

It did not take Mother long to realize what had happened and, worse yet, what was about to happen if I participated in the scheduled championship events. She was not aware of the date or the event, but the consequences of my participation were clear to her from the stone and the note. Without a moment's hesitation, she picked up my running shoes and my sports uniform from the desk, rushed out of the room and threw them all into the burning kitchen stove, while I stood helplessly looking on.

I spent the rest of the evening on the phone with the two Borises and with Mosia. They suggested that I stay home until the next morning and that I then come quickly outside – but only after making certain that all three of them were there, standing by my window. Mosia told me that another set of spike shoes and a new uniform would be waiting for me at the stadium. Out-maneuvering Mother with a skein of lies, I left home the next morning accompanied by my friends and closely followed by several roughnecks from the Russian opposition.

Had I been walking alone, there is little doubt that the hooligans walking behind would have made sure that the threatening note that flew through my window would be followed by an assault on my person. However, seeing the four of us, they chose to avoid a direct confrontation. And so I reached the dressing room of the stadium, changed into my sports uniform and tried on the spikes Mosia had borrowed from someone in Betar. Everything fit to perfection!

As I walked out to the track, I glanced at the spectators' gallery and could not believe my eyes: It seemed that everyone in the Jewish community knew of the event and had come to cheer for their own. No longer was this a competition between two sportsmen – it was now a contest between "them" and "us," between White Russians and Jews! In the meantime, as expected, Iza easily defeated her competition and walked away, crowned "Champion of Harbin in the Women's Category."

Now it was my turn. To this very day I remember every moment of the race, every meter covered, every breath taken from beginning to end. I recall clearly the sound of the starting gun and that I had managed to take off in a perfect start, placing myself a shoulder in front of Protasoff. With every muscle, with every step, I was determined to keep this advantage till the end of the race. I could hear Protasoff's heavy breathing on my right, as he seemed to be catching up to me with his long and smooth strides. Imagining him slightly in front of me, I decided to pump my hands, to stretch my steps, to give every last iota of my strength to synchronizing my movements, in order to accelerate my speed.

Only moments after crossing the finish line did I notice a sea of white and blue flags waving in my direction from the stands. Not all were proper Jewish flags, for some spectators had brought white and blue paper, while others simply waved the white-and-blue Betar t-shirts that had been brought in quantity by the sports committee. Many viewers stood on their seats, shouting my name and that of Betar. Only then was I certain that I had won the race – and with it the city championship. My official time in the race was 11.1 seconds, a new record for the city and for Betar as well.

Within hours, my parents knew of my victory. Although my father was proud and excited, my mother was less forgiving and continued to oppose my strenuous participation in sports. She was convinced that it was not good for my heart – a claim that she reiterated. For the next twelve years or so, I did not heed her protestations but tried to sustain my achievement in track.

Due to the war and travel restrictions incumbent upon it, my parents' dream of an American university education for their son could not materialize. Instead, I was sent to Tokyo, to spend one year preparing to enter the famous Waseda University of Japan. I was convinced that my parents' decision, though well meaning, was mistaken, but I had to concede to their wishes.

As in previous years, my mother accompanied me to Tokyo and made all the necessary arrangements concerning my studies, room and board. Once again we left Harbin by train for Dairen, from there to sail on a Nippon Kissen Kaisha (NKK) passenger vessel, directly to Yokohoma.

The entire journey took three-and-a-half days, every hour of which (except for sleep, meals and an occasional chat with my mother) I spent recollecting the myriad of episodes involving laughter and tears, frustrations and achievements, failure and success that I was leaving behind. Above all, I thought of my friends.

At the time I did not suspect that I was leaving Harbin – "my Harbin" – for the last time.

TOKYO INTERMEZZO

Upon disembarking, we proceeded at once to the earthquake-proof Imperial Hotel in Tokyo. Mother immediately secured my room and board and signed me up for the preparatory class for the University. I accompanied mother in her search for a place among Tokyo's Russian families. Eventually, we found a middle-aged widow and her mother who owned a house in the Meguro section of Tokyo. Another Jewish student from Harbin also rented a room from these women. Onia Paley, three years my junior, later became a dear friend.[1] Onia's father and uncle were well-known furriers from Harbin who only recently had moved to Shanghai. Onia was studying at a Japanese school in Tokyo and wore the school uniform and skinhead haircut. To the amazement of all around him, he spoke fluent Japanese.

Two of my Harbin friends as well were living and studying in Tokyo. One was Mara Raznoschikoff and the other was Misha Kogan, a student at Waseda University. Like Onia, he, too, was amazingly fluent in Japanese.[2]

---

1. Onia died at a relatively young age in Israel, leaving behind a lovely wife and three children.
2. After spending the war years in Tientsin, Misha married Asia Kachanovskaya and went to Japan. There he operated the largest nickelodeon business in the country. He died of a heart attack in Los Angeles.

I was less successful in enrolling in the Waseda preparatory class. Evidently, even here only students with a minimal knowledge of the Japanese language were accepted and, at the time, I had no fluency whatsoever in Japanese. Lacking an alternative and on Dad's insistence by cable, I hired a private tutor in Japanese and a second tutor in accounting. As a result, when Mother returned to Harbin, I discovered that I had much time to spare and began spending it in ping-pong parlors and, occasionally, at the newly constructed Tokyo stadium. I relished my visits to this magnificent arena that had been built for the Tokyo Olympic Games of 1940 and then cancelled on account of the war.[1] Here I watched the best Japanese runners and was invited to take a few starts with them and even to participate in an occasional 100-meter sprint. My walks also took me to the Dai-Ichi Hotel, which had been specially built to accommodate the Olympiad athletes and amateur sportsmen. It was now open to the public and gradually seemed to be losing its initial glamour. Both my accounting and Japanese studies progressed slowly and not too impressively. However, my ping-pong game was improving rapidly and well.

By this time, another friend from Harbin arrived, who also intended to matriculate at the Waseda preparatory class. He, too, had to settle for lessons in the room he rented from another Russian family but a few blocks away. Pavel Smushkovitch and I became close friends, and spent most of each day together.[2]

Pavel and I concentrated on ping-pong during the day and mixed movies and nightlife, depending on our budget, during the evening hours. At the beginning of each month, when spending money would arrive from our parents in Harbin, we would be able to indulge in the luxuries of Tokyo's bachelor delights. In fact, we found the most sought-after

---

1. The 1964 Olympic Games were held in Japan, and to my great pleasure, I was able to attend all of them.
2. Pavel competed successfully in Harbin's yacht races on behalf of the "Maccabi." He later joined us in Israel, where, until he left for Rome, we continued our friendship. There he established a prosperous jewelry business.

"paradise" in Yokohama, a thirty-minute train ride away. There, we discovered a picturesque site atop a small mountain looking down on the Sea of Japan where, hidden away by trees and gardens, stretched a street of two-story exclusive hotels. These provided Japan's high budget entertainment, including ballroom dancing to a live band, food, girls and plush bedrooms. Some forty *yen* or ten dollars, almost half of our monthly budget, and about ten times more than a regular brothel fee for the night in downtown Tokyo, brought us this indulgence.

Prior to and after the war, Yokohama was known for its excellent port facilities. In fact, Pavel and I had occasion to visit Yokohama once, during the day. Philip (Lipka) Materman, a mutual friend in Harbin, telegraphed us advising us that he was en route to America and that his ship would be docking at Yokohama for almost twenty-four hours. We met Phil by the docks as his ship approached the pier and took him off for a pleasant evening in the city, which included a dinner, a nightclub with dancing girls and a show. Late in the evening when we all returned to the ship, Phil suggested that we join him in his cabin for the night, since it had three empty beds and the ship was not scheduled to sail until nine o'clock the next morning.[1]

There was no difficulty getting on board the vessel, as the guards did not suspect well-dressed Caucasians to be either saboteurs or stowaways. We slept well and decided to stretch our luck a bit further, by going into the dining room together with Phil and sitting down at the table for breakfast. I was halfway into my second boiled egg when the dining room captain approached us, and asked rather aggressively whether we were passengers. Upon learning that we were visitors, he pointed to the door and said resolutely: "O-U-T!" So we parted with Lipka and returned to Tokyo.

---

1. Phil Materman emigrated to the United States, where he worked for the federal government. He married Mira Liberman (no relation to me) from Harbin and the couple settled in Hawaii, where they lived with their children for almost two decades. They presently reside in San Diego, California.

We deserved to be expelled. Although we were living in a country that was inevitably approaching the abyss of war, I never experienced any personal animosity directed toward me during all my time in Tokyo. Neither did we encounter an excess of friendliness or fraternization. Anti-Allies propaganda was heavy, and suspicion of foreigners was evident everywhere. Both Pavel and I concluded at the time that no Japanese girl would dare be seen in the company of a stranger, and we decided not to put this conclusion to the test. Besides, Yokohama was an attractive substitute.

At this time, thousands of refugees escaping the Nazi domination of Europe were reaching the shores of Kobe, a nine-hour trip from Tokyo by train.

The year was 1940. European Jewry was on the verge of mass annihilation. Polish Jews and Jews from Austria and Germany were bombarding consulates for visas, visas of any kind: entrance visas, tourist visas, transit visas. None were made available. In Lithuania, a Dutch Jew discovered that, based on a stamp in his passport, which read, "No entrance visa required for Curaçao," he was able to get a transit visa from the consul of Japan. The word spread like wildfire among the large refugee community of Kovno, Lithuania. Eventually thousands received their papers and were in a position to book passage on boats that would leave Europe and reach the shores of Kobe, Japan. These escapes were dependent on the goodwill, courage and humanity of the Dutch Consul, Jan Swartendyk, and the Japanese Consul, Sempo Sugihara. These two Righteous Gentiles not only saved thousands of lives, but also established an important historical fact, demonstrating that even in the midst of a degenerated human society, a spirit of decency and beauty can shine.

The transit visas were good for twenty-one days. What then?

A tiny group of Jews from Harbin and Shanghai who had established businesses in Japan created a small Jewish community, with its own little club, a place for services and a dining room for meetings and meals. The group took upon itself the mammoth task of assisting their brethren in time of need. In constant communication with the larger communities in Harbin, Tientsin and Shanghai, Kobe Jewry organized themselves under the name of "JEWCOM" and began welcoming and assisting the thousands of Jewish refugees reaching their shores. The president of the community, the businessman, Anatoli Ponve (Poniversky), in later years became the organizer and leader of the post-war Tokyo Jewish community and subsequently helped to establish and finance the World Center for Jewish Immigrants from China, in Tel Aviv, Israel. Working closely with Anatoli Ponve were Leo Hanin,[1] Mosia Moiseev, Sania Triguboff and others. An old friend of Harbin's Jewish community, Professor Katzuji, rendered practical assistance, facilitated introductions and helped with governmental and international relations and translations.

Funds were immediately made available, committees formed, authorities approached, dormitories rented, kosher kitchens organized, guarantees for extensions of stay issued and arrangements made for most of the refugees to proceed to Shanghai. There, under difficult conditions, they nevertheless lived and survived the war!

Several members of the Polish Betar were able to receive their visas for Palestine from Kobe. Only one of these visas was genuine – the rest were fake. While I shall never know precisely all who were involved in this operation, I do know one of them – my very dear friend from the Harbin Betar, Milia (Michael) Ionis.[2] His job was to sign the completed documents

---

1. Leo was a prominent leader of Betar in Shanghai. He subsequently became a successful businessman, and then he retired in Los Angeles. Leo and Riva Hanin were an active couple, and their family was very popular in China.
2. Milia (Michael) Ionis first joined Betar in Harbin. After spending a year in Kobe signing visas for the British Consul, he proceeded to Shanghai where he became head of the Shanghai Betar. He married Risa Tukachinskaya, cousin of Yosef Tekoa, Ambassador to the United Nations. They emigrated to Israel in 1949. Milia and his family subsequently went to Tokyo and finally to the United States, where he succumbed to cancer.

on behalf of the British Consul General in Kobe. As a result, more than a dozen Betarim from Kobe landed in Palestine and eventually participated in Israel's War of Liberation.

It was now the end of spring, 1941. Japanese-American negotiations were intensely bitter and the world was bracing itself for an all-out conflagration. Hitler succeeded in winning several decisive victories in Europe, while the Dunkirk rescue of the British defenders of France was the only "success" the Allies could register. The entire Jewish population of Europe was helplessly locked up in prisons, concentration camps and ghettos. Escape or rescue was now next to impossible. England and, to some degree, the United States shared the moral responsibility for the destiny of European Jewry. They had discouraged all rescue attempts and had kept their gates solidly shut to the desperate escapees. As for England, her leaders found this to be an appropriate time to exercise a total ban on the issuance of certificates for Palestine. Only the Japanese military government, a government accused (rightly) of war crimes and atrocities, together with the hospitable people of China, opened the doors of Shanghai to some 40,000 Jews of Europe. There they were able to survive the war and to start life anew after the defeat of the Axis and the resolution of hostilities in the Pacific Theater.

In the meantime, my parents had moved to Shanghai, where my father opened his office in partnership with a Japanese businessman whom he had known from Harbin. They at first imported piece-goods from Japan and subsequently exported scrap iron to Tokyo. Dad gave up the office and (in partnership with Zukerman of Harbin) opened the "Mars Café." There, on the Nanking Road at the corner of Szezhuan Road, in the commercial center of town, his business flourished from its opening day.

In Shanghai, my parents rented an apartment on Avenue Foche, in the French concession, where I arrived in early June to begin another epoch of my life – in Shanghai!

~~PREPARATORY COMMISSION~~
INTERNATIONAL REFUGEE ORGANIZATION — FAR EAST
106 WHANGPOO ROAD, SHANGHAI

联合國國際難民組織遠東局

上海黄浦路一〇六號

IN REPLY REFER TO:

TEL. 40070

DATE 21 December 1948

TO WHOM IT MAY CONCERN

Please be informed that Mr. Jacob Lieberman has been appointed as Group Leader of the s/s "Wooster Victory" by the Far East Office of the Palestine Bureau and that this appointment is recognized by this office.

It will be appreciated if all authorities concerned will give facilities and assistance in the performance of his duties and permit him to land while ship is in port.

G. Findlay Andrew,
Director,
Shanghai Branch Office,
IRO Shanghai Branch
Office

Mr. J. Lieberman
is permitted to
go on shore

COMANDANTE

COMMISSARIO

Letter appointing the author as leader of the first transport, carrying 893 Jewish immigrants from China to Israel, 1948.

Page 4 THE JEWISH HERALD Friday, January 21, 1949

892 Chinese Jews Dock At Cape En Route To Israel; Betar Leader In Charge

ON Monday morning, the S.S. Wooster Victory docked at Cape Town with 892 Jewish refugees from Shanghai who are on their way to Israel. Mr. Harry Hurwitz, General Secretary of the South African U.Z.R.P., was among those who had the privilege of greeting the refugees. Below is his report on the arrival of the ship.

It was an unforgettable day for South African, and particularly for Cape Town, Jewry. It was a memorable day for 892 Jews from China travelling to Israel. And it was a wonderful and inspiring day for the Movement of Jabotinsky.

From the moment the s.s. Wooster Victory entered Cape Town Harbour against the background of the majestic Table Mountain to the moment it steamed out accompanied by the strains of Hatikvah and the Betar Anthem, a powerful wave of Jewish national solidarity swept right through the Cape Peninsula and even further afield. And it seemed that the new spirit of Jewish independence and dignity knew no barriers and limitations.

Scenes unknown in the life of South African Jewry were witnessed during the 12 hours' visit of the s.s. Wooster Victory, as the immigrants on board and thousands of their South African brethren on the dockside merged to create an amazing picture of happiness and comradeship.

There is no doubt that the smartly-uniformed members of the Chinese Betar stole the limelight and gave the whole event a real national colour, as they personified to the vast crowd of onlookers Jabotinsky's challenge which was prominently displayed on the decks. "Let us liquidate the Galuth before the Galuth liquidates us." It is in this spirit that the whole transport has to be viewed.

The whole Cape Town Press, both English and Afrikaans, made special reference to "this group of young Jews belonging to the Berit Trumpeldor (Revisionist Youth), who introduced a spirit of Jewish patriotism with their songs, flags and banners. In reply to a question about their plans when they arrive in Israel, these Betarim answered, 'Every one of us who can hold a weapon will don the uniform of the Israeli Army, for we are determined to participate in the struggle for the Hebrew State both in war and in peace.'"

SPONTANEOUS CHEERING

The central figure on the ship was Qatzin Jacob Liberman, a member of the Netzivut of the Chinese Betar, who, as a representative of the Palestine Office of Shanghai, was Commander of the transport with Mr. Toni Gaberman, another member of the Chinese Betar Netzivut, as Second-in-Command. A great deal of the organisation and efficiency on board the vessel is undoubtedly due to these very fine leaders. That the passengers and Cape Town Jewry recognised this fact was proved by the spontaneous cheering for Mr. Liberman when the boat was about to leave Cape Town.

None of the passengers was permitted to leave the vessel and only a few South African Jews who had relatives on board and a few representatives of various organisations were permitted to board it. Towards the late afternoon, however, arrangements were made for Jacob Liberman to disembark and it was my great pleasure to take him to the Betar Hall in Cape Town and show him a little of the city.

Mr. H. Hurwitz, general secretary of the South African Revisionist Party, with a group of Betarim on board the Wooster Victory. On his left is Mr. Liberman and on his right Mr. Gaberman, second in command on the ship. Behind Mr. Hurwitz is Jacob Shtedfman, head of the Tientsin Betar who left China shortly before the fall of that city.

These two babies were born on board. The group on the right represents three generations of Revisionists. The baby's father is a member of the Betar and his grandfather (in the centre) is Mr. Zimmerman, chairman of the Revisionist Party in Hongkong.

EVACUATION OF CHINESE JEWRY

The s.s. Wooster Victory is a 7,600-ton vessel built in 1945, and is under charter for the International Relief Organisation which, in consultation with the American Government, the Government of Israel, and the Jewish Agency, is arranging for the evacuation of Chinese Jewry. The ship which was expected to arrive in Cape Town on Sunday, was delayed 24 hours. Hundreds of people had assembled at the docks in Cape Town on Sunday, not knowing of the delay.

By 6 o'clock on Monday morning Cape Town Jews began to stream into the dock area again. Among the first to arrive were families who were looking forward to the prospect of meeting relatives whom they had not seen for many years.

The most interesting case, which was given considerable prominence in the Cape Town Press, was that of Mrs. Stackel, who was eagerly waiting to meet her brother, Mr. Traub, whom she had not seen for 40 years. When the boat eventually arrived, however, she learned to her bitter disappointment that Mr. Traub was ill in the ship's hospital and she was among the first people to go on board.

At approximately 7 a.m. the words "Wooster Victory" could clearly be seen on a ship escorted by Cape Town tugs, and the onlookers at the dockside made a scramble for positions near the waterfront to give them a first glimpse of the incoming vessel. A great cheer went up from the crowd and the passengers on board when the ship was close enough for the people to be seen.

HAPPY FACES

The moment the Wooster Victory docked the passengers began shouting the names of friends and relatives whom they were hoping to meet in Cape Town, and the people at the dockside in turn began enquiring whether any of the passengers came from particular towns in Europe. It was as if thousands of members of a family were reunited. On board could be seen men and women, old and young, and many happy faces of little children. Cape Town Jews in their enthusiasm began throwing on board whatever they could lay their hands on. The morning papers were in particular demand, for the immigrants had been at sea for 24 days and were eager for news about Israel and China, where many had left their families. And they were thrilled to receive the latest issue of the "Jewish Herald," which was specially flown down over the week-end. One Cape Town Jew, in his eagerness, removed his jacket and threw it aboard.

But soon the large crowd was attracted to the centre of the vessel, where a group of young, happy-looking Jews, wearing the uniforms and badges of the Betar were singing some of the songs which Jabotinsky had written for the new generation of Jews. Press photographers and newspapermen recorded this inspiring scene and paid tribute to the national spirit which was now predominant.

As I approached these Betarim and informed them that I had come to greet them on behalf of the Revisionist Party and Betar of South Africa, their faces lit up as if they had met with some long-lost brothers, and I was at once introduced to Jacob Liberman, the Commander of the transport, who in spite of his youth, lent a colour of dignity and efficiency to the vessel.

Although there were many complaints and protestations against the refusal to allow visitors on board, in retrospect it is proved that the Italian captain of the s.s. Wooster Victory made a wise decision, for it would have been impossible to control the thousands of Jews from Cape Town and all corners of the Peninsula who wished to make contact with their brethren from the Far East.

Only 20 people were permitted on board, and I was fortunate to be among them and to have the opportunity of spending an unbelievable day with the passengers generally and with the Revisionists and Betarim in particular.

As I entered the ship I was immediately surrounded by the Betarim, who remained at my side throughout the day and made certain that I did not miss anything of interest or importance on board the vessel and the stories which were told by the passengers.

We were taken to the lounge of the ship for an official reception by the committee headed by Jacob Liberman and Mr. Gaberman. Sitting among Mr. Gitlin, the veteran South African Zionist, Rabbi Abrahams, Mr. Zvi Infeld, of the Zionist Federation, with whom I had travelled down to Cape Town, and Mr. Max Spitz, Chairman of the S.A. Jewish Appeal, Qatzin Jacob Liberman told the story of the "Wooster Victory."

Mr. Liberman explained that there were less than 10,000 Jews left in China, and that it had been decided to liquidate the Chinese Diaspora. The Government of China was giving its favourable support in the scheme and with the good office of I.R.O. and the Government of Israel, who had instructed its representatives to grant a visa to every Jew in China desirous of settling in Israel, it was possible that the plan would soon materialise.

The "Wooster Victory," the first of the two I.R.O. transports, has an Italian crew of 130, carries the Panama flag, and had 890 passengers on board when they left Shanghai. Since then one of the older passengers passed away and two children were born at sea to bring the total up to 892. Twenty-five per cent. of the passengers were born in China and come mainly from Shanghai, Peking and Hongkew, and a few succeeded in leaving Tientsin before the city fell in the present civil war. 30% are of Russian origin and the remainder came to China as refugees during the war. There are 136 children under the age of 10 on board ship. The vessel left China on December 24th and will reach Genoa, Italy, in three weeks, from where they will be transhipped to Israel by the Israeli Government.

ONE HAPPY FAMILY

A few days before their arrival in Cape Town, a Zionist advisory committee was set up, including representatives of the various parties, but Mr. Liberman stressed that in spite of the vast differences among the passengers, who come from all parts of the world and speak a multitude of different languages, the passengers on board are one happy family.

The command of the ship has organised an Israeli press which gives the latest news of their future home and also has its own radio service. Concerts and other forms of entertainment are organised for the passengers and daily synagogue services are held. Six Sifre Torah are housed in special Arks in the lounge of the ship. Facilities are also arranged for the education of the children and for studying Hebrew during the voyage. Among the passengers are a number of efficient physicians and nurses who have proved a valuable asset to the Italian medical corps.

The Betarim in particular are responsible for discipline and order, keep guard, and ensure the security of the ship. They also help the crew and assist in the kitchen and engine rooms.

Although conditions on the ship are by no means luxurious, the passengers are making the journey pleasant through their co-operation and joyful spirits.

When I spoke to Mr. Liberman privately he said that at first some of the passengers complained against the control which the Betarim exercised on board, but a few days before their arrival in Cape Town, the same people were full of gratitude, for they realised that without the Betar discipline and efficiency there would have been chaos, and instead of the ship presenting a picture of the first free voluntary immigration of Diaspora Jews to Israel, it would have been just another disorganised passenger vessel.

FUTURE IS BRIGHT

Concluding his address to the delegation who had boarded the ship, Mr. Liberman said: "In the first half of our journey we had to break the chains of Galuth, but from now on we are facing the happy future. I am confident that the future is bright and I know that we will participate in the struggle and upbuilding of our free and independent Hebrew State."

We were taken to the main deck of the ship, where Rabbi Abrahams, on behalf of Cape Town Jewry, Mr. Spitz on behalf of the Jewish Appeal, and Mr. Infeld on behalf of the S.A. Zionist Federation and as the Israeli immigration officer in the Union, extended a welcome to the passengers. Mr. Liberman replied in an impressive short address which he read on behalf of the 892 people on board.

On the dockside there was pandemonium as Cape Town Jews, and even non-Jews, began flocking to the ship with parcels containing almost everything that a person could wish for. Food, clothing, medical supplies, toys and sweets for the children, newspapers and magazines were passed through the Customs officers and handed aboard by a chain of Betarim who, to the accompaniment of their happy songs and laughter, managed to cope with what became an endless supply of gifts.

The S.A. Zionist Federation, the Board of Deputies and S.A. Jewish Appeal had arranged in advance to place on board additional food-supplies, and tons of meat, fruit, and children's food were loaded on board throughout the day. To add to the confusion there commenced a scramble for souvenirs from the "Chinese Jews," and Betar badges and the smart caps which the Betarim wore were at a premium.

I think many of the onlookers were a little disappointed because they expected to find yellow-skinned, slant-eyed Jews, speaking Chinese; instead they were faced with people like themselves, most of whom spoke perfect English with a very noticeable American accent.

People travelled from all corners of the Peninsula to see the immigrants and holiday-makers at Muizenberg rushed to the dockside to see the "Wooster Victory." By the time the vessel was scheduled to leave at 6 o'clock, thousands of people had congregated and joined in the singing, to the accompaniment of the ship's orchestra.

Again the Betarim were the centre of attraction and many South African Jews joined in the Betar songs with fervour and enthusiasm. Just before the gangplank was raised, Jacob Liberman addressed his final message to South African Jewry and expressed the deep appreciation of all the passengers for the magnificent reception which had been extended to them.

"We are going home. We are [illegible] who have themselves decided to break the chains of the Diaspora and enter the Holy Motherland. We know what we are going to and what will be expected of us in our free and independent State. We shall do our duty well. Long live the free Jewish people and the free Jewish State!" he said.

THUNDEROUS APPLAUSE

When the thunderous applause which greeted "Jack's" words died down, the orchestra struck up Hatikvah, which was sung by the people aboard and those on the dockside. As the Hatikvah died down, the Hebrew flag was raised by the passengers, and as the "Wooster Victory" slowly left the dockside the Betarim on board ship began to sing the Betar Anthem, and although the people on the dockside did not know Jabotinsky's immortal words of the song which he gave to his new generation of youth, they joined in the tune with enthusiasm and heard the last strains of the anthem as the ship moved away.

Somehow the South African Jews did not want to leave the scene of one of the most inspiring experiences they had undergone. They remained on the dockside in little groups endeavouring to discuss all that had happened during the day, but few of us will really be able to recount or to write the story of the "Wooster Victory" to South Africa, and the wonderful demonstration of the Jewish will to live in freedom and independence to which China Jewry with the rest of world Jewry aspire.

Few will forget the picture of "Jack" Liberman, Toni Gaberman and the other smartly uniformed Betarim who did justice not only to their nation as a whole, but also to Jabotinsky's Movement [illegible] "national sport."

MESSAGE TO SOUTH AFRICAN JEWRY

This is the text of the speech delivered by Jacob Liberman, Transport Commander aboard the s.s. Wooster Victory, in welcoming delegates of South African Zionist organisations and South African Jewry.

THIS vessel, in every sense of the word, represents China Jewry itself. Aboard this vessel we have men, women and children who were born in China, lived there and prospered. We have representatives of other groups—groups which have been carried to China by a wave of misfortune, a wave of tragedy and inhuman persecution.

Yes, it is true that, as in the case of other communities, our Jewish communities in China made a home for themselves, some a good home, some a poor one. Indeed, it was a case of a typical community with chains of Galuth thoroughly attached and binding.

But the call of logic by Dr. Theodor Herzl, Max Nordau, and Vladimir Jabotinsky was for most a voice in the wilderness. The uprising of the modern Maccabees, the heroic struggle of our ironclad Yishuv and the historic sacrifices at the barricades of Warsaw and other ghettos had lit the torch of independence and pride in each and every one of us.

All through the war, behind the wall of the Hongkew ghetto, in the clubs and associations representing China Jewry, in the heart of every Jew, a new sentiment swelled up—unity of Jewry in China, unity with world Jewry, unity with the Hebrew forces of liberation in Eretz Israel.

Following the termination of the war, the aliyah from China was opened by organised groups of our youth, who managed to break through the barricades and join our forces of freedom. Lately, however, the gravity of the situation in China threatened the possibility of continuing small-scale immigration and it had become imperative to organise big-scale repatriation, the beginning of which you are now witnessing.

We take just pride in being members of the first transport of China Olim, the first to sail from the Orient to our historic homeland. But we are only the vanguard. More are to come from China. More are to come from Japan, Korea, and Manchuria. More from every part of East Asia.

On this vessel, due to the co-operation of all, we were able to organise ourselves into a small city. We are learning to live together, work together, and mould ourselves into a unit prepared and ready to do all required of us in the upbuilding of our Hebrew State.

We do not go to seek greater individual welfare and security. We take pride in receiving the opportunity of joining our Yishuv in creating a homeland worthy of the suffering, the courage, the determination and the historic right of the Hebrew people.

The past is behind us, buried in blood and tears and human misery. With us is our present, the beautiful present, the glorious present of a rejuvenated nation. This is our aim, our only justification in joining our brothers and sisters in Israel, in the war of liberation, in the war of upbuilding, in the war of creating a new psychology, a strong psychology of a proud Hebrew nation spreading its wings of freedom over the historic boundaries of our sacred Motherland.

Long live the victorious Hebrew nation, long live the might of the new Hebrew generation, long live our conquering armed forces, long live our sacred independent Hebrew State!

Qatzin Jacob Liberman, one of the leaders of the Betar in China who was in charge of the party on the Wooster Victory.

SECOND IRO SHIP

THE Jewish Herald has just received a cable from a group of Revisionists and Betarim on board the second I.R.O. ship, s.s. Castel Bianco, which left Shanghai with 900 passengers at the beginning of January.

The Castel Bianco is expected to pass through Cape Town over the week-end and arrangements are again being made for the members of the National Movement to be welcomed officially by the South African Organisation.

OFFICIAL WELCOME FOR REVISIONISTS AND BETARIM ON "WOOSTER VICTORY"

MR. BARRY HURWITZ, General Secretary of the S.A. United Zionist Revisionist Party and a member of the S.A. Netzivut Betar, flew down to Cape Town last week to meet the group of Revisionists and Betarim on board the "Wooster Victory."

As reported elsewhere on these pages, the Betarim led the "Wooster Victory" transport—and they had a special deck which they used for their educational work.

Mr. Hurwitz had the opportunity of meeting them all at a special Assembly on the "Betar Deck," where he conveyed to them the greetings of the Revisionist Party and the Betar in South Africa. They were pleased to hear of the activities of the organisation in this country, and were looking forward to meeting the former South African Betarim and Revisionists in Israel.

Representatives of the Chinese Movement told Mr. Hurwitz that the Revisionist Party and Betar were the leading organisations in all fields of Zionist endeavour in China. They produced a fortnightly publication, "Tagar," and expressed deep gratitude for the "Jewish Herald," which they had been receiving regularly for many years and which has helped them immensely in their educational and political work.

A number of Chinese Betarim are already in Israel, having gone there by air in the last few months, and those who had remained behind are now making arrangements to leave as soon as possible. The head of the Betar in China is Miss Judith Hasser, who attended the last Zionist Congress in Basle and is held in the highest regard by all members of the organisation. She is expected to leave for Israel very soon.

Prominent among the large group of Revisionists on the "Wooster Victory" was Mr. Zimmerman, the chairman of the party in Hongkew. Besides his great joy at going to Israel he has had the additional pleasure of becoming a grandfather on board ship. In a conversation with Mr. Hurwitz, Mr. Zimmerman spoke of the success which the Chinese Revisionist Party had in the last Congress elections, when they emerged as one of the strongest and best organised parties. They sent two delegates to the last Zionist Congress.

The Betarim and younger Revisionists intend entering the Army of Israel if their services are required, and most of them seem confident of being able to adapt themselves to the new conditions without much difficulty. As most of the Betarim speak English quite fluently they would be happy to join any Anglo-Saxon Betar settlement scheme which the Movement may plan.

Almost every one of them has a profession or trade, and Mr. Hurwitz was advised that almost any occupation one can think of is represented by this group. An interesting Betar leader was Jacob Shtedfman, head of the Betar in Tientsin, who left the city during the present clash of the Chinese armed forces. The Betar in Tientsin has been completely evacuated.

The Wooster Victory enters Cape Town Harbour.

The South African press warmly greets the pioneers of the exodus from China.

The Wooster Victory docks at Cape Town, South Africa. More than a thousand Jews of South Africa welcome this first transport.

Харбинъ, - Синагога
Charbin, - Synagoge.

The old Harbin Synagogue, erected on Artillery Street, Harbin, China, in 1907.

Chief Rabbi Kiseleff of Harbin, seated in the front row, among members of the Jewish community, in 1917. Standing second from the right is Dr. Abraham Kaufman.

*Aunt Sarah and the author's
parents on her left. Harbin, 1928.*

*The author, posing in the backyard of the
Liberman's Birch Street home, with his new
bicycle, and wearing a cork hat. Harbin,
1932.*

*The author, age eleven, while on
vacation, in the uniform of the Shanghai
Public School. Harbin, 1932.*

Harbin Betar rescue units during the big flood of 1932.

The author with Joe Wainer in Pyongyang, Korea, prior to the conversion episode. 1939.

Friends of Betar, together with the Betar sports committee, at the opening of the Betar sports grounds. Harbin, 1936.

Abram Milichiker, head of Betar, Harbin, front row, center, surrounded by senior Betarim and some prospective pioneers, 1936.

The Hotel Moderne. Harbin, 1936.

The opening of the Betar sports grounds. The fence in the background divides the facility from the adjacent "ploshchadka" (summer camp and Commerical School). Harbin, 1936.

Parade of Harbin's Betar, marching on Chinese Street. Harbin, 1938.

The Harbin Young Dramatic Troupe performing in Chekhov's The Wedding. Front, left to right, the author, Ura Horosh and Lucy Bogdanovsky.

Wedding portrait of Lea and Yana
Liberman. Shanghai, 1948.
Yana is in his Betar uniform.

Gisia and Sema Liberman – the author's
parents.

The
"trailblazers":
Arie Marinsky
(left) and
Shmuel Muller.

Standing, third from left, the author. Clockwise: Izia Lias, George Aranovsky, Frank Ognistoff, Mark Malchinsky, Leva Olshevsky, Joe Wainer, Bob Freiman, and Mark Lifshitz. Shanghai, 1946.

Greeting the New Year. Shanghai, 1942.

Lea and Yana under the wedding chuppah, together with Rabbi Ashkenazi, who conducted the ceremony, 22 June 1948.

Betar and Irgun on parade, marking the birth of the State of Israel. Shanghai, 1948.

Rabbi Ashkenazi with his daughters Esther and Mania. Shanghai, 1942.

The Shanghai synagogue, established by S. A. Hardoon in 1927.

The Betar naval unit, being inspected by Chief Rabbi Ashkenazi and leaders of the Shanghai Jewish community. 1938.

Shanghai Betar senior girls' group on parade. Commanding officers: Pana Samsonovich and Sima Leimanstein. 1938.

A parade of the Shanghai Volunteer Corps Jewish Troop led by Robert Bitker. 1939.

The opening of a Betar branch in the Hongkew ghetto for European Jewry and Hans Dreyer, its first leader. The tall figure in the center is Michael Ionis, leader of the Shanghai Betar, during World War Two.

Dedication of the Tientsin synagogue with Rabbi Levin, Betarim in uniform, and community leaders. 1939.

Rabbi Levin and Cantor
Krimchansky at the opening
of the new synagogue in
Tientsin.

Tientsin Betar on parade. 1947.

Shanghai Betariada. 1947.

CESS TO THE BETARIAD—SPIRITUAL AND PHYSICAL
UNITY OF OUR FAR EASTERN MOVEMENT!

From Mehoratai (My Country), as performed by Betarim of Shanghai. The author is pictured in the box of the accused. 1948.

Mordechai Olmert and his friends during his mission to China. 1948.

PART TWO

SHANGHAI

Chapter 1

1897-1941. THE JEWS OF SHANGHAI

For more than a century, Shanghai had been an international kaleidoscope of dozens of different cultures. Large in area, huge in population (Shanghai had some nine million people living within its borders during the early forties), the city was loosely divided into concessions administered by the British (the International Settlement), by the French (the French Concession) and by the Chinese (the municipality of greater Shanghai), including Hongkew. The International Settlement was established in 1843 and the French concession in 1850. Each of these ethnic enclaves differed not only administratively, but also in architecture, clothing, the arts, sports and nightlife.

At the very end of the nineteenth century, a few Jewish families from Bombay became a part of this colorful metropolis. They claimed an ethnic origin that could be traced back to the Sephardic community of Baghdad.[1] As successful Jewish entrepreneurs and international merchants based in Bombay, they gradually developed and expanded their business interests to Hong Kong and Shanghai.

In the early years of the twentieth century, the Sassoon family moved to Shanghai to establish a business in this promising port city, on the

---

1. Spanish-Portuguese Jews and their descendants.

southeast coast of China. While Jacob Sassoon was organizing his office and bringing in Jewish employees from Bombay, Nissim Ezra, together with Silas Hardoon, established the first Jewish School in Shanghai and – a few years hence – with the help of Jacob Sassoon, built a magnificent synagogue that they named "Ohel-Rakhel" ("The Tent of Rachel"). Eventually the school moved to the synagogue compound on Seymour Road in the International Settlement and became one of the better-known foreign schools in the city.

By 1910, this first Jewish community in Shanghai had claimed itself to be an organizational entity under the presidency of David Abraham, who remained its titular head for the next thirty years. Well remembered among these Jewish community pioneers in Shanghai was Silas Hardoon. The Chinese citizens of Shanghai honored him on every occasion, because he generously devoted time and money to non-Jewish causes. Married to a Chinese woman and a Buddhist, Silas supported Buddhist charities and other native causes. When Hardoon and his wife realized that they could not have children of their own, they adopted a dozen or so boys and girls of different nationalities and backgrounds. When the children became teenagers, it was rumored that each child had been given a million dollars as "a start in life."

Zionism was not especially popular among the Baghdad Jews, who were inclined to be more loyal to the concept of British colonialism than to the Jewish dream of a homeland in Zion. Nevertheless, between 1904 and 1936, Nissim Ezra succeeded in publishing and editing an English language Zionist paper called *Israel's Messenger*, that became the official organ of the Shanghai Zionist Association and the Jewish National Fund. Eventually, many sons and daughters of these pro-British pioneers became ardent and active Zionists.

Although after the Bolshevik Revolution, many Jews had emigrated to China from Russia and some from Poland, the Ashkenazi Jewish community in Shanghai was established only in 1937 and built its first synagogue soon thereafter.

In 1938 some 10,000 Jews lived in Shanghai, the vast majority of whom were Ashkenazim.[1] While they lived side by side in relative peace and harmony, the two Jewish communities in Shanghai were nevertheless united only by a thin cord of Zionist activity. In religious, charitable or social affairs, the two groups lived a totally separate existence.

On the other hand, when the chips were down and the Jewish tragedy in Europe began to touch the shores of the Whangpoo River, the leadership of both communities found a way to work together in order to assist their brethren in their hour of need. A mass effort at improving the lot of the European refugees resulted in the organization of special joint committees to collect funds and assist in arranging affordable lodging and centers for food distribution for the needy. Collectively, the Shanghai community represented the Jewish refugees before the appropriate authorities. Largely through the monumental efforts of the JOINT and HIAS,[2] aid began to pour in generously from Switzerland. However, as the clouds of war thickened over the Pacific, it became ever more difficult to receive this aid and more and more responsibility fell on the shoulders of the two local Jewish communities. Indeed, the Ashkenazi community of Shanghai was in constant touch with the Jewish communities of Harbin and Tientsin. Everyone was involved and everybody shared in the overall effort.

The Jews of China became terribly anxious. Those with visas left for the United States while others sought to relocate in areas of China where they might live out these tense months in relative comfort and safety. Many persons traveled from one city to another, since friends and relatives, who had been in quest of economic opportunity, were scattered between Harbin, Tientsin and Shanghai. When the war eventually did

---

1. Jews of German, Polish and Russian origin.
2. Hebrew Immigrant Aid Society, founded in New York in 1909.

erupt in the Pacific, many of them were cut off from one another for its duration.

During the pre-war years, Jews traveled freely and enjoyed peaceful interaction with their fellow Asians and a rich communal life. Shanghai was no exception. In fact, its Jews lived under the illusion of great security, due to the presence of foreign concessions and a significant number of Allied military personnel.

Jewish organizational life was structured around the Shanghai Jewish Club and the Jewish Recreation Club (JRC) that was especially active until 1940. The Jewish community also actively collected funds for charitable institutions to support the poor, the sick and the old, assisted in funding education for worthy youth and catered to the social, cultural and religious needs of its members.

Due to the enthusiasm and devotion of Nissim Ezra, Zionism had made its early entrance into Shanghai. Ezra continued his Zionist efforts courageously and stubbornly with a small following. His *Israel's Messenger* spread the gospel of Zionism to the Jews of Shanghai and even reported on the drama of the First Zionist Congress convened in Basel, Switzerland, in 1897. By 1903, Shanghai Jewry was already represented by a delegate. Zionism acquired a large following in Shanghai with the arrival on the scene of Russian and Polish Jews shortly after the Great War of 1914-1918. Zionism flourished during the thirties, when other Ashkenazi Jews arrived in Shanghai from Harbin, and Zionist thought began to occupy a significant place on the Jewish agenda, especially among the Ashkenazi community.

Ezra deserves credit not only for keeping the flame of Zionism burning in the early years of the twentieth century but with bringing the ideology of Zionism to the attention of the great Sun Yat-sen – the father of the Republic of China. It is in response to Ezra's appeal that Dr. Sun Yat-sen wrote:

> I have read your letter and the copy of *Israel's Messenger* with much interest and wish to assure you of my sympathy for the

movement – which is one of the greatest movements of the present time. All lovers of democracy cannot help but support the movement to restore your wonderful and historic nation, which has contributed so much to the civilization of the whole world and which rightfully deserves an honorable place in the family of nations.

I am, Yours very sincerely,

(signed)

Sun Yat-sen[1]

Ezra also merits recognition for his pro-Zionist publicist work. On the other hand, the Zionist organization he headed did not accomplish a great deal. I cannot stress too strongly that it was not until the advent of the Ashkenazi Jewish community in Shanghai that Zionism there began to flourish. And this was due, to a large extent, to the enormous success of the Revisionist Party and its youth movement – the Betar. But, it must be mentioned that even during the thirties, there was a record of the existence of three Zionist outlooks in Shanghai: the Revisionists, the General Zionists or the "Kadima" and the small group of the Sephardic community who called themselves the "Ezra Zionists," in honor of their leader in Shanghai.

In 1931, only a few months after organizing themselves, Betar and the Revisionist Party became the undisputed leaders of the Zionist movement in the city. Young people joined its uniformed ranks in large numbers, while parents and older Zionists became either "Friends of Betar" or active members of the Revisionist Party.

The early leaders and founders of Betar in Shanghai included Lela Kotovitch, Reuven Slossman, Fred Fuchs, Leo Hanin, Judy Hasser, Pana Samsonovich, Misha Leimanstein, Sarah and Mara Morguleff, Yosef Gurin, Julius Feldstein, Eric Gabriel and many others. They, in turn, brought in businessman Robert Bitker, who became the *netziv* (leader) of

---

1. Panguang, *Zionism in Shanghai*, p. 5.

South China Betar and an ardent supporter of the Jewish platoon of the Shanghai Volunteer Corps, an international volunteer contingent, organized for the protection of life and property in the city.

History will record that it was Kotovitch who actually established this youth movement in Shanghai. He arrived from Harbin and Tientsin where he had gained firsthand experience of Betar's activities and its ideology. It is doubtful whether his efforts would have borne fruit without the enthusiastic support he received from the local youth, who were eager to unite all young Jewish men and women into a strong, nationally conscious organization. The names of several of those who belong to this group of Shanghai Betarim already have been mentioned. The very first Betar council included: Lela Kotovitch, Mara Bach, Senia Emburg, Julius Feldstein, David Hanin, Leo Hanin, Mara Morguleff and Pana Samsonovich. Eventually the leadership expanded to include Fred Fuchs, Eric Gabriel, Misha Leimanstein, Reuven Slossman, Eric Levin and Robert Bitker, who became leader of the Shanghai branch and its *netziv*. It is doubtful that Betar in Shanghai initially would have succeeded were it not for the generosity and devotion of Genia Korf, a true friend of the Shanghai "Jabotinsky Family," Gita and Grisha Klebanoff, the respected and loved leaders of the Jewish community, and Sava Yabroff, one of the early leaders of the Betar of Southeast China. Toward the end of the thirties, Sarah Morguleff, Erik Levin and M. Yosilevitch (Avinami) also joined the ranks of leadership of the Shanghai branch of Betar.

Betar's early activities were devoted to education and physical development. Its members also acquired some military training by being placed in the ranks of the Shanghai Volunteer Corps. This was the only Betar branch in the world that could officially and professionally train its members in military warfare. Due to its enthusiastic efforts and national pride, Betar persuaded the high command of the SVC to allow Jewish volunteers to establish its own Jewish platoon. Its beloved commander was Captain Noel Jacobs, a man of dignity and honor. Betar also organized a "Sea Brigade" that received elementary naval training. Several members of the SVC and of the Betar Sea Brigade volunteered for the

British army and navy during the war, losing their lives in combat against the Japanese.[1]

During the early thirties, Betar organized basketball, volleyball, ping-pong and boxing teams. A number of these teams competed successfully in international sporting events of the city and, as a result, the Betar Menorah symbol (the seven-branched candelabra) became a familiar sight to be reckoned with and respected.

Betar and the Revisionist Party in Shanghai published an English-language bi-weekly, *The Jewish Call*. The magazine catered to the entire Jewish community and presented Revisionism with a forum from which to combat the slander of the Zionist Left as it waged its relentless campaign against the Revisionists.

As some younger Betarim progressed to become instructors and leaders in Shanghai, others joined their comrades from Harbin and Tientsin to become pioneers in Palestine. They included Bitker himself, Sarah and Mara Morguleff, Lela Kotovitch and Nelli and Mark Avinami.

In 1941, a new leadership, (*netzivut*) were appointed. Heading the group, Vulia Zubitsky (Shanon) became the new *netziv* of Southeast Asia. A Russian Jew, who had several relatives already residing in China, Vulia and his wife Larisa reached Shanghai from Rumania. Well-informed and highly intelligent, he soon won the unanimous approval of the Betarim, adding eloquence and class to the already popular and highly respected organization. Concurrent with Zubitsky's appointment, Leo Tomchinsky, a businessman from Harbin, became head of the Friends of Betar and a leader of the Revisionist Party.

In the summer of 1941, as Europe was devastated, Shanghai Jewry was living in conditions of safety and comfort. Daily life was inexpensive, labor cheap and luxuries abundant. No one imagined that within the

---

1. J. Ben Eliezer, *Shanghai Betar*: China Memorial Publication, 1969, Tel Aviv.

boundaries of modern Europe the stage was being set for the greatest tragedy ever encountered by the Jewish people throughout their history. Nor did the Jewish community of Shanghai anticipate that in another six months Shanghai would become part of a war-torn world.

It was to this city that I came from Japan in the summer of 1941, and it is this community that shaped my life for the next seven-and-a-half years.

Chapter 2

1941 SUMMER-FALL. "MY SHANGHAI"

The summer of 1941 was a time of defeat and devastation. It was also one infused with a glimmer of hope as the Soviet Union was forced into the Allied camp. In these months a final stand would have to be made against the forces of evil bent on bringing destruction and doom to the world.

With this feeling of "a common effort against a common enemy," the democracies sided with the Communists, and the Zionists fought alongside the British colonialists – all to defeat the prime menace of the world: Hitler and his Nazi murderers.

As German tanks crossed the Russian border and the German air force entered the Russian skies, Winston Churchill spoke to the world in words that might have been well applied to any Zionist leader of the world in relation to Britain itself:

> "The Nazi regime is indistinguishable from the worst features of Communism. It excels all forms of human wickedness in the efficiency of its cruelty and ferocious aggression. No one has been a more consistent opponent of Communism than I have for the last twenty years. I will unsay no word that I have spoken about it. But all this fades away before the spectacle

which is now unfolding... Any man or state who fights on against Nazidom will have our aid. Any man or state who marches with Hitler is our foe."[1]

As this barbaric war machine was poised to march through Europe and part of Russia, the United States of America was slowly but surely approaching the point of no return in negotiations with Japan. In another six months the American isolationists would be jolted into reality by the shower of bombs that would rain on the Pacific fleet at Pearl Harbor.

Meanwhile, I was on a ship slowly maneuvering between the *saipans* and the rowboats leading to the glamorous metropolis of Shanghai. Stench and dirt plugged up my nostrils as I stood on the deck of the Kobe Maru. The foul air drifted with me townward, until I reached the purer air of the French concession.

My parents met me at the pier and brought me to our apartment in the French Concession on Avenue Foche, corner of Route Say-zoong. A modern apartment, it had one bedroom, a living room-dining room area with an alcove (my bedroom-to-be) as well as servants' quarters and a garage. This was to be my home for the next eight years.

As the reader will recall, I had been in Shanghai before and spent most of 1933, 1934 and 1935 studying in the Public and Thomas Hanbury School while living with my relatives. But I was not even a teenager then and my impressions of the city were limited, as were my experiences with the social and political life of the Jewish community.

Now, different horizons were opening before my eyes and I was presently showing a deep interest in events, situations and circumstances that during my earlier visits I had not even known existed. Virtually upon my arrival I was surrounded with friends, boys and girls of my age, most

---

1. Winston Churchill, *The Grand Alliance* (Boston: Houghton Mifflin Co., 1951), p. 371.

of whom I had known from Harbin. Our shared experiences brought us even closer together than we had been before, and these friendships, intimate and genuine, have survived the test of time.

We usually met on the roof garden of my parents' apartment, or at the King Albert Apartments, where many of my peers resided. Hundreds of Jewish youngsters of my age were then living in Shanghai. In addition to those who were unaffiliated with any social organization there were many who were actively involved in the YMCA, some in the Soviet Club and others in Betar.

At this time, there were two such Jewish crowds in town that often combined activities, New Year parties, dances and the like. Most of us belonged to Betar and participated in every activity the organization had to offer.

For some reason, our crowd was known as "Jack's crowd." Comprising some fifteen to twenty members, the group revolved around seven intimate friends, whose lives were completely intermingled. Our friendships, however, were not built in a day and were not spared either tears or heartaches. During the first summer after my arrival in Shanghai, George Terk and I lost our dear childhood friend, Boris Koffman (whose father had been kidnapped in Harbin). Boris contracted infantile paralysis in a public swimming pool and died within twenty-four hours! We were long in recovering from this loss.

As our circle of friends expanded, we were joined by Joe Wainer and then by Frankie Ognistoff, Leva Olshevsky, Mark Malchinsky and Izia Lias.[1] All of them occupied a warm and permanent place in my heart, and

---

1. During the War, Frankie fell in love with a beautiful girl, one Nadia. They became engaged just before Frankie left on a student visa for the United States. When Nadia was refused an entrance visa to the States, she chose instead to sail to Canada to be close to her fiancé. They married at the United States-Canadian border. After their son was born, they made their home in Vancouver, British Columbia, where they live happily to this day. Our friendship continues unimpeded by distance. Izia (Izzi) Lias, with whom I spent many years in China, was instrumental in my choosing San Diego as a retirement home setting. Here, despite years of separation that disrupted our friendship, some forty or more years later, we and our wives continue to sustain our warm relationship.

all played an important part in shaping these years of my early adulthood. Gradually the group came to include Milia Ionis, who had just arrived from Kobe and soon became my close friend and ideological comrade; Onia Paley, who also came from Japan after graduating from a Japanese School in Tokyo; Abe Fradkin; George Aranovsky; Mark Kaptzan (my excellent setup man in volleyball); Velia Litvin (who eventually emigrated to the Soviet Union and died there from cancer); and Izra Klurman, whose father was also kidnapped and murdered in Harbin.

We met daily, went to Betar meetings, enjoyed movies and sports and organized dance parties. We also shared our dreams, our feelings and our desires and ambitions. We were, and most of us remained, close and dear friends for life. All of these friends succeeded and became good citizens of the countries in which they later lived, and respected members of their professions.

The same can be said about the other group, which was known by the uncomplimentary name, "the zoo crowd." I truly do not recall how such an epithet stuck to such nice young people, some of whom even came to lead exceptional lives. Among them was Joe Tukachinsky, the firstborn son of a wealthy piece-goods manufacturer and trader who had emigrated to Harbin from Poland during the thirties. Joe then moved to Shanghai with his parents, his brother, Mark, and sister, Ducia. In his late teens, Joe had shown himself to be a brilliant student, a talented speaker, conversant with Jewish history, the Talmud and the Hebrew language. Eventually, he became a prominent debater in school and a regular speaker at public meetings of Betar. During the war years and immediately thereafter, I shared the Betar platform with Joe, who spoke in English, while I gave my talks in Russian.

Eventually, Joe left for the United States, where he graduated from Harvard, and then embarked on a brilliant career with the Israeli Ministry of Foreign Affairs. At one time, Ambassador to Mexico, Joe became Ambassador to the Soviet Union, Israel's permanent representative in the United Nations, and finally, Chairman of the Board of Be'er Sheba University in Israel. Then on one of his many visits to the

United States, Joe died of a heart attack. Having served his country with brilliance and pride, he died as Yosef Tekoah, one of Israel's most talented and eloquent representatives.

Joe's close friend in Shanghai, Izia (Cherry) Chernomorsky, had come from Harbin to study at St. John's University.[1] There he resided with his aunt and uncle and three of their children – the Jacobs family – in the French concession of Shanghai. Izia was active in Betar in both Harbin and Shanghai and when the war in the Pacific started in earnest and there was no place for Betar activities within the walls of a sadly congested Jewish Club, Izia donated a top-floor apartment of his father's house on Avenue Joffre to us as a clubhouse. The Betar Club remained at that location throughout the years of the Second World War, until such time when, once again, it might occupy a very spacious facility within the large, new compound of the Shanghai Jewish Club on Route Pichon. In Betar, Izia became my assistant in instructing a younger group of Betarim, ages nine to twelve. My other assistants were Lily Frank, Onia Paley and Mark Tukachinsky (Joe's brother).[2] Working together, we shaped a large group of young Jewish patriots, most of whom eventually participated in the overall effort of building the Jewish State.

My happiest hours were those spent with my friends, at my work and among my Betar peers. The remainder of my time I devoted to my studies at St. John's University. My father was busy with his new business and gave freely of his leisure moments to the Jewish Hospital. He was elected

---

1. After the War, Izia returned to his family in Harbin, where he married Joe Wainer's cousin, Bella Wainer. In 1949, together with their firstborn daughter and Izia's brother, Milia, they were among the first to leave for Israel. Izia and Bella established a successful antique business in Tel Aviv, which allowed them and their two daughters to live in comfort and luxury, surrounded by many close and dear friends. Izia died of a rare infection, following routine gall blader surgery.

2. Lily, after a stay in Israel, emigrated to Canada. There she became an esteemed director of the Zionist Women's World Hadassah.

vice-chairman, in which capacity he served for many years under the able chairmanship of Israel Kogan. Mother, too, was active in social work. Together with many other Jewish women in town, she was a member of several auxiliary committees that collected monies for the local Jewish charities. My uncle, Joseph Oppenheim (my cousin Bertha's father), was a very devoted president of the "Shelter House," an organization that provided basic assistance to the destitute minority of the community.

Two smaller Zionist organizations were in existence at the time. One was the "Kadima" of the general Zionist organization. The other was the "Mizrahi" of the religious Zionist group. However, here, as in Harbin and in Tientsin, the Revisionist Party and its youth organization, Betar, predominated among Zionist groups.

At the center of Jewish life in Shanghai were the synagogue, the Ashkenazi Jewish Communal Association and the Shanghai Jewish Club. Even in 1941, two autonomous Jewish community structures were fully operative in Shanghai. One was the Sephardi community of Shanghai, the true pioneers of Jewish life in this city; the other was the Ashkenazi community that began its existence with the arrival of refugees from the Russian Revolution and evolved into the largest Jewish community in Shanghai during the twenties and thirties. The two communities rarely united in any joint efforts, with the exception of aiding the absorption of thousands of refugees from Hitler's Europe. Boats were filled with refugees coming in from Japan and by train from Siberia and northern China. They soon outnumbered the local Jewish population of the city. By 1940, some forty thousand Jews lived in Shanghai, the vast majority of whom were recent arrivals from Europe. Once a part of the glorious Jewish communities of Germany, Austria and Poland, they were now a community of transients, who remained in Shanghai only for the duration of the Second World War.

Religious life for the Jews of Shanghai was essentially limited to synagogue attendance on High Holy Days and occasional Bar Mitzvahs and weddings. Only a small percentage of the community was considered to be Orthodox. None of us knew much about either Reform or Conservative Judaism. However, despite our estrangement from the ritualistic and traditional demands of *halacha*, the legal texts of traditional Jewish literature, most of us united with our fellow Jews in attending synagogue service on the High Holy Days. We all respected religion, loved our rabbi and found strength in belonging to the community and its house of worship. Indeed, Rabbi Ashkenazi was a highly motivated man, respected and loved by all, as were his wife and two daughters. Their younger daughter, Esther, was an active participant in the "zoo crowd," and a good friend and a regular guest at our parties and celebrations.

Beyond a doubt, the liveliest focus of Jewish activity was the Jewish Club of Shanghai. Although most members spent their time at the Club card tables, others enjoyed bowling, billiards or snooker, table tennis, the Club's dining rooms and its library, as well as the musical and theatrical performances. During the 1930s and 1940s, the offices of the Betar Youth Movement as well as those of the Revisionist Party were housed gratis on the premises of the Jewish Club. Betar had a separate entrance with an adjacent sports field, rooms for meetings, a hall, an office and a dressing room with showers. This proved again the degree of acceptance and popularity of the organization within the entire framework of the Jewish community.

When I arrived in Shanghai in 1941, I found the best attended functions in the Jewish Club to be those organized by the Russkii Literaturnyi Khudozhestvennyi Kruzhok (The Russian Literary Artistic Circle). During the forties, however, as its ranks widened and its programs multiplied, Betar almost completely took over the Club's cultural activities. In the summer of 1941 when it still functioned under the auspices of the *Kruzhok*, I was invited to take the lead in a Russian drama titled, *The Morals of Pania Dulskaya*, about a wealthy snobbish Polish family. The play was directed by the well-known Russian actor-dancer Seroff, and evidently I performed my part quite successfully for a month later I was approached by a professional troupe of Russian actors to undertake the role in their presentation in the famous Lyceum Theatre. Reluctantly, I rejected this opportunity to make my debut on a highly visible, professional stage.

Certainly, not all members of the Jewish community could afford membership in the Jewish Club. Although the synagogue was open to all free of charge (only reserved seats on High Holy Days had to be booked in advance and paid for), membership in the Shanghai Jewish Club was quite expensive. As a result, many were occasional guests while most belonged to such other clubs as the YMCA or the Soviet Club for those bearing Soviet passports. These Soviet passports were the only available passports for all Russian-origin residents of China.

Although Soviet passports were easily obtained and were important documents facilitating travel both within and outside of China, many of us Jews, including my parents, refused to take up Soviet citizenship and managed to survive with our "stateless documents" that indicated our former "Lithuanian" citizenship.[1]

The popular president of the Shanghai Jewish community was the mild-mannered, energetic Boris Topaz, who lived in Shanghai for many years with his wife and daughter and who was a successful and highly respected businessman. A religious Jew, he presided over the Jewish community until his arrest and brutal torture by the Japanese conquerors during the Pacific War.

Women prominent in the Jewish community included Bertha Levin, Rebbitzen Ashkenazi, Gita Klebanoff and dozens of others. Among the men, I recall Boris Topaz, Grisha Klebanoff, Leo Deutch, Robert Bitker, Paul Kraslavsky, Sima Hessin, Grisha Shifrin, Leo Tomchinsky, Yosef and Walter Citrin, Izia Magit, Boris Solomonik, Vulia Zubitsky, Joseph Oppenheim, Saul Tukachinsky, Sema Liberman, Israel Kogan and many[2]

---

1. Lithuanian passports sold for a thousand dollars in Harbin and were recognized by the Japanese until 1941, when all "Lithuanians" became stateless again.
2. Alas, circumstances have not been kind to my personal archive, and I regret that I no longer have on record the complete list of all activists of the community.

more. These men and women, devoted to the cause of Jewish unity and safety, kept the community alive and alert.

In the summer of 1941, although we were only nine months away from impending catastrophe, Jewish life in Shanghai continued to thrive. Each segment of community activity seemed to throb with vitality and excitement. Communication facilities were superb. Up-to-the-minute news was brought to every home by radio as well as by the daily press. The Russian and English morning and evening dailies flourished. They were supplemented by two Jewish bi-weeklies, *Unzer Lebn* (*Our Life*), edited by David Rabinovitch, and the Revisionist-Betar magazines *The Jewish Call* (until 1940) and *Tagar* (*The Struggle*) that served the community from 1941 until the end of 1949, when most of the Jewish population of Shanghai had left the city.

Also linking us to the rest of the world were our many opportunities to participate in international sports competitions, debating, theater, and the like. Jews were prominent in all of these activities and, as a result, enjoyed an exposure and a popularity in Shanghai and elsewhere.

When I arrived from Japan, I discovered that the French Concession and the International Settlement were seething with preparations to join the Allied war effort. This is not to say that there were no enemies of the Allied Powers stationed in Shanghai, including the rather dejected Germans and Italians. In fact, Italian military barracks were still operative in Shanghai. Their presence resulted in occasional bloody skirmishes in the city's nightclubs and provided the setting for numerous night battles between Italian sailors and American marines.

Other aspects of our daily lives were not affected by the war in Europe. Dog racing and horse racing alike drew crowds, cinemas and nightclubs were filled to capacity, and the local theaters offered outstanding Russian and English plays and musicals, operas and ballet.

As a student at St. John's University in Shanghai, I, like my peers, had a bicycle, our transportation from one end to the other of this vast city of nine million souls. Although most of us were economics majors studying for a baccalaureate degree, two girls were preparing to become biologists, while the Katzenelson brothers, Alex and Daniel, ambitious and determined, were preparing to enter medical school.[1]

At this time, to the regret of my parents, I, alas, was too deeply engrossed in my dreams of a Jewish state, in my participation in Betar activities, sports and socializing to seriously pursue my studies. My one goal in life was to go to Palestine to help my people establish an independent Jewish state. Everything else seemed irrelevant.

I was not, however, immune to romance. Through my friend George Terk, I met Annie Sherman, who became my first sweetheart. To this day, she remains my dear friend, even though she left me brokenhearted some six months into our dating and began looking for someone who was interested in a "serious relationship."

The sexual mores of my generation were far different from those of the 1990s. It was permissible for us to kiss and "to neck," but to go "all the way," one went to a brothel or found himself "one of those girls," (a non-Jewish girl of loose morals). While I was recuperating from the painful loss of my first girlfriend, my friends were also engaged in girl hunts of their own. Some were more successful than others, but we had all reached that age where male companionship alone was insufficient. In between dates, we often accompanied one another to the better known and more hygienic brothels in town.

At this time in our lives some serious relationships leading to marriage began to mature. Eventually Mark Kaptzan (my friend and volleyball partner) met and married Mira Treyman;[2] Mark Tukachinsky (Yosef Tekoah's brother) met and later married Luba Shifrin; and Joe Wainer

---

1. Today, Alex, a prominent bone specialist and professor of medicine, and Daniel, a well-known pediatrician, both live in Israel.
2. The Kaptzans have a beautiful daughter, Anya. Mira and Mark, however, are divorced and happily remarried to partners, who are also part of Jewish emigration from China.

met Dora Zegerman, whom he later married, and who would bear him two daughters.

In the meantime, Milia Ionis, the "British Consul" of Kobe, arrived in Shanghai. Together with his father, he opened a small fur store on Avenue Joffre, in the French Concession. The store immediately became the meeting place of all our friends. Milia soon met and fell in love with Risia (Ray) Malchinskaya-Tukachinskaya and eventually married her. Risia too belonged to the "zoo crowd." She was a dear friend of both groups and a sister of Mark Malchinsky, who was a member of our "intimate seven."

In the same summer of 1941, the Shanghai Jewish Club and, with it, the Betar moved to a new compound on Bubbling Well Road, in the International Settlement, previously occupied by the American marines. The new facilities had a bowling alley, a badminton court and rooms for small meetings and large assemblies. It was here that I organized my first Betar Purim Ball, learned to bowl, played volleyball and gave my first important speech (in Russian) on the anniversary of Ze'ev Jabotinsky's death.

Our volleyball instructor and coach was Mark Avinami (Yosilevitch), who can be credited with my initial success on the volleyball team. Mark and his wife Nelli had two young daughters and a small son, all of whom were active members of my young group in Betar.[1]

Together with Milia we worked on improving the educational level of the Shanghai Betar. Out of his vast experience in Harbin's *Ha-degel*, Milia popularized the idea of a high-quality Russian-English bi-weekly magazine. It was due to his initiative that the *Tagar* was born. It would become one of the most widely read Jewish publications in town. While Milia edited the Russian section of *Tagar*, Judy Hasser took over the editorship of the English-language edition. Soon *Tagar* served as a living

---

1. Mark Avinami died of a heart attack in Tokyo in the late 1950s. His wife and two daughters live in Israel. His son lives in South America. Naomi, his youngest daughter, married our friend Onia Paley. He died in Israel, in the late 1980s, of diabetes.

link between Shanghai, Eretz Israel and the centers of world Jewry, in New York, London, Paris and Johannesburg.

By early winter of 1941, I had settled into my new life in Shanghai, made new friends and joined the leadership of the Shanghai Betar organization. Late at night, on December 7, we all awoke to the pounding of heavy guns from the direction of the Whangpoo River. Pearl Harbor had been attacked a few hours earlier, and now Shanghai was being taken over by the navy of His Imperial Majesty, the Emperor of Japan. The war in the Pacific Theater had begun!

Chapter 3

1941. JEWISH LIFE IN SHANGHAI AFTER PEARL HARBOR

Opposite the broad boulevard known as the Bund, a British frigate lay at anchor on the Whangpoo River. When the Japanese navy bombarded the frigate, it fired a token self-defensive salvo and made a gallant exit from the harbor. Bloodless and well-planned, the Japanese takeover of the city was swift and painless as well.

For the foreign population of Shanghai, the major effect of the war was the large-scale creation of camps for "enemy nationals" and a ghetto in Hongkew for Jewish refugees escaping the curse of Nazism in Europe. But this displacement of peoples was not put in place until late 1942. Until then, enemy nationals were ordered to wear red armbands, while the Jewish community feverishly preparing to assist its European Shanghai Jewish brethren, organized funds and arranged for health care and rented all available spaces in Hongkew for public service offices, free dining rooms and spartan dormitories.

Under the directives of the Japanese authorities, a central committee of Jewish leaders was formed to deal with problems related to the needs of these more than thirty thousand Jewish refugees. Named SACRA (South Asia Central Refugee Association), this committee was chaired by a Dr. Cohen. Hitherto unknown, of Turkish descent and fluent in

Japanese, Cohen surfaced when the Japanese took control of the city, and then, after the war, vanished as suddenly as he had appeared.

Although many prominent and highly respected leaders of the Jewish community of Shanghai participated in SACRA, on account of the latent mistrust of the motives of its initiators, namely, the Japanese military authorities, its legitimacy was questionable. Rumors circulated regarding the mishandling of funds, since it seemed that large sums of money had passed through private companies dealing in international trade, firms that had been intermediaries in currency transfers from the Joint Distribution Committee in Switzerland to SACRA in Shanghai.[1] However, these allegations were never followed up, and no proof of any wrongdoing ever materialized. It is quite possible that SACRA simply fell victim to ugly rumor born of hatred and nurtured through bitterness and suffering.

All too soon, days of sorrow and separation descended on the foreign population of Shanghai. Thousands of enemy nationals, friends and relatives were bussed away to internment camps in the remote outskirts of the city. Overnight, their daily routine of comfortable living turned into a nightmare of rat-infested barracks and filthy partitions of sheets and mud-caked blankets separating families. The food was bad and insufficient, the hygiene was nonexistent. Every attempt at normalizing life and creating an acceptable routine was usually frustrated by the sporadic brutality of the Japanese guards and their commanders. Similar scenes would occur in Tientsin.

Among the interned were many members of the Jewish communities. In Shanghai they included the Betar leaders, Sarah and Mara Morguleff, who, as citizens of Palestine, possessed British papers. For almost four long years we were bereft of their wisdom and guidance while they and their young son Yuda and baby daughter Shulamit suffered the indignities of internment.[2] In Tientsin, the Japanese interned my cousin, Ella

---

1. The JOINT provided funds to Jewish refugees before, during and after World War Two.
2. Yuda now resides with his wife Zvia in California. He has been an enthusiastic supporter of this project and, in fact, to him belongs the credit for my writing this book.

Shluger, who was born in Chicago and returned to China with her parents several years before the outbreak of the Pacific War. She was later exchanged and repatriated to the States and spent the war years with her aunt in Chicago.

Soon, the tragedy of separation, barbed wire fences and the curtailment of freedom became the lot as well of our Jewish brethren who had arrived recently from Germany, Austria and Poland. Even those who had created their modest living quarters on the outskirts of Hongkew were now being forced either to move out again or to share their quarters with others, in order to be within the limited borders of the designated area and occupy not more than their designated space. Because of their status as "refugees" rather than "enemy nationals," they were not as restricted in their movements. Those with jobs or business opportunities outside the restricted area were usually given entry and exit permits. The relative misery of those passing through the control points with such passes was predicated on the mood and character of the guard commander on duty. Seldom a day would pass when a Jew passing the control point would escape being pushed, slapped or beaten.

The head of this operation was a Japanese man named Goya, short in stature but long in brutality and gall. Goya would jump onto tables in order to look down on the innocent human being trembling before him and then spit venom and abuse at him, before climbing down to molest him physically. On occasion, Goya had been known to mock rabbis and cut off their beards before allowing them passage through the gates of the ghetto. Goya liked to call himself "the king of the Jews." At the end of the war he was snared by a group of Jewish youngsters and given a royal beating. He was last seen being dragged off by the United States military. Months later, rumors circulated that Goya was an American agent but this (strangely) was never officially confirmed or denied.[1]

In the meantime, two devastating blows, one after the other, befell the Jewish community of Shanghai. Its president, Boris Topaz, was arrested

---

1. Rena Krasnow, *Strangers Always* (Berkeley: Pacific View Press), p. 58.

and incarcerated in the infamous Bridge House. Shortly afterward, another prominent leader of the community and a highly respected businessman, Grisha Shifrin, was also taken into custody by the Japanese military. To everyone's relief, Shifrin was soon released unscathed. Topaz left the Bridge House, a seriously sick and broken man who would never regain his health or his strength. His was another war crime that passed unpunished in this cruel and indifferent postwar world.

With the arrests of Jewish community leaders, the harsh treatment of Jewish refugees in Hongkew and the brutal abuse of power by the occupants of the city, it could be expected that Jewish life would become less assertive and more covert. Surprisingly, such was not the case. On the contrary, Jewish communal life grew stronger, and its practical achievements soared to an unprecedented high. In both the Shanghai Jewish Club and Betar, this vitality was especially remarkable.

Even in the Hongkew ghetto, life continued apace, and despite its discomfort, frustrations and fear, our brethren there were able to create a miraculous semblance of normalcy within its outdoor coffee shops, restaurants, theaters and markets. Amidst the degradation, our China's European Jews built a civilized haven that no longer existed in Europe itself! Among the refugee colony there were thousands of talented and innovative people who helped to organize high-standard musical recitals, plays, operas and other forms of entertainment. Athletic teams participated victoriously in Shanghai's outstanding sports competitions.

Political parties were in full swing. On one street there was a tiny office of the religious Zionists, "Mizrahi," and on the other "Poalei Zion," representing the Labor movement in Palestine. Further into town, you would find the General Zionists and somewhere in between, the Revisionist Party and the Betar Youth Organization. All were active, all had members and all considered themselves more successful than the others.

There were also several sports organizations in Hongkew and they all carried the white-and-blue banner with pride. Among the better-known sportsmen was Kurt Jeffris, a ping-pong champ. The J.R.C.'s formidable boxing contingent included the heavyweight Sam Levco. He created a sensation by knocking out a Japanese professional champion, brought especially from Tokyo to demonstrate the power of the nation of the conquerors!

In early 1942, it was decided to organize a second Betar branch in Hongkew. Initially, it was located on the upper floor of the Ward Road synagogue and in later years it moved to larger premises on Chungkong Road. The task was facilitated by the numerous members of the Polish Betar, as well as of Betar branches in Austria and Germany, who were now living within the restricted area of the Hongkew ghetto. With help from the first Betar branch in town, the second soon became well established.

Visiting Betarim often brought the two Hongkew branches of the organization together. Lectures would be exchanged, sports competitions held and frequent parades of uniformed Betarim would pass through the narrow streets of the ghetto. In its founding period, the Hongkew branch of Betar had been led by a Betari from Berlin, Hans Dreyer. Under his leadership, the branch expanded its activities to include debates, political discussions, theatrical presentations and a wide variety of sports. The Zimmerman family, young and old, also contributed to improving the standards of our Hongkew Betar. They were joined by such devoted Betarim as Paul Adler, Rudi Adda, Kurt Seiden and the Spiegel family.[1]

Most Betarim, as was true of the majority of the residents of the Hongkew ghetto, had no desire to ever return to Europe, and they eventually found their way to the United States and Israel. A very small number proceeded to Australia and to Canada; almost none went either to Europe or to any of the South American countries. They left with

---

1. "Betar-Shanghai," in *Bulletin of the Igud Yotzei Sin.* [Tel Aviv] (March 1973).

different memories, some bitter, some sweet, but they all left behind a legacy of survival, of fortitude and of creativity.

At this time, the pioneering Sephardic community was coming to an end. Predominantly British subjects, they had either been interned or evacuated and only a few remained behind. On the whole, they were unable to function any longer as an active community. Indeed, it was depressing to witness the disappearance of this once vibrant and productive Jewish community.

Fortunately, the Ashkenazi community was spared a similar fate. Composed primarily of stateless Russian emigrants and of some possessors of Soviet passports, the Ashkenazi Jewish community and its leaders by and large managed to resist political change and to hold high the banners of both Judaism and Zionism.

Almost immediately upon taking over the city, the Japanese set their sights on a handsome building in the very heart of the former International Settlement on Bubbling Well Road. To the chagrin of its members, the building housed the Shanghai Jewish Club! Within weeks, the board members found another building on Avenue Road, that at one time had belonged to the Freemasons. Sufficiently spacious to cater to the various needs of the club, Masonic Hall housed a restaurant, a billiard parlor, card rooms, a sizeable auditorium with a stage and a library. Alas, it had no rooms to spare nor an adjacent garden and so, to our disappointment, it offered no place for Betar.

Izia Chernomorsky's generosity and care saved the day. He made it possible for Betar, driven by the optimism and enthusiasm of its members, to move to its new home on a small rooftop apartment on the Avenue Joffre. After appropriately decorating the main hall and organizing the office, meeting room and the "wall newspaper," we realized that an additional hall might be required for our popular Sunday activities. Once again, we were assisted by the Jewish Club, whose board agreed to provide us with their auditorium for drills, sports and large meetings. There, we held our regular Purim and Hanukah Balls, public debates and open meetings. It was also in the Jewish Club where our senior members studied Jewish history with a "Labor Zionist," the well-known and highly respected Mr. Ivri.

Some months prior to the relocation of both the Jewish Club and of Betar, Vulia Zubitsky, a veteran member of the Revisionist Party and of Betar, arrived in Shanghai. He was at once invited to take over the leadership of our youth movement. Vulia, who was of Russian origin, and his wife, Lara, a native of Rumania, had a cousin, who was one of the leaders of Betar in Tientsin, and another relative, Ara Prejensky, who had been a highly respected leader of the Tientsin Betar for many years. Well-educated, Vulia added eloquence and class to the Betar organization. At the same time, Leo Tomchinsky, a businessman and a Revisionist leader from Harbin, became the head of the Friends of Betar group and took a very active part in the leadership of the Revisionist Party in Shanghai.

Withstanding the hardships of the Japanese occupation of Shanghai, the Jewish community braced itself for whatever lay ahead. Somehow, most of us felt that, no matter what, we would survive!

Chapter 4

1941-1944. THE WAR YEARS

With the opening of the Pacific front and the relinquishing of their concessions by both France and Great Britain, the administrative rule of greater Shanghai swiftly changed. We soon felt the lack of foreign "imports", from the lack of some favorite food items and imported garments to the disappearance of all Hollywood movies from local cinemas.

Although the Soviet Union was solidly within the Allied camp, it did not declare war on Japan until early August 1945.[1] As a result, the local foreign population was able to receive up-to-date news on events in the Far East. This information was transmitted through two local Russian newspapers, a Soviet radio station and the *Soviet Movietone News*, which was shown in the Soviet Club and on the screens of some select movie theaters in town.

Due to the relentless efforts of Avram Kaufman in Harbin and the leaders of the Jewish communities in Shanghai, Tientsin and Harbin, Jewish life as well continued without significant interruption. The Jewish Club, in its more modest quarters on Avenue Road, continued to offer daily card games, mahjong for the women, dance parties on weekends and

---

1. The Russians made their declaration on 8 August, at which time they invaded Manchuria.

occasional performances by amateur and professional groups. Betar organized the traditional Purim and Hanukah Balls in the main auditorium of the club, and held bridge and snooker championships.

Gambling was limited for the most part to charity contributions. This did not mean that the amounts involved in dollars and cents were insignificant. At one especially successful Betar Purim Ball, immediately following an amateur program, a group of wealthy businessmen placed enormous stakes on a snooker game in progress. The players included Boris Solomonik, Mike Bellinki, Senia Robin and Kolia Yappo. From their forty-minute competition, Betar raised sufficient funds to cover its expenses for the next two years. Many others found various ways to contribute to their favorite Jewish charities in Shanghai.

The synagogue at Tenant de la Tour was packed to capacity on all Jewish Holy Days. Some came to pray, others to listen. All were there out of a feeling of solidarity and their own need to be a part of a larger community.

War had its negative effect on the earning capacity of some of Shanghai's Jews. The recipients of Shelter House assistance increased in number and in necessity. The Jewish hospital dispensed more and more services, as the level of poverty in the community increased. Due to the high standard of its professional staff, the hospital catered to many affluent patients who helped to provide the necessary funds.

Betar settled into its small rooftop apartment in the Chernomorsky house and began to expand both its activities and its membership. The group of young Betarim under my command soon reached a record high. In fact, the group became so popular that one day, during a specially organized festive parade, our good friends Dora and Mike Medavoy presented Betar with its own embroidered flag.[1]

In 1943, Leo Tomchinsky became the new leader of the Southeast Asia Betar, while Mike Ionis was appointed head of the Betar in Shanghai. My

---

1. The Medavoys moved to Los Angeles after the War. Dora and Mike became successful in business, and their son Michael became a cinema mogul in Hollywood.

own responsibilities now included the organization of our annual Purim and Hanukah Balls, and of our weekly "wall newspaper." I was also head of the sports committee, and general secretary of the Revisionist Party. Of all my duties, I enjoyed preparing programs for the Hanukah and Purim evenings the most. I surrounded myself with lovely people and real talent. I wrote and staged plays, and arranged for ballets and skits that had hitherto never been presented on the stage of the Shanghai Jewish Club. Especially talented were the singing Treyman sisters and Freda Gabriel, who could easily have gone on to discover a promising theatrical career. Countless others performed dangerous pyramids or danced ballets based on subjects from Jewish history.

Our sports program at this time was dominated by volleyball tournaments in the YMCA, where Betar heroically but unsuccessfully competed against the White Russian ROS team (the Russian Sport Club) and the all-powerful Soviet Club. However, in ping-pong, track and boxing, Jewish teams did very well, indeed. In addition to such veterans as Kurt Jeffris from Hongkew, Norman Soskin and Joe Feller from Shanghai, a young man unexpectedly drew attention to himself by the brilliant way he played ping-pong and the regularity with which he defeated one champion after another. At age fifteen, George Kanzepolsky became the undefeated ping-pong champion of Shanghai and a captain of the Betar team.

The Japanese-controlled English-language press continued to trumpet reports of victories in Southeast Asia, in Africa and on the Russo-German front. But the language of these reports noticeably changed, and often we would read such phrases as: "strategic change of venue," or "the Allies have suffered heavy casualties." Soon we could decipher these propaganda reports and distinguish genuine victories from defeats.

Daily routines differed. The less affluent members of Shanghai's Jews frequented a Russian émigré club that provided occasional movies and bingo games. Others spent time at the Jewish Club or visited one another's apartments for a game of *rummy*,[1] poker or mahjong.

I recall my mother's friends gathering at our house in the early afternoon hours and playing cards or mahjong until their husbands came home in the evening and joined them until midnight, when they would all leave. Sometimes these day-and-night games took place during a period of stifling humidity and record high temperatures. There were no air conditioners, and fans were the only relief from Shanghai's unbearable humidity. In despair, the ladies would strip to the waist and pursue their games with added vigor. Occasionally, I would enter the apartment unannounced only to be greeted with cries and commotion, as the ladies ran for "cover."

Evenings would be spent at inexpensive coffee shops or deluxe restaurants – the names of "The Renaissance" and "The Kavkaz" stand out. "The Mars," "The Victoria" and "DD's" were equally popular places where one could enjoy a meal or cup of coffee without having to be wealthy. This was not the case with the better nightclubs of the city, that became the haunts of the well-to-do businessmen of the Jewish community. Most such nightclubs were located on Yu-yen-Road and carried exotic names such as "Ali Baba," "Farrell's" or "Ciro's." Students and youth of my age would rather have spent a free evening by going to a movie, to a Chinese restaurant (such as the "Sun-Ya") or to a dance parlor, where a girl was paid a few pennies for a dance.

Occasionally, my friends and I would meet at the famous Lyceum Theatre where top Russian actors and actresses performed in plays and musicals. The musicals never failed to attract full houses. The names that are etched in my memory include those of Rosen, Slabotskoy, Sovielev, Katia Orlovskaya and Larissa Anders. The war robbed Shanghai of the

---

1. *Rummy* is played by four persons. Ten cards are dealt, and when his turn comes, each person may exchange a card. The game ends when one person has a full hand of the required card combinations.

great talent of Valin, who became the president of the Soviet Club and abandoned his successful theatrical career.

We were reminded that we were living in wartime, when in early 1944 the American Air Force carried out occasional bombing raids. Very rarely did we see any of the attacking P-51s or the B-29s. But each raid was accompanied by earthshaking thuds that indicated direct hits on the outskirts of the city.

At first, the wildly gesturing and shouting Japanese security police created panic as they ordered everyone indoors and watched for any open window curtain that might reveal the city's whereabouts to the enemy. Perhaps the Japanese did not believe this themselves, but that is what they were ordered to tell the population. Soon, however, calm settled in and the air raids became just another routine of the war days in Shanghai.

Through all this, our group continued to meet, to study, to attend Betar meetings and to party. We now welcomed into our intimate ranks an old Harbin friend. Leva Olshevsky had spent several years studying in Tientsin, and he was now spending his university years with all of us at St. John's. At the same time, the beautiful Monica Pogrebetskaia arrived from Tientsin. As I had no current girlfriend, many who knew Monica predicted that she and I were bound to become an "item." And we did.

Monica's parents rented an apartment only a few blocks away from where I lived, and it was very convenient for me to pedal up to her place. Monica's father was a Jewish financier, and her mother of the Russian Orthodox faith. Since religion did not play a part in the lives of Monica's family, both she and her sister Irene grew up indifferent to Judaism and Christianity alike.

Monica attended St. John's University with all of us. She was a bright girl and very sexy for her age. Although our romance had all the makings of a torrid love affair, I restrained myself and took care of my sexual needs elsewhere. Since ideologically, she was more familiar with Communism than with Judaism, and had had no exposure to Zionism, I missed being able to discuss my Betar activities and problems of the day with her. But, being so impetuously in love, I must confess that whenever I was with Monica, passion overcame my Zionism as well. Our romance lasted two years.

Several months passed after we broke up, and my friend George timidly asked if I was still interested in Monica. When I assured him that there was not a chance for us to resume our previous relationship, he inquired if I would mind if he courted Monica. His consideration reflected the integrity of our friendship.[1]

The war devastated St. John's University. The best professors either escaped to America or were arrested for their anti-Japanese activities. The new professors were for the most part inferior and contributed to lowering the educational standards of the University.

In psychology, a subject required of all students, Joe Wainer and I were assigned to Professor Chang, a new member of the faculty. Clearly, he was not a born teacher. Instead of lecturing to us out of his expertise, Professor Chang simply stood and read from various textbooks, insisting that we take notes. This inauspicious situation was further compounded by the fact that Professor Chang read in a heavily accented Chinese, that was virtually incomprehensible.

Bored and rebellious, Joe and I would bring a baseball and glove to the class and seat ourselves on opposite sides of the huge classroom. The moment Dr. Chang's head would turn toward the chalkboard, to the delight of all the other equally bored students, one of us would pitch the ball across the room. Finally, we were caught and summoned to appear before the professor.

Anticipating a circus, the whole class remained behind to witness the confrontation. After a moment of silence, Dr. Chang addressed me first:

---

1. Monica and George were not together for very long. Eventually, she emigrated to the United States, where she married and had two children. Circumstances kept Monica from sustaining friendships with anyone in our crowd.

"Liberman! Do you have a diary? Never mind! Mark down in your diary: 'In ten years, you sure, criminal!'" Then, casting a glance in Joe's direction, Dr. Chang declared: "Wainer – you – failure in life!" I wonder where Dr. Chang is today and what he is doing. Joe Wainer is an exceptionally successful businessman, whose firm ships wheat to Japan and the former Soviet Union.

Our 1944 New Year's party was especially festive. It was becoming clear to all that the German armies on the Russian front were being wiped out. The Allies stood on the threshold of the second front. The Germans suddenly ceased announcing their "historical victories." The mood was full of anticipation of a better tomorrow. In this frame of mind, each of us faced the arrival of a new year.

Celebrating on the thirty-first of December, we continued our festivities into the next day with a fancy-dress party. Each celebration included members of Jack's crowd and the "zoo crowd," as well as several "neutrals" from the YMCA and a few unaffiliated young people. As was the case on such occasions, much food was served, and we feasted on fancy cakes, fruits, nuts and ice cream, and a variety of alcoholic beverages. Most of the boys smoked either cigarettes or pipes, but the girls partook of neither alcohol nor tobacco. Our crowd had not taken up drugs then and we never missed them later.

In between dancing to the music of phonograph records, we played such games as "Monks," in which a couple would go to an empty room and confess to sins, which were, of course forgiven, after cleansing the sin with a kiss; "Spin-The-Bottle"; and competitions in which couples standing on chair-tops opposite each other would kiss with their hands behind their backs. At all times, we treated our girls with gentleness and respect. Even the remotest form of a sexual proposition would have been considered a grave insult by our girls – an insult leading to a permanent breach in the relationship.

Although we young people attempted to live by certain group standards, it would be incorrect to surmise that morality was always high in every sector of the Jewish community. In fact, among the young married couples of the so-called *nouveau riche*, infidelity was the rule rather than the exception. However, although many of us were aware of the existence of these fast-living young men and women, they did not represent a significant part of the Shanghai Jewish community.

During the 1940s, well-established business enterprises were forced to close down. Import and export trading to Europe or the United States had halted, shrinking the job market. Many Jewish families in town experienced financial difficulties. However, with mutual assistance and an enterprising effort, some found substitute work and others began business ventures of their own.

My father was among the fortunate ones. Restaurants and coffee shops all did well during the war days in Shanghai and as a result my dad prospered. The fur trade also flourished, and many Jews in China imported skins from the Chinese provinces which they sold wholesale to the many fur stores in the city. Several of these stores, including some of the most luxurious fur salons in town, were owned by Jews. Among the successful fur-traders, the names that immediately come to mind are those of the Soskin family, the Deutch family, the Boxers, Abrasha Ifland, Valia Koffman, Shura Shvetz, Leo Tomchinsky, the Tsinghause family and Gita and Grisha Klebanoff.

Young entrepreneurs also successfully engaged in trading in films, cameras, sugar, paper, spices or skins. Among them were numerous good friends, all of whom I had met through Betar. They included Sima Karlikoff, Elia Rosenberg, Eric Gabriel, Pana Samsonovich and Grisha Nissenbaum. Out of Betar emerged businessmen who had established their firms before the war. Not only were they wealthy and successful, but they were also generous and helpful to all Jewish causes as well, and especially to Betar. Some of their names may not be remembered, but their deeds will be cherished forever. Among them are my dear friends Izia Magit, an outstanding leader of Australian Jewry today, and Vova Rifkin and Grisha Tsipris, who also live in Australian retirement, where they are surrounded by local and "Chinese" friends.

Others embarked on a risky though honest road in order to provide the necessities of life for themselves and their families. Commuting on the Shanghai-Tientsin Railroad to carry out their trade ventures, they earned substantial income, due to the difference in exchange rates as well as in the cost of cigarettes, alcohol or toiletries. On one such voyage, during the Allied bombing raid of a commuter train, Boris Krimchansky, the handsome, talented son of the highly respected Tientsin cantor, was killed weeks before his scheduled wedding to Alla Krinkevitch of Tientsin. In a similar incident, a Jewish merchant from Shanghai was also killed returning from his business trip to Tientsin, leaving behind a wife and two lovely daughters.

For the Jewish population of China, fortunately, the fatalities of the war were limited. A tragic exception was the loss of life by Hongkew's refugee population, when Allied planes bombed ammunition stores close to the ghetto. Thirty Jews perished and several hundred were left wounded and homeless in this badly miscalculated bombing attack.

Many Jews could not eke out a living, no matter how hard they tried. Some of them were assisted by the well-organized welfare institutions of the Jewish community. Others, however, were too proud to admit any need for assistance or to request help. As a result, they subsisted in cramped rooms with no hot water and barely enough money for food. Few knew of their plight, which they bore stoically and in secret. Little wonder that it was these destitute families who composed the very first groups for evacuation to the Soviet Union. Those who remained behind were able to settle finally in Israel, the U.S., Canada and Australia into a new and better life.

In the meantime, we all carried on with our regular daily routines, waiting and hoping for an end to the world conflagration. The end would not be long in coming.

Chapter 5

1945. THE BURDENS OF PEACE

Some days before Japan surrendered, a few of my close friends had an inkling that this momentous event was about to happen. During the final months of the war, we would meet regularly at George's apartment, go to his room, pull out a shoebox from his closet and tune in to the forbidden Voice of America or the British Broadcasting Corporation, for the latest developments. Had we been caught, we could have been summarily executed without trial. However, we assured each other that the Japanese were too busy with more important problems. Luckily, we were right.

Finally, Emperor Hirohito publicly announced Japan's unconditional surrender. The entire city seemed to be out on the streets waiting for the long-anticipated victorious Allied armies. No such thing happened. The Japanese continued to remain on guard over public buildings and bridges, as the native population mocked, spat and pelted them with stones. Eventually, to avoid beatings and possible loss of life, the sentries were withdrawn to the barracks and there seemed to be no one left to take over the responsibility for law and order in the entire city.

The multitudes on the streets searched the skies. Others gathered at the Bund, the broad boulevard that is Shanghai's gate to the Whangpoo River, and the city's center of commerce and banking. Here they stood peering at the horizon hoping to spot a naval flotilla coming in to claim victory. Instead, we began to notice several funny-looking, roofless toy cars carrying smartly uniformed American airmen, smiling and waving to the crowds. With them, on conventional vehicles, came military administrators, who flew in to supervise the surrender of the Japanese forces in the city.

It took us a few days to become acquainted with the military toy-sized cars that eventually flooded the streets of Shanghai. Soon enough, the jeep became a popular, easily recognized vehicle and to drive one was considered a prestigious mode of transportation.

Gradually more and more American airmen and GIs entered the city, which now anxiously awaited the arrival of the 7th Fleet. In the meantime, the new Chinese administration, representing the Kuomintang Government of Generalissimo Chiang Kai-shek, began to round up the Japanese commanders allegedly responsible for atrocities committed during the war against the civilian population of Shanghai. They were all brought before military tribunals and immediately sentenced. Some received prison terms, others the death penalty. Capital punishment, a bullet in the head, delivered in view of the entire citizenry, was carried out virtually on the day of judgment.

I witnessed one such summary execution. Riding through the city on my bicycle, I noticed a large crowd following a slow-moving truck. On top of the truck stood a uniformed, blind-folded Japanese officer, tied to a wooden block with Chinese letters indicating his name, rank, crime committed and verdict received. I followed the truck until it came to an open field. The prisoner was helped out and marched into an adjacent field. A uniformed Chinese official came up to the prisoner and, at close range, put a bullet through his head. As the victim of the execution dropped to the ground, the huge crowd of citizens cheered and applauded wildly. After a few moments, the crowd dispersed and we all proceeded to our original destinations. Surely, the execution was just, I mused, as I returned home, visibly shaken by what I had seen. Certainly, the crimes committed by many Japanese commanders and officers were brutal, inhuman and deserving of the death penalty. But I had never yet witnessed a killing of a human being and it was an experience I would never forget.

The arrival of the fleet was a very special day in the history of Shanghai. The entire Bund area and the adjacent northern end of Nanking Road swarmed with spectators of all ages, as the 7th Fleet majestically entered the Whangpoo harbor and dropped anchor directly opposite the main segment of the Bund. Within hours, the river was dotted with motorboats transporting weary, happy sailors to the shores of Shanghai.

Within weeks, the ever-enterprising Shanghailanders closed up shops and opened girlie bars in their stead, transforming Avenue Joffre from a sophisticated shopping area into an alley of corruption and vice. The few beautiful young girls of Shanghai reserved themselves for the military men of higher rank, while the thousands of ordinary men in uniform desperately searched for female companions. And soon enough, we all witnessed the magical workings of the supply-and-demand theory of economics: old women, maids and streetwalkers – all became lovers of the Americans in uniform. Some of these girlie-bar romances even ended in marriage! The American soldiers and sailors, airmen and marines flooded the city with love, U.S. dollars, American cigarettes, chocolates and nylon stockings! With these treasures, they remained unchallenged for months.

Even young Chinese boys, begging on street corners, were influenced by the benevolent powers of the United States military machine. Instead of displaying their decaying wounds or pointing to their dying parents, they ran around grabbing foreigners by the arm, shouting: "Do you want a girl, mister? One dolla. Do you want a virgin? Two dollas!"

But the most far-reaching metamorphosis took place in the character of the Chinese themselves, or at least in the makeup of many persons. Once subject to the domination and brutality of a cruel occupying force, the native population reacted to its newly gained freedom with an unbecoming arrogance and a bias of its own. This attitude was soon directed at foreigners, including those who had been their own allies during the war.

After taking over the concessions, the government of Chiang Kai-shek at once set in place its own judicial system, municipal government and police. Very soon it became evident that a foreigner "would have no chance in court" and that even a short imprisonment was a death sentence, given the atrocious sanitary and dietary conditions of the local jails.

Attendant on Chiang Kai-shek's return to Shanghai was the citywide spread of graft. Wealthy merchants were approached for protection money or simply bribes. Kickbacks in business became a legitimate business transaction, and outright arrests or threats of imprisonment cost the victim anything between one to ten gold bars.[1]

Hunger for money and personal enrichment afflicted not only the government but also the military. Generals and low-ranking commanders were often caught selling military hardware to the Communists, who were bent on capturing city after city in their quest for complete control of the people and the land.

With the gradual surrender of the Japanese, the detention camps for "enemy nationals" began to be evacuated. However, even before the inmates could complete their registration and leave, the camp gates were opened for free entrance and exit. Upon hearing the news that the camp would be open to visitors, our group of friends left the city on our bikes to visit the Morguleff family, our closest friends among the inmates. To reach the Lunghwa Camp, we had to pedal forty-five minutes, but it was worth all the effort. We were Sarah and Mara's first visitors, and we all

---

1. The Chinese Reserve Bank paper money (the CRB) was worthless and became devalued daily. Gold bars were the only stable currency available. Citizens would carry their salaries in suitcases.

had many stories to exchange. The Morguleffs, courageously and with no obvious ill effect, survived the hardships of camp life. They recounted their sufferings under the strict regime of the Japanese conquerors and we, in turn, related to them the goings on in the community, the news we received from Palestine and the daily gossip of Jewish life in Shanghai. By the time we left the camp, it was late in the evening and we were all emotionally drained by our reunion.

Soon the Morguleffs were back home in their apartment in the former French Concession. It did not take long before they renewed their active participation in Betar and Revisionist activities and in the life of the Jewish community as a whole.

Meanwhile, a delegation had been formed by the Shanghai Jewish community to meet the newly arrived Jewish chaplain, Rabbi Alvin Fine.[1] To my delight, I found myself selected as a member of the delegation.

Rabbi Alvin Fine, young and dapper, proved to be an inspiring personality and a charming host. During his first visit to the Jewish Club, we spent several hours discussing the life and activities of the Shanghai Jewish community. During our subsequent conversations, we agreed to establish a Jewish Welfare Board office in the Shanghai Jewish Club and to organize services for Jewish men and women of the United States armed forces in our Tenant de la Tour Synagogue. We also decided that a second Passover Seder be organized in our club for Jewish military personnel. Chaplain Fine, in turn, was to provide the prayer books and other necessities, free of charge to the entire Jewish community. For more than a year, until his final departure from Shanghai, I sustained a warm friendship with this gracious and urbane military chaplain.

---

1. Rabbi Alvin Fine (b. 1916) served as senior rabbi at Congregation Emanu-El, San Francisco, from 1949-1964. He currently enjoys a productive retirement and the devotion of a following that claims him as one of San Francisco's most beloved clergymen.

The liberation of Shanghai by the American forces brought an end to the apprehension that the foreign population had endured throughout the years of the Japanese occupation. However, for all of us, especially for those without passports and visas, a gnawing uncertainty and feeling of anxiety set in. Should we leave? If so, where should we go?

At this time the Soviet Consulate in Shanghai announced Stalin's amnesty to all "misguided" Russian émigrés. Our anti-Communist sins were forgiven. All who strayed away from the homeland might now return. Citizenship would be granted immediately, together with passports and all necessary travel documents! And so, thousands of Russians – White émigrés and stateless residents of Shanghai – all dashed to the Soviet Consulate to receive the promised passports: red booklets of the Union of Soviet Socialistic Republics! Among them were some Jews of meager financial means who had no hope for an immediate alternative.

With the exception of Leva Olshevsky and myself, all of our close friends applied and received student visas for the United States. One by one, they began to leave Shanghai, and to reassemble in the United States. Leva and I, however, were determined to wait for our permits for Palestine.

In the meanwhile, my parents, my relatives and friends of our family all began applying for visas to whatever countries were open to refugee immigration. Due to new quota regulations, bureaucratic red tape and an indiscriminate ascription of Communist affiliation to China's Jewish population, it was extremely difficult to obtain a visa for entry into the United States. Dozens of instances came to light of Shanghai residents who telephoned the American Consulate, only to be advised that "Mr. So-and-So" was a Communist. An applicant's chance for a visa was doomed on the spot. So personal scores were settled. My dad was a victim of one such unscrupulous informer who now lives in South America. Many years later, when the United States authorities examined my own visa application, the story unfolded. (At that time, in 1956, the World Betar Headquarters had sent me to the United States on a Zionist mission.) Not only did we learn the name of the informer, but apologies were submitted to us in person, and duly accepted on our part.

During these days of desperate search for new havens, all such refusals became personal catastrophes. To compound their first visa refusal, my parents faced another. This time, they applied for a visa to Australia. Within two or three months, they were invited to the Australian Consulate, shown a file of their son's anti-British speeches and a photo as he was delivering one of them and they were promptly refused entry to Australia! Devastated, my parents sought and finally received visas for Cuba, while I stubbornly refused to leave Shanghai, optimistically awaiting my opportunity to go to Palestine.

The hysteria of exodus began to take its toll on the entire stateless community, as well as on many citizens of the United States, England and France. Everyone was leaving. Some today, some tomorrow or the next year – but with no one seriously planning on staying behind.

By now, a second large wave of Soviet citizens was about to embark on a return journey to Russia. However, rumors from the first wave already began to trickle in to Shanghai. Dangerous as it was to write negatively about the conditions in Soviet Russia, enterprising individuals still managed to spread the word that no one should hurry to join them. In fact, the following anecdote began making the rounds: Two brothers decided that one would go to the Soviet Union and the other would stay behind to wait for his brother's reaction. Since one could not risk criticizing the Soviet Union openly, it was agreed that if the letter was written in blue or black ink, it would mean conditions were indeed favorable and that the brother who was left behind should follow immediately. If, however, the letter was written in red ink, it would signify that life was awful and the brother receiving the letter must not even dream of joining the brother who wrote it. After much waiting, the letter arrived. It was written in black ink. At the very bottom of the letter, however, a barely noticeable P.S. had been scribbled. It read, "Sorry, searched all over Siberia but couldn't find red ink." Thousands left for the Soviet Union, and many lived to regret their decision. But not all.

The exodus mode was now irreversible, and all embassies and consulates were flooded with desperate requests for entrance visas. As a result, thousands succeeded in leaving for the United States, Canada, Australia, Cuba and Argentina. Among them were many members of the Shanghai Jewish community. This scenario began to unfold in late 1946 and it continued for the next three years. In 1945, during the first weeks of peace, the world was not preoccupied with tomorrow – it was too busy celebrating the delivery brought forth by today. Such was not the case with the Jewish world, however.

In Shanghai, members of the Jewish community looked up to the Zionists for leadership and guidance. Much needed to be done and young people had to be prepared for struggle and sacrifice, without which neither freedom nor independence could be achieved. This task was the assignment of Betar's current leadership. Our leadership consisted of many new young men and women. However, with every change in the headquarters of Betar, the names of Sara and Mara Morguleff and Pana Samsonovich were always included, to assure the stability and continuity of purpose of the organization.[1]

The end of the war exposed a smoldering revolution at our very doorstep. It also reopened communications between Shanghai and the world at large. It was then that the full horror of the Holocaust became known to the Jewish communities of China, and with it the realization of how decimated, how tragically orphaned, we had suddenly become.

---

1. Pana Samsonovich, his wife Musia and their two children, reached Israel on the first vessel to leave Shanghai. The Samsonovichs settled in Tel Aviv, where Musia worked for many years in the municipal government. On the last day of the Six-Day War (June 1967), their son was killed. Abrasha's tank received a direct hit, and he was killed on the spot. He was the youngest immigrant from China to give his life in the defense of his new country.

Chapter 6

1945. A SMOULDERING REVOLUTION

As Western Europe slowly recovered from the devastation of war and Eastern Europe submitted to the clutches of Communism, China began to pass through a smouldering revolution. From the very first, this internal power struggle was confined to minor skirmishes and major raids. Both parties in the conflict were reluctant to involve outsiders. Neither the party of Chiang Kai-shek nor the Communists could count on mass support were it to prostrate itself before a foreign power. Even the Communists carefully avoided openly displaying Stalin's assistance. In addition, the administration of President Harry S. Truman was reluctant to take sides in what it considered to be an internal matter. Instead, American diplomacy was geared to mediation, a policy that eventually proved fatal to Chiang Kai-shek's government.

This sudden dislike of outsiders was not a question of a capricious social dynamic. For decades, China had been subjected to one form or another of foreign domination and control. Europeans, and especially the British, had exercised their colonial prerogatives with notable arrogance. As a result, the Chinese people lived in servitude and subordination. The foreigners not only rode the rickshaws, but occasionally kicked the rickshaw-man in order to achieve a speedier trot. Native pedestrians hit by passing cars of foreign residents would rarely bother to complain to the police of either the French Concession or the International Settlement for fear of being additionally injured by the baton-wielding policeman. With few exceptions, the many foreign clubs in Shanghai were forbidden ground to the native population. Only on very rare occasions were known personalities or high-ranking government employees accepted as members at these "whites only" institutions.

Little wonder then, that with the end of war and the defeat of the Japanese, both the leaders and the populace of China were fed up with foreign intervention and colonial rule. Once the guns of war finally had been silenced, it was only natural to find a less hospitable attitude toward foreigners than had prevailed earlier.

On the other hand, the Kuomintang government of Chiang Kai-shek remained dependent and totally reliant militarily on the United States. Seemingly without serious apprehension, the Nationalist Government of China was gradually being drawn into an all-consuming confrontation with the Communists of Mao Tse-tung.

It was difficult to imagine that the victorious American-trained army and air force of Generalissimo Chiang Kai-shek, backed by the multimillion arms arsenal from America, would eventually succumb to the ragged revolutionaries of Mao Tse-tung and be forced to seek refuge on the island of Taiwan. No doubt, the fault lay not only with the Nationalist leadership, which included elements that betrayed its own comrades, but with the United States and its allies who had failed to back the Nationalist effort wholeheartedly. Instead, General Marshall, President Truman's Secretary of State, concentrated his efforts on a peaceful solution and fervently tried to create a coalition government wherein the Communists would share power with the Nationalists.

This was a typically naive policy that betrayed a total lack of understanding of the political, social and psychological background of the conflict, as well as the parties involved in it. No similar experiment had worked in Europe and there was much less reason to expect it to work in faraway China.

As it turned out, while the Nationalists were asserting themselves in the south and southeast, the Communists were slowly encroaching and widening their control from the northern mountains and Manchuria southward into the direct line of confrontation with the Kuomintang armies of Chiang Kai-shek.

Even before the final round was fought between the opposing Chinese armies, it was blatantly clear that China had emerged as an independent power and was not about to return to the days of Western domination and control. In *Westerners in China*, Nigel Cameron notes that after World War II, the only familiar part of China was its scenery and architecture: "There was the inescapable knowledge that the West was no longer the master of the East," states Cameron.[1] Surely, this is the way it had to be.

It is difficult to determine at which particular juncture the smouldering revolution graduated into a conflagration of destruction and blood. However, with the capture of important northern cities within earshot of Tientsin, it soon became clear that the days of the Kuomintang were numbered.

By that time, however, most of the Jews of China were on their way to new homes. And on reflection, many of us realized that throughout all the years of Jewish life in China, no serious effort had ever been made to create contact and to maintain a relationship with either the interior or the foreign ministries of this country.

The only incidence of such an attempt resulted in Dr. Sun Yat-sen's warm response to Nissim Ezra's letter.[2] Now in the turbulent aftermath of the war's end in the Pacific, another serious effort was being made. Judy Hasser, the energetic last *netziv* of the Shanghai Betar, actively sought appropriate contacts. Finally, through business acquaintances, she was

1. N. Cameron, *The Face of China* (Philadelphia: Philadelphia Museum of Art, 1978), p. 155.
2. See Part 2, chapter 1, below.

able to meet various government officials who helped her contact Dr. Sun
Fo, the Vice President of China, and Dr. George Yeh, its acting foreign
minister. Corresponding with Sun Fo, in her capacity as chairperson of the
political wing of the United Zionists Revisionists of China, she received
the following note: "In reply to your letter, I wish to state that the Zionist
movement is championing a worthy cause. I am glad that the late Dr. Sun
Yat-sen's sympathy for, and support of, the movement has produced
results. As a lover of democracy, I fully endorse my father's views."[1]

Unfortunately, at a later time, China did not vote in support of the
establishment of a Jewish state in Palestine. However, the Revisionist
Party in Shanghai, led by the efforts of Judith Hasser, had done all that
was humanly possible to avoid the setback.[2]

In Tientsin the situation was no better, and the city's foreigners were to
depart as soon as it was expedient to do so. There, as in Shanghai, foreign
consulates were overwhelmed with applications from the dispossessed,
and from persons lacking a country and a passport, people with no state
to protect them and nowhere to go.

Further north, in the once gay and active city of Harbin, where the
main foreign population consisted of White Russians and émigré Jews,
stateless and desperate, they, too, were reluctant to accept the invitation
of the Soviet State to repatriate to Russia. However, all accepted
citizenship, for Soviet citizenship came with a passport that allowed them
to travel in the event they could obtain a visa for any other destination on
earth. But this was not easy. And in the meantime, most of the foreign
population of Harbin was pitifully a part of an empire that was now
extending its borders into Manchuria as well. As a result, the majority of

---

1. From Judith Ben Eliezer, *Shanghai Lost, Jerusalem Regained* (Tel Aviv: Steimatzky), p. 348.
2. Judith Hasser left for Israel by plane in 1948. She married Arie Ben Eliezer – a leading figure
   in the Israeli Knesset (Parliament) and a former close friend and colleague of Menachem Begin.

the Russian émigrés and a minority of Jews decided to risk repatriation to the Soviet Union.

The bulk of Harbin Jewry, however, optimistically waiting for better days, stayed behind. It was to be a long and difficult wait of three years before the establishment of an independent Jewish State permitted them to leave.

These developments unfolded over the course of several years. They began with the first toasts to victory and ended with the complete evacuation of all foreigners from Shanghai, Tientsin and Harbin. For the Chinese multitudes, the historic changes enveloping their ancient land began with the evacuation of the hated enemy and ended with a revolution that changed every life beyond recognition. Whether all the changes brought about were for the best is something history will have to judge – history and the people behind it.

As for the Jewish community of Shanghai, this short period between victory and mass evacuation was rich in developments, achievements, concerns and excitement. Whereas to others the day of final victory invited days and weeks of celebrations and festivities, we Jews again embarked on a period of unprecedented national mourning. Within days, we were informed of the great tragedy that had obliterated one third of our people. Plunged into desolation and despair, we understood that without our own Jewish state, there could be no future for the Jewish people.

Chapter 7

1946. DAYS OF MOURNING AND GRIEF

Shortly before the end of the War, I decided to drop out of St. John's University. Before finding a job, I assisted my dad in keeping books for his "Mars" restaurant on Nanking Road. My friends, however, continued their courses, hoping to graduate by the time the war ended and to use their diplomas to facilitate entrance to the United States with a student visa. Since I had no such plans and intended to leave for Palestine at the first opportunity, the diminishing standards of my university were of little concern.

At this time, I took on an additional assignment in the Revisionist Party. Appointed general secretary, I ran the office and took care of the administrative work of the New Zionist Organization of Revisionists in Shanghai. My able and devoted secretary was Amalia Tsipris, who with her brother, Grisha, was active in the Revisionist Party and in the Friends of Betar organization.[1]

---

1. Amalia married Al Goldberg, who succeeded me as secretary of the Revisionist Party in Shanghai. The Tsiprises and the Goldbergs subsequently resettled in Australia, where they have continued to be active in Zionist causes.

One morning after the tumultuous celebrations on the streets of Shanghai, just as I had arrived at the Revisionist office, I was handed a cable from the New Zionist Organization in Paris. It read:

> We regret to inform you, that it has now been officially established that 6,000,000 of our brethren were brutally murdered in the death camps of Auschwitz, Dachau, Treblinka and others. Orphaned and in deep mourning, we will continue our struggle for a free and independent Jewish State. Organize meetings and join the struggle so that the sacrifice of our martyred brothers and sisters, mothers and fathers, sons and daughters will not have been in vain.
>
> Signed: Shimshon Yunichman,
> Executive Committee, Political Department,
> Zionist Organization, Paris.

This cable burned itself into my memory. To us, the victims were total strangers, and yet the pain of loss was as real as a death in the family. Suddenly, we felt bereaved and orphaned, emotionally drained and spiritually devastated, left alone to continue our trek to eternity bearing the burden of history, culture, tradition and faith.

In Jewish practice, before attending to one's own grief, anger, frustration and desire for revenge, one is required to attend to the needs of the victim. It was this obligation that made it incumbent upon Jews everywhere to attend memorial services for the dead before staging protest meetings or attempting to seek justice from the silent world. Now throughout the world, Jews gathered in their houses of worship to pray for the souls of the massacred innocents – the men and the women, the young and the old. And so it was in Shanghai. The prayers were held at the Tenant de la Tour Synagogue. There was no room to accommodate even a quarter of all who came for the services. On the next day, similar prayers were held in Hongkew, where many were mourning blood kin, known to have been murdered in one of the death camps.

Only after attending to the blessings of the souls of these millions of victims of the Holocaust, did agonizing questions begin to penetrate our minds: Why? How? Who was responsible? We tried to find answers to some of these painful questions at our protest meetings held in the Jewish Club and in Hongkew. During the meeting organized by the Revisionists and Betar, I read Yunichman's cable word for word to the hundreds of Jews assembled in the main hall of the Shanghai Jewish Club, and then added: "To some, these days are days of thanksgiving and celebrations – to us, the Jewish people, these are days of sorrow and mourning. We have been decimated and orphaned and our 'trophies of victory' are the ash piles of Treblinka and Dachau. Let us not rest until our brethren are avenged. Let us not forget nor forgive. Let us – the remnants of world Jewry – become the last generation of slaves and the first generation of free men!"

These sentiments were well accepted by all present and it did not take long before the Jewish community proved its loyalty to Zionism with its own generosity, sacrifice and devotion. Shortly after this meeting, another was held in Hongkew that was attended by several thousand people. The main speakers were Aron Kalmanovich and Joe Tukachinsky. They both delivered powerful and eloquent orations, again calling on Jews to participate in the rebirth of a Jewish State.

Several months passed before the Nuremberg Trials were flashed on screens around the world. In Shanghai, a special two-hour feature covering the trials was shown at the fashionable Roxy theater, located on Bubbling Well Road in the former International Settlement. Many of the Jewish community stayed away from this showing, but I did not. The film displayed only a handful of the murderers of the Nazi era. Thousands, however, had found safe havens in South America or were living incognito elsewhere in the world. When I entered the Roxy theater, I did not know what to expect.

Before judging me naive, the reader must realize that in China, we were totally unfamiliar with Nazism. Fate and geography had conspired to protect us. Living within the splendid isolation of the Jewish communities in China, we had been spared visual as well as physical contact with the military personnel and former administrators of Hitler's Germany.

Not that life in China provided us with immunity against anti-Semitism or protected us from physical clashes with organized gangs of Jew-haters. But all of these encounters had been confined to the White Russians and its fringe Fascist groups that were notoriously rampant in the city of Harbin. And so none of us had ever met or seen a "real" Nazi.

I was therefore totally unprepared when, sitting in a luxurious movie theater, I was compelled to stare into the faces of the top echelon Nazis as they sat on the benches of the accused during the civil proceedings of the Nuremberg Trials. Observing the accused in that courtroom, meticulously dressed, neatly combed and well-groomed, I could not help but wonder at how normal they looked. As I watched them rise, speak calmly, smile to their lawyers and return to their seats, I observed their eyes, the window of the soul, and I saw nothing. And I began to wonder whether this might be an inseparable part of the tragedy of the Holocaust and a warning to the entire human race. Could it be that this was another weapon of their success, the very fact that most of them looked so human? There, in the darkened theater in Shanghai, I began to wonder how many more Nazis were walking the streets of the civilized world. And how many might be born tomorrow to continue the evil deeds of their fathers when, once again, the world would watch in total silence.

As these questions formed in my mind, I observed the images of the Nazis on the screen, and once again I was reminded that to prevent repetition of the Nazi horrors, we must never forget the past. We must forever hunt down both the perpetrators and the apologists of the Holocaust. If we do, perhaps coming generations will be spared the sight of the Devil with a human face!

Together with the rest of the Jewish world, we gradually learned to live with our pain and our agony. But accursed be the day when we forget the lessons of the Holocaust. If we forget, we shall no longer be worthy of existence as a nation.

At the very same time, when audiences were viewing the Nuremberg Trials on the silver screen of the Roxy theater, the Shanghai Jewish Club received notice that it could no longer occupy the Masonic Building for its activities. Again a search committee was established and again an appropriate compound was found, at 20 Route Pichon, the site of the former French Concession. This was a magnificent location with spacious grounds on which were set a number of buildings.

It was immediately agreed that Betar would be given possession of the smaller building and the adjacent grounds. Moving from our crowded headquarters in the Chernomorsky building, we happily reestablished ourselves. Meanwhile, "Cherry" (Chernomorsky) returned to his family in Harbin, and for several years we were separated from each other by the Communist Bamboo Curtain.

In late 1946, my closest friends began to leave Shanghai. For a while, I seemed to be spending more time on the Whangpoo wharfs than in the city. Our farewells were emotional and depressing, marking a total change of life for us all, and no one knew what to expect. We were about to turn our backs on the halcyon days of youth, to face the awesome responsibilities of adulthood.

By early 1947, the last of our intimate group had left Shanghai, and even Leva Olshevsky, who stayed behind with me, returned to Tientsin to wait his turn for a travel visa to Palestine. Earlier, two Betarim from Tientsin had arrived in Shanghai and immediately became active in the organization. One was Chaim Werreck and the other Leo Kiachko. Both of them very quickly became my close friends and our friendships have lasted a lifetime.

At this time I was also drawn into a circle of peers from the ranks of Betar who were one or two years my senior. Among them were such talented and devoted people as Shura Litvin, Judy and Dodia Volovick,

Joseph Feller, Grisha and Freda Nissenbaum and Joseph Krupnick. They were unassuming young men and women with talents in sports, commerce and the arts. There were others, too numerous to mention, who attained their highest achievements only after leaving China. Some became famous diplomats, journalists, architects, doctors and artists. But more importantly, they all were and remain good, decent, honest and sincere human beings, whose companionship enlivened the last months of my life in Shanghai. That period would be marked by a change in my own fortune.

Chapter 8

HOLLYWOOD COMES TO SHANGHAI

In a sense, the turn in my personal story that I am about to recount is a part of the turn in fortune of the Shanghai Jewish Club and Betar. At 20 Route Pichon, Betar now had ample space for clubrooms and offices, a spacious auditorium, a full-sized volleyball court, a dressing room and showers. In fact, the volleyball court facility could accommodate scores of spectators.

Before moving to its new premises, Betar decided to hold another Hanukah Ball in the old Masonic Auditorium. As it happened, this would be the last Hanukah Ball that I would organize, and it turned out to be a huge success. The evening began with a ballet, the scenario of which featured a heroine who represented Israel. Her male partners, dressed in Nazi uniforms, throw her acrobatically all over the stage in a choreography suggestive of violence and rape. Suddenly, two other dancers, in British uniforms, rescue the maiden, only to violate her themselves. Finally, two dancers, dressed as Irgun fighters, engage the British attackers in a life-and-death battle that concludes with the rescue and freeing of the heroine-Israel. The next number displayed the prowess of the Betar athletes, who paraded onto the stage in sports attire and formed daring pyramids that reached the ceiling of the theater.

The third number was a comedy: The mise-en-scène caricatured the Jewish Club itself. On the window sill of each window a humorous figure could be seen sitting, but instead of painted heads, arms and legs, holes had been cut out and filled with the heads and bodies of our amateur actors. Everyone participated in this skit that included verses sung to the accompaniment of a band and depicted the problems of Jewish organizational life in Shanghai. One actor, for instance, representing the Hevrah Kadisha, explained in song and verse that the cemetery was filled, and he urged the Jewish community to cooperate with this crisis by not dying. The evening was a huge success, and Betar collected significant funds to enroll new friends and members into its popular organization.

The next day, I was surprised to receive a phone call from Alex Caplan, the local manager of Warner Brothers Films. A guest at the Betar Hanukah Ball, Mr. Caplan invited me to visit his office the next day, at my convenience. The upshot of that interview was that I was asked to become manager of the publicity department of Warner Brothers, Shanghai. I loved my job from the very first day and enjoyed the complete independence that accompanied it. I was free to promote Warner movies in any way I saw fit, and the results were rewarding. On one occasion, while working on a publicity campaign for *This is The Army*, the premier performance of which was donated to the retired soldiers' fund of the Chinese Military Forces, I met Madame Sun Yat-sen – the widow of the founder of the Chinese Republic.

Movies in China were as popular as rice, or so it seemed. Like most other Asians, the Chinese preferred martial arts and military actions, accompanied by scenes of devastation and destruction. Smaller foreign audiences, however, gravitated to films based on popular novels or simply to movies featuring the big names. Not surprisingly, in the English- and Russian-language press, to attract a Western audience, we publicized the romantic flavor of a film, but for the Chinese-language publications, we magnified the scenes of violence in movies that in fact focused on love stories and emotional crisis.

During a publicity campaign for the film *Sergeant York* I received the cooperation of the Shanghai police, whose captain delegated some hundred men to participate in a street parade with banners advertising Gary Cooper as Sergeant York. I, in turn, organized a target-shooting competition for the entire police force with prizes and free tickets to the show.

However, my most memorable piece of publicity work was the stunt that I created to accompany Ronald Reagan's film, *King's Row*. Atop a canopy of the Grand Theater on Bubbling Well Road, a giant book was displayed. Out of it came the voice of a storybook character, saying, "I am So-and-So, and this is what happened to me. What would you do in my place?" The voice was recorded in Chinese and a hidden Chinese worker was employed to turn the pages of the book. After seeing to it that all was ready, I left instructions to activate the display at noon, when the streets would be crowded with traffic and lunch-hour pedestrians. I slipped away to the Revisionist office to take care of the incoming mail.

By one o'clock, police cars with sirens were driving up to the Jewish Club compound, in search of "Mr.-Warner-Brothers-Liberman." On the back of a police motorcycle I was taken to the Grand Theater, and there I could not believe my eyes: thousands of people were gaping at the display above the canopy. Dozens of street cars and buses, cars and pedicabs, all had come to a halt. No one was able to cross the street. I was instructed by the police to stop the motion and the sounds of the display and to request that the Chinese worker come down from his position atop the canopy. I obeyed reluctantly. The incident, nonetheless, increased publicity for the movie and I must say that *King's Row* enjoyed an unprecedented success with Chinese and foreign audiences.

I earned very little money at Warner Brothers, but since I lived with my parents, my salary didn't matter. The benefits of my job were sufficient compensation: I was free to move around at will, even to travel to Tientsin and miss several days of work; I could attend any movie in town, free of charge; I was constantly meeting interesting people and becoming well known in the film industry both locally and among the publicity personnel of Warner Brothers Studios in Hollywood. Above all else, I found my work interesting and enjoyable.

Many of my friends, meanwhile, found jobs with the United States military. Whether in their Post Exchanges or in other civilian departments, they were well compensated and some were able to earn more than one hundred dollars per month.

Toward the beginning of my second year with Warner Brothers, my chief, Alex Caplan, was offered a very promising position with Walt Disney Studios. He was replaced by Jack Dagal, a Jew of Sephardic origin, with a Hindu background. A pleasant man, tactful, kind and a workaholic, Jack Dagal quickly realized that the future of our publicity department depended on focusing on the Chinese public. Therefore, he suggested that we devote our main thrust toward Chinese-language publicity campaigns.

Soon thereafter, Jack was preparing my Chinese assistant to take over my job, and I, in turn, was being geared to move to sales, possibly to serve as manager of our Taiwan office. In the winter of 1946, as each new day unfolded, it became clearer and clearer that unless I was prepared to take on the Taiwan assignment, I would be out of my job by September of 1947. Realizing that I was determined to stay in the Orient and to await my permit to travel to Palestine, my parents insisted that I take up the offer and work in Taiwan until my papers for Palestine arrived. They could not leave me alone in Shanghai jobless and without an apartment. The argument had merit, and we began to plan accordingly.

Although I enjoyed my work as head of Warner Brothers' publicity department and appreciated the warm letters of gratitude that I received from my superiors at the Hollywood studios, my mind and heart were with the heroes of the Irgun Underground in Palestine. Led by the former head of Betar in Poland, Menachem Begin, these young women and men were sacrificing their lives for the cause of the freedom and independence of the Jewish people.

We were especially happy to hear that the bitter strife between the Nationalist and the Leftist elements of the Yishuv was subsiding, and that some form of understanding and cooperation was beginning to emerge. News now reaching us in Shanghai was of the gallant attempts of the Haganah to bring shiploads of illegal immigrants, the remnants of European Jewry, to the shores of Palestine. We learned of the valiant struggle of the Irgun against the brutal and arrogant mandatory regime. Indeed, there were signs of Jewish unity everywhere, and, as if to confirm this fact, we were advised, again by cable, that the New Zionist Organization had decided to reenter the World Zionist Organization and combine efforts in order to reach a successful conclusion to the Zionist dream of Jewish statehood! Once again, we became Zionists – Revisionists and members of the World Zionist Organization.

The Betar organizations in Tientsin and Harbin were informed of various activities surrounding the struggle for Jewish independence, but nonetheless they were isolated from important details and personal contact with us. It was still difficult to travel within China and the safest means of doing so, by air, was extremely expensive. Thus, the most powerful and reliable link between our Jewish communities was our bi-weekly magazine *Tagar*, skillfully edited by Milia Ionis (in Russian) and Judy Hasser (in English).

It was impossible to reach Harbin, but Tientsin was another matter. Our organization was as keen as I was to reestablish contact. To do so, I decided to seek the assistance of my friend, Chaplain Alvin Fine, who asked me if I would be prepared to fly out to Tientsin at a moment's notice, should he arrange my transportation via an Air Force transport plane. I replied in the affirmative and informed my parents and my office at Warner Brothers that I would be visiting the airport each morning until a flight materialized. When it did, I stated that I would be away for five to seven days and would return home on a civilian flight. (The Revisionist Party was willing to pay for a one-way ticket for me.)

As luck had it, Chaplain Fine was successful on the first try. I flew out on a two-engine transport plane that carried a jeep and some cases of equipment. Seated alone, next to the rope-fastened jeep, I held onto the rope for dear life, whispering a prayer for safe landing. In some two hours we reached Tientsin and I was driven from the airport to the home of my dear friend, Levchik (Arie) Olshevsky. With his help, I was introduced to the Jewish community and met its leaders – the former Betar *netziv*, Leo Piastunovitch and the Jewish community head, Zelia Bellokamen, as well as Ara Prejensky, the then-current leader of the Tientsin Betar and his assistant, Yasha Shtofman. I met other prominent leaders of the community and the Revisionist Party: Grisha Zubitsky (cousin of Vulya Zubitsky of Shanghai), Yasha Blinik, the talented poet, Monia Pirutinsky, Joe Pittel, Zelik Bellokamen and many others. Only toward the end of my visit, did I meet two young Betarim, Arie Marinsky and Samby Muller, with whom I would develop a long-lasting and deep friendship.

In Tientsin, my goal was to reach as many members of the Jewish community as possible and to transmit to them all the details of the current struggle for Jewish statehood; to forge unity between our communities; and to assure members of Betar that everything would be done in order to assist them in reaching Palestine, as soon as possible. I also used the opportunity of my visit to discuss with the Betar leadership the possibility of organizing another Betariada – in Shanghai.

While there, I would visit different organizations, meet people and bask in the warmth and unity of yet another wonderful Jewish community in China.

Chapter 9

1947. TIENTSIN

Situated geographically between Shanghai and Harbin, Tientsin is a one-hour train ride from Peking, the ancient and modern capital of China. Nonetheless, in recent times, it has been corrupted by internationalism, divided by concessions and force-fed with Western culture and the Western way of life almost as much as Shanghai.

Dating back to the first decade of the twentieth century, Jewish life in Tientsin has been firmly rooted in the mores of the Harbin Jewish community. At the time of its first settlement, its Jewish population consisted of the few Russian Jews who had trickled in from Manchuria, but by 1904 the Jews of Tientsin actually had bought some land for a cemetery and registered the Jewish community with the Russian Imperial Consulate in Tientsin. As the majority of early Jewish settlers in town were relatively poor, they created the Tientsin Hebrew Association, a mutual aid society for the purpose of extending interest-free loans to its members.

Although the Jewish population seemed to be growing rapidly, the Tientsin Jewish community was by far the smallest of the three and at no time exceeded three thousand members. Its undisputed founder and long-term president was Leonid Gershevich. Many others assumed the initiative and became exemplary communal leaders. Among them were Abba Izgur, Leva Piastunovitch and Zelig Bellokamen.

In 1925 Tientsin Jewry established the Tientsin Jewish School that subsequently became one of the best schools in town. A Jewish Club, "Kunst" (Art), was founded in 1928 and soon, with its large hall well-suited for theatrical performances, became the heart of the Jewish community. It boasted a library, a reading room, a popular restaurant and many smaller rooms for card games and meetings.

At one time, the community published a bi-weekly newsletter page in one of the Russian-language newspapers. For news of the wider region and for world Zionist information, the community relied on the Zionist publications that arrived via Harbin and Shanghai.

Whereas Jews in Shanghai were evenly scattered around the major residential areas of the city, the foreign community of Tientsin was concentrated in the British Concession. Here the leading trade offices were located and the most important international business was transacted.

One of the most popular and successful business ventures toward which Jews gravitated was the fur trade. A variety of fur skins were purchased from nearby provinces, including those in Manchuria, sorted and processed in Tientsin and shipped out to the world.

Jewish organizations spread and multiplied. "Charity begins at home" was not just an empty slogan for the Jewish communities in China. Once the new settlers increased and began to establish businesses, they, like their brethren in Harbin and Shanghai, attended to the less fortunate and provided all the necessary care for the poor, sick and destitute. By 1939, the Jewish community of Tientsin proudly opened its own synagogue, a majestic building, centrally located on Davenport Road in the British Concession, and large enough to accommodate the religious needs of its congregation.

As organizations grew and developed, Zionism in Tientsin came to occupy a prominent place in the kaleidoscope of Jewish activities in the city. Parents were eager to see their children join a Zionist organization that would create a basis for Jewish identity and ethnic pride. Before long, the most prominent organization to attract the mass of Tientsin youth was Betar. Around it, older people were organized into "Friends of Betar" committees as well as into the ranks of the Revisionist Party.

The distinct honor of founding the Tientsin Betar branch goes to Lelka (Lev) Kotovich. Not only was he an initiator of the Betar branch in Harbin in 1929, but two years later, he became instrumental in the founding of the Shanghai Betar as well. Subsequently, the more organizationally and ideologically experienced Betarim from Harbin helped other branches to grow and mature.

Jewish youth, ranging in age from twelve to sixteen, were the first to join the ranks of the Tientsin Betar. They came primarily from the Tientsin Jewish School, where they had already received a basic knowledge of Judaism and Jewish history and an initial introduction to the Hebrew language. In Betar they became steeped in the history of Zionism, the ideology of the Zionist movement, the twists and turns in modern history that included British betrayal of the Balfour Declaration, and they came to revere Jabotinsky's struggle for an independent Jewish State. They also acquired a serious understanding of the catastrophe experienced by European Jewry. These young people, in turn, brought with them a most remarkable enthusiasm and esprit. But they were not mere bookworms – rather, they demonstrated a notable proficiency in a wide diversity of individual and team sports as well.

Among the older Betarim was Ara Prejensky, who had formed the first Betar executive council that commanded the Jabotinsky Movement in Tientsin and who subsequently became a prominent leader of the Jewish community in the city. However, the overall leader and *netziv* Betar in China was Leo Piastunovitch, who in his later years became the beloved head of the Jewish community as a whole. Resolute, honest, fearless and determined, Leva had the characteristics of a born leader. He devoted all of his time, energy and health to the needs of the Jewish community of Tientsin. A mild-mannered man full of life, enthusiasm and creativity, he devotedly served many Jewish causes. However, he loved Betar above all other groups and in turn was greatly beloved by the Betarim. In 1949, with his wife and young son, Teddy, Piastunovich emigrated to Israel and, there too, he assumed the leadership of the Association of Jewish Immigrants from China.[1]

In the early forties, another loyal Betari from Harbin came to assist with the leadership of Tientsin Betar. Girsh Nehamkin was a devoted worker who eschewed the limelight and overt power. There is hardly a soul who ever entered the ranks of Betar in either Harbin or Tientsin who did not have a good word to say about this extraordinary man – the embodiment of Jabotinsky's concept of *hadar*. In many ways he reminded me of Abrasha Milichiker, another Betari from Harbin.

The heads of Betar in Tientsin, under *netziv* Leva Piastunovitch, included Ara Prejensky (1931-1935 and 1943-1946), Misha Hutaransky (1935-1940), Grisha Zubitsky (1940-1943), Yasha Shtofman (1946-1948) and Ara Shprahman (1949). Many others made their lasting contributions by serving on the executive council, in training athletic teams, in teaching and in collecting funds for organizational expenses.

Tientsin Betar served the community well. It participated honorably in all-Tientsin sports events, protected Jewish property from pillage by gangs of hooligans and anti-Semites and added pride and cheer to every Jew in the city, when in their smart uniforms its members paraded on the streets of Tientsin to the sound of bugles and drums.

During the devastating flood of 1939, Betar became a household word in numerous families, Jewish and gentile alike. The Betarim worked tirelessly day and night, transporting stranded citizens, delivering food and caring for the old and the sick. Nothing could illustrate better Betar's contribution to alleviating disaster and the appreciation of total strangers than the following story of the flood. It is recounted by an elderly émigré from Russia, a non-Jew.

---

1. In 1951 Leo Piastunovitch settled in Japan where he became an employee of a business magnate. Suddenly, one evening at home in Tokyo, he was struck with a massive heart attack and died. With his death, the entire Jabotinsky Movement lost a loyal and devoted member and friend.

"My wife became ill. There was no food in the house. I decided to look around and went out to wade in the water outside. The water was about to reach my belt and even higher. Where would I find food? Well, I figured, the end has come! I will go back in, take my old woman and we shall both put an end to our misery by drowning. Suddenly, a rowboat approached: 'Where to, Grandpa?' the rowers asked. They took us home and gave us bread, sugar and a can of sardines and the next day delivered milk for my wife. They did not forget us, but continued to bring food to our door until the waters finally diminished. I shall pray for those Jewish boys in their Betar uniforms the rest of my life."[1]

In competitive sports, Betar boasted excellent teams in boxing, volleyball, ping-pong and other forms of athletics. Mike Boyarsky, one of Betar's best all-around sportsmen, represented his city in international soccer games held in Shanghai. Extremely mild-mannered, Mike was adored not only for his achievements but for his personality as well. Fortunate were those who knew Mike, and greatly enriched were they who counted him among their friends.[2] Mike's older brother, Itzhak Boyarsky, devoted much time to training Betarim in track, volleyball and basketball.[3] As a result, the Tientsin Betar volleyball team managed to beat the acknowledged Chinese champions, the Kun-chan University team of Tientsin. The Tientsin Betar ping-pong team, led by Tientsin champion, George Kanzepolsky, became a formidable opponent, and pugilists of the caliber of Bob Shmerling and Muller became known as the best boxers in town. These achievements helped to establish Betar as one of the better-known sports organizations in Tientsin, and they became a source of happiness and pride to the Jewish population as a whole.

Perhaps the best illustration of Betar's popularity and wide acceptance came a year after my brief visit to Tientsin. In May 1948, a public announcement invited Tientsin's Jewry to the synagogue to

---

1. "Tientsin Flood – 1939" from *Betar in China 1929-1949* (Tel Aviv, 1973).
2. Mike Boyarsky died in June 1949 of a sickness that had incapacitated him in World War Two years.
3. Itzhak Boyarsky emigrated to Israel from Tientsin in 1949.

celebrate the Declaration of Independence of the State of Israel. The announcement carried portaits of Theodore Herzl and Ze'ev Jabotinsky. Below Herzl's portrait, a caption had been included from his speech made to the first Zionist Congress in Basel: "Here I have founded a Jewish State. I do not know when it will be fully realized. Perhaps in a year. Perhaps in five years. Certainly in fifty." Below Jabotinsky's portrait another quotation taken from one of his addresses had been placed, and it read: "Jewish People of the World – give us the power and the courage and we shall liberate you!" So on this most joyous day in modern Jewish history, Tientsin Jewry side by side, commemorated the achievements of Herzl and Jabotinsky.

This was the Betar that I came to visit one evening in the spring of 1947. It was here that I met Harry (Arie) Marinsky and Samby (Shmuel) Miller who, in their unswerving loyalties to Betar, would become fateful in my life as well.

Chapter 10
1947. THE TRAILBLAZERS

After meeting with the leadership of the Revisionist Party in Tientsin and the executive council of Betar, I was led to the main hall where I addressed the Betarim and the guests who had flocked to the Kunst Club to hear news from abroad. When the meeting ended, we proceeded to Betar quarters for further talks and discussions. It was there that I was stopped at the staircase by two seventeen- or eighteen-year old youths who peered at me – was it with disdain, was it a conspiratorial sign? I could not tell. They spoke abruptly and seemed decidedly unfriendly. Nor were they impressed with my seniority or status as a dignitary and guest.

Arie (Harry) Marinsky introduced himself and his comrade Shmuel (Samby) Muller.[1] Their message, too, was brief. They had decided to go to Palestine via Europe and to enter the ranks of the Irgun Tzevai Leumi, the Jewish Underground. There was nothing that I or the *netzivut* (the national council) could do or say to dissuade them from executing their

---

1. Arie Marinsky became a prominent lawyer in Israel. He married and had two sons. In the 1980s he developed a brain tumor, to which he succumbed at a relatively young age. Shmuel Muller married Chana Litvin from Harbin, who bore him three children. During the Yom Kippur War, their son Shulik served in the paratroopers unit on the Southern front. Leading his men over the Suez Canal, Shulik was hit by a sniper's bullet. He died instantly. Today, the Mullers live in Kfar Shmeriahu, Israel, where Samby is the owner of an international trading company.

plan. Their one request was that we pass on to them some addresses in Europe and a letter of introduction.

I was immediately impressed with the determination of these two young men who stood before me. I explained that I would be the last to interfere with their intentions. However, in order to achieve better results, I suggested that they plan on a short stay in Shanghai where I would introduce them to Judy Hasser, who would definitely support their plan, even if the rest of the leadership might be cool to this attempt at an unauthorized activity.

Marinsky and Muller went to Shanghai within a week and met with Judy and me as well as with other members of Betar and of the Revisionist leadership. In spite of the rather tepid support these Tientsin boys received from the majority of the movement's leaders in Shanghai, no one actually stood in their way. The European leg would be difficult and dangerous since in addition to legitimate Polish passports in their possession, they would be carrying false visas, or rather visas improperly obtained. Their letters of introduction from Shanghai were, of course, genuine, but given some of their ports of call, promised to become more of a hindrance than a help.

It did not take them long to reach Paris and to make contact with the Revisionist Party office. There they were introduced to the Irgun's contact man and were placed in an Irgun training course in Italy. In his memoirs, printed in the jubilee issue of *Betar in China*, Arie writes: "What impressed us most was the spiritual and physical strength of the Irgun recruits. I had imagined that in Europe we will find remnants of a once glorious European Jewry – hungry, depressed, weak and humble. Instead, we found young men and women, strong, determined, motivated and brave."[1]

Midway through their training, our friends asked the commander if he knew the whereabouts of Ilushka (Eliahu) Lankin. By this time, Lankin had been captured by the British, taken to a prison camp in

---

1. Arie Marinsky, "Memoir", *Betar in China*.

Eritrea from which he had escaped and was put in command of the Irgun's European branch. At the mention of Lankin's name, the commander paled and scolded Shmuel and me, prohibiting us from ever mentioning his name again. Lamely, the boys explained to their commander that Eliahu Lankin came from Harbin, China, and that his family was anxious to know about his well-being. Within days, Arie and Shmuel were summoned to appear at a certain street corner in Paris, carrying two newspapers under their arms. Marinsky recounts this meeting in another paragraph of his memoir: "The newspapers under our arms were superfluous," recounts Marinsky. "Someone tapped me on the shoulder, and as I turned around, I saw Ilushka standing there right in front of my eyes."[1] After a warm embrace and a few moments of nostalgic reminiscing, they continued their Russian conversation and their unique relationship that was special to the Jews of the Far East.[2]

On Eliahu's personal instructions, Arie and Shmuel were to return to China to organize an Irgun contingent there and either to prepare it for marine sabotage operations against British shipping in Hong Kong and Singapore (in the event the British did not leave Palestine on the day promised to the United Nations) or else to ready these units to defend the newborn State of Israel from an imminent Arab attack.

Before long, Arie and Shmuel were on their way back to Shanghai, bringing secret orders sewn into their jackets, appointing Judy Hasser, Tony Gaberman and me as commanders of the Chinese branch of the Irgun. Together with these orders came other official instructions from the Betar headquarters signed by Aron Propes, appointing Judy as netziv Betar of China and me as head of the Shanghai Betar. By now the age difference between Arie, Shmuel and myself became insignificant and we became the best of friends. We were destined to spend the best and worst days of our lives together.

---

1. Arie Marinsky, "Memoir."
2. As this book is being prepared for publication, I learned that Eliahu (Ilushka) Lankin, aged eighty, passed away suddenly from a massive heart attack at his home in Jerusalem.

Before leaving for their assignments in China, Arie and Shmuel had the misfortune of experiencing fraternal strife, a phenomenon that none of our Betarim from China could ever accept or excuse. This hatred was carried out and inspired by the left-wing labor parties that were in complete control of the administrative arm of the Jewish Agency and of the Va'ad Leumi (the National Council, acting as the official representative of the Yishuv). Stoicism in the face of severe provocation was the answer of the Irgun, whose commander-in-chief, Menachem Begin, constantly warned his soldiers to avoid fraternal strife at all cost and under any circumstance.

Suddenly, all efforts to achieve unity of the Yishuv failed, and the Haganah continued its previous tactics of hunting down the Irgun fighters, all over the country. "We were sitting in the Café 'Noga' near Mograbi Square in Tel Aviv with two Irgun contacts," writes Marinsky, "when a man came up to Muller and told him that someone was asking for him in the street. For a long while we waited, but Muller did not return. I was not too disturbed, because I knew how good a boxer Shmuel was. Nevertheless, curious about his absence, I decided to go and take a look outside the café. As I stepped into the street, I was attacked by several men, tied, gagged and driven away. Soon enough I found Shmuel – he was a Haganah prisoner together with me. We spent a couple of days in detention, while Haim Landau, commander of the Irgun in Tel Aviv, using every available means at his disposal, finally rescued us from our ordeal."[1]

No doubt our boys from Tientsin experienced much physical discomfort and possibly pain, while the Haganah men tried to extract information from them. Neither Shmuel nor Arie talked much about the episode. They also shied away from conversations on the subject of their suffering and deprivations during those trying times. Indeed those were days when heroic deeds were commonplace, and sacrifice – a way of life.

---

1. Haim Landau became a member of the Knesset and served in that capacity until his death from cancer. He was a Minister of Transport in the first "wall-to-wall" coalition government of Israel.

While their papers were being prepared for the long trip back to China, Arie and Shmuel participated in several military actions of the Irgun. But finally when the day of farewells approached, Haim Landau came up to the boys and warned them with a smile: "Don't you dare to become dead martyrs of our cause! You fellows cost us a fortune to train and to transport – you better stay alive!" Gratefully, they did.

Marinsky and Muller were exemplary representatives of the China Betar. They came from warm, loving and well-to-do families. They lived in comfort, surrounded by friends and tranquility. Nevertheless, like those before them, with them and after them, they chose danger and hardship, deprivation and sacrifice, in order to participate in the historic struggle for the liberty and independence of the people of Israel and the land of Zion.

Without any doubt, Arie and Shmuel were worthy followers of our first waves of *halutzim* (pioneers in Palestine) from China. They were also models of our postwar mass *aliyah*.[1]

While Shmuel and Arie were packing for their journey, I was struggling with boredom and loneliness in Taiwan (Formosa) as a representative of Warner Brothers. None of us back home was aware of how Muller and Marinsky were faring, of what had happened to them and of their immediate plans. In fact, except for the occasional messages indicating that they were both in Palestine, and that they were well, we had no contact with them.

Back in Shanghai, some days before Harry and Samby left for their trailblazing trip to Eretz Yisrael, the Jewish community was excitedly preparing for the announced visit of the first postwar emissary of Keren Kayemet, the Jewish Agency National Fund. Gedali Zhuhavitsky was a high-ranking employee of the Fund and a prominent member of the Labor Party in Palestine. His Socialist background did not make a bit of difference with the general membership of the Shanghai Jewish community. From Sima Hessin, the current president, to the Chief Rabbi

---

1. In Hebrew, *aliyah* means "ascent" and refers to immigration to the Land of Israel.

and from the religious Zionists in Hongkew to the last Betari and member of the Revisionist Party, Zhuhavitsky's visit was enthusiastically awaited.

Every member of the Jewish community of Shanghai was eager to welcome its first visitor from the land of our dreams – the Land of Israel!

Chapter 11

1947. DAYS OF VIOLENCE

The year 1947 was a very difficult one for Zionists everywhere. And after the Holocaust, who amongst us, except for some extreme Communists, was not a Zionist?

Despite rumors to the contrary, President Truman's administration was not overly enthusiastic about the creation of a Jewish state. Europe seemed preoccupied with postwar rehabilitation and reconstruction. Britain was rapidly distancing itself from the contractual obligations of the Balfour Declaration concerning the establishment of a Jewish National Home. Moreover, immigration to Palestine came to a standstill and most "illegal" attempts to bring in Jews from Europe resulted in searches, arrests, deportations and drownings.

In Palestine itself, the Mandate authorities ruled over the Jewish population with the "Law of the Gallows." Tragically, the short period of cooperation and attempted unity between the conflicting political forces of the Jewish Yishuv in Palestine was weakened by the Socialists' hunger for undisputed power.

Given this abominable state of affairs, augmented by the constant betrayals of the Irgun soldiers by the Haganah, by kidnappings, beatings and the vicious incitement of the Labor press against the Revisionists and the underground movement, the Jews of Israel were on the verge of internecine warfare.

During this time the British had arrested Dov Grunner, Yehiel Dresner, Mordechai Alcoshi and Eliezer Kashani, all soldiers of the Irgun Tzevai Leumi. For months, humanitarians and Jewish communities everywhere had been appealing to Britain's sense of fairness and reason. Ignoring these protests and pleas, the Mandate authorities, in the middle of the night, took their prisoners – fighters for independence – and executed them in secrecy.

As Menachem Begin explains in his memoir, on April 16, 1947, the Israeli population had tuned in to an early morning radio news broadcast. In a tear-choked voice, the announcer stated: "This morning at Acre jail, Dov Gruner, Dov Rosenbaum, Mordechai Alcoshi and Eliezer Kashani were executed on the gallows." According to the broadcast the soldiers were not even permitted last rites by a rabbi. In addition, the regulations required that the condemned men stand to hear the sentence. The four Irgun soldiers, apparently, defying both the occupying army and its laws, refused to rise. The hangman tried to raise them to their feet, and the guards who were present dealt them blows. But the soldiers did not capitulate – even in their last moments, they resisted and, as the report has it, went to the gallows singing the national anthem – "Hatikva," (The Song of Hope)."[1]

Until the last days of the Mandate, British attitudes toward the rejuvenation and statehood of Israel remained negative and hostile. It was at this time of frustration and anger that the Jewish community of Shanghai was happy to learn that Gedali Zhuhavitsky of the Jewish National Fund would be arriving shortly. When Zhuhavitsky arrived, he was enthusiastically received by the entire community and assured assistance and support. He was a polished speaker and his various talks

---

1. Quoted and paraphrased from Menachem Begin, *The Revolt* (New York: Nash Publishing Co., 1951), p. 354.

resulted in generous pledges to the Jewish National Fund from all strata of the community.

On April 18, we received a cable from Paris headquarters, informing us of the hangings in Palestine. Immediately, the Revisionist Party and Betar (of both the former French Concession and the Hongkew branches) announced a mass meeting of protest to be held in the open sports field in the Hongkew area. The meeting attracted the largest Jewish gathering ever witnessed in Shanghai. Some estimates claim that more than five thousand people attended. Our main speaker was Ari Kalmanovich, who spoke in Yiddish, the popular language of this gathering. Joe Tukachinsky would have been the speaker in English, but on the eve of his departure for the United States, he left Betar and joined the B'nai B'rith organization. In his place, I was selected to deliver the speech in English.

Betarim from both branches attended in full uniform, escorted by an honor guard led by our tall, handsome flag bearer, Leo Kiachko. The organizers of the event invited our guest from Palestine, Gedali Zhuhavitsky – to say a few words. And he did!

In an emotional speech, Zhuhavitsky "calmed" the large audience by telling them that in Palestine the Yishuv does not mourn today; rather it sings and celebrates! "Perhaps," he noted, "this will put an end to insubordination of the small terrorist groups." He ended his remarks by suggesting that we not be provoked by the "desperate outbursts of the Irgun."

His was a typical voice of the Labor movement in Palestine, expressive of its attitude and approach. But Zhuhavitsky miscalculated; he was in Shanghai, where the community fervently supported its underground heroes and had come to the meeting in order to express its fury and to mourn its loss.

I pleaded with our leadership to call another meeting in the former French Concession, possibly in the Jewish Club, and to declare a boycott of Zhuhavitsky's campaign, to protest his ill-mannered and vicious outburst of the previous day. My colleagues felt that it was best to speak to the people individually so as not to be blamed for any possible divisiveness that might result from the proposed action.

I did not concur, and since time was running out and payments on pledges would soon be coming in, I decided to act independently. I composed a leaflet in Russian, accusing our visitor of desecrating the memory of our Jewish heroes and of misusing the speaker's platform offered him in his capacity as guest from Eretz Yisrael. The leaflet was printed gratis by our old Revisionist friend, Avraham Shor, whose son and daughter were active members of Betar, and it was distributed by several of my friends.

Many older people who were involved in assisting Zhuhavitsky in his campaign took offense, suspecting that the entire campaign had been carried out with the blessing of the Betar and the Revisionist organizations. For days people would inquire, "Have you read the leaflet?" At once payments on pledges stopped and what was a promising campaign trickled down to an embarrassing failure. At the meeting of our executive council, I took full responsibility for the leaflet and its distribution. As a result, my friends were faced with a dilemma. I left the meeting voluntarily, in order to facilitate their deliberations and awaited their verdict in the reading room downstairs.

After almost an hour, the meeting adjourned, and I was notified of their decision – suspension from all Betar activities for a period of two weeks. I accepted this penalty without remorse. Nor was I angry with my friends and colleagues. I understood their position vis-a-vis the Jewish Club and the community as a whole. They were eager to show their distance from my leaflet, and there was little else they could have done.

Upon reflection, I was quick to realize that mine was an immature, unsophisticated endeavor, albeit one undertaken in reaction to an act of moral violence – an indispensable weapon of Labor Zionists of the period which led to a dangerous and self-defeating Jewish confrontation.

Zhuhavitsky left, and the incident was soon forgotten. The Jewish community was solidly united again and anxious to lend its full support to the cause of Zionism and the resurrection of the Jewish State. But such was not the case in Palestine and in other parts of the Jewish diaspora. The curse of division was accelerating and leaving hatred and anger in its wake. Indeed, these were days of violence and fury, from which we, in Shanghai, were fortunate to find refuge in the fraternity of our ranks and in the righteousness of our cause.

For several years now, I had been considering the possibility of organizing a sports meet with as many Betarim as possible from every corner of China. It was not only an important event in its own right, it would also serve as a pretext for stimulating a wider comradeship and in establishing a framework for collective training and an eventual mass immigration to Eretz Israel. We were also waiting to hear from Marinsky and Muller and from our European headquarters. In the meantime, something had to be done to maintain interest and to promote productive activity within our ranks. It was at this point that I officially presented a recommendation to organize Betariada II, another sports meet between the Tientsin, Shanghai and Hongkew branches of Betar.

Regretfully it had to be held without the participation of Harbin, which by then was isolated by the Iron Curtain and by Communist China. The date was set for July-August 1947. Shanghai was to host the Betariada, while I was placed in charge of the organizing committee. We began preparations at once for this important fraternal event.

Chapter 12

1947. BETARIADA II

Shortly after the end of World War Two, when the Japanese no longer dominated the Asian shipping industry, a small Chinese company was moving passengers and cargo between several coastal cities of western China. The owners of this shipping company had never dreamed that one day, on a small and dingy vessel, they would transport a dozen young Jewish men from Tientsin to Shanghai! But this is exactly what happened, when, in the last week of July 1947, Betar's Tientsin contingent braved filth and seasickness on its way to compete against its fellow Betarim of Hongkew and Shanghai in the second Betariada to be held in China during the past fifteen years.

Among those teams competing at this event were runners, jumpers, discus throwers and volleyball and ping-pong players, as well as comedians, singers and musicians. Most of them combined more than one talent. A happy, enthusiastic group, devoted to the ideals of Zionism, they were all loyal followers of Betar's founder, Ze'ev Jabotinsky.

On board ship, despite many obstacles, they trained continuously while in the evening, supplied with accordions and a dozen good voices, they sang Betar songs, popular modern melodies and naughty limericks, some of which were authored on the spur of the moment.

These young men took their mission seriously and were determined to do their very best. It was wonderful to travel with old friends and to be given an opportunity to make new ones, whose aim was to win, to bring trophies of victory back to their city, their community and to their Tientsin Betar!

In the meantime, the Hongkew and Shanghai branches of Betar became beehives of activity. While the sportsmen trained, practiced and exercised, abiding by the strict dietary and social regimes imposed by their trainers, the rest of the community was caught up in the excitement. Bets on winners were waged by many. Some contributed new and better sports equipment, while many donated money, cups and silver shields for winners of the various events.

The organizers had to prepare homes for the sportsmen arriving from Tientsin, order uniforms for their teams, prepare grounds for different competitions and plan programs for social occasions. Special care and effort went into preparations for the festive opening and closing ceremonies.

Finally, the Tientsin team arrived and was met by hundreds of Betarim from Shanghai and Hongkew. Within minutes, the new arrivals and welcomers who only moments ago had not even known each other's names, blended into one blur of young people.

In the evening, the first social took place in the main hall of the Shanghai Betar Club. It could barely contain the participants, the team managers and the coaches. Everyone else had to wait for other functions that would be held in the larger auditorium of the Shanghai Jewish Club. This first evening was spent in song, music and toasts of welcome, toasts of friendship, toasts for an early reunion in Eretz Israel. Were this warm and enthusiastic gathering of friends, inflamed by the ideal of Jewish nationalism all that the evening conveyed, the Betariada would have been worth organizing. But the evening was merely a prelude to what followed.

The next day, the front grounds of the Shanghai Jewish Club were the scene of the festive opening of Betariada II. As sportsmen from Shanghai,

Tientsin and Hongkew marched with their respective banners, hundreds of Jews from all walks of life gathered to applaud these young athletes.

Not surprisingly, most of the participants of this meet chose to remain in Shanghai, to camp in Betar dormitories, receive military training and eventually become the pioneering groups to reach the frontline in Israel and join the battle for its liberation. But I am getting ahead of myself. Now the second Betariada presented us with many exciting days, crowned by high achievements, infused with great joy, albeit mixed with disappointment for others. Despite its esprit and valor, the young, poorly trained contingent from Hongkew, for instance, could not come close to the better trained teams of Tientsin and Shanghai.

The organizers and participants in the meet were amply rewarded by the devotion of the entire Jewish community: Hundreds of spectators attended each event. As usual, the one-hundred-meter sprint, the 4x100-meter relay and the final volleyball competition between Tientsin and Shanghai drew the largest crowds. Although I did not have much difficulty in winning the one-hundred-meter race, the relay was quite another matter. Our Tientsin friends did unexpectedly well and led by several meters. As anchorman for the Shanghai team, I had to make a truly extraordinary effort to catch up and beat my friend Leva Olshevsky, who anchored a Tientsin quartet.

The total scores of the two leading teams were so close that the final outcome hinged on the victory in the last event of the Betariada – the best out of three games in volleyball, played on the Jewish Club grounds. A seesaw game from start to finish, before the final whistle the score stood at one game each, with a fourteen-to-twelve score in Shanghai's favor in the third game. After the serve changed hands several more times, the host team finally secured a victory, and with it, first place in the Betariada!

Following the final parade and distribution of prizes, we began a week of outside competitions, in which combined Betar teams challenged Shanghai champions in volleyball (teams and doubles) and in ping-pong. With the addition of such Tientsin stars as George Kanzepolsky, Billy

Bellokamen and Vova Gurvitch, Betar won most of their games and added to their already enviable prestige as a major sports organization in China.

Finally, after the last of the volleyball doubles ended with Betar's unexpected victory, the participants began to pack away their sports gear and head for their respective homes.

By now, many Jews had left Shanghai and we felt the loss everywhere, in restaurants, in clubs and in the movie houses. My own home by now had become a way station, as my parents made final preparations to emigrate to Cuba and to pack me for my short flight to Taiwan.

It was agreed that I should precede my parents by a few days. My belongings were to be stored at my cousin Bertha's place, where I was invited to stay during vacations and holidays or when I was on my way to Palestine.

On my last evening in Shanghai, after bidding farewell to all of my friends and acquaintances, I decided to set out on the walk from Betar to my house, a thirty-minute excursion at the most. It was a typical late September night, the air was extremely humid and the temperature high. Most citizens took refuge on roof-gardens and windy street corners.

As I walked down the Avenue Joffre, passing fur stores and dress salons, all locked for the night, I recalled how (only two years before) they had served as temporary pleasure havens for the hungry and thirsty GIs, *gobs*, to use the war-time slang, airmen and marines. Life was returning to normal. Most shops were as empty during the day as they were now, at eleven o'clock at night, which only added to my feeling of slight depression and insecurity. My parents had been invited to a small dinner party next door, and I knew that they would be coming home late, so I continued my leisurely walk home, stopping by displays and indulging in reminiscence. One of the better known boutiques displayed a large sign: SOLD.

These were not the best of times for shop owners or restaurateurs, especially if they were foreigners and employers of local Chinese staff. Everyone knew that the foreigners intended to depart, sooner or later, and the employees wanted to make certain that they would receive abundant compensation. Although there were no professional labor unions in Shanghai, government agencies supported workers' demands. With a few notable exceptions, the average Chinese employee was out to make a killing off his foreign employer, before the latter sold out and departed. In some cases, the workers actually demanded more than the total worth of a given enterprise and the proprietors had been known to hand over the keys of the business in order to avoid being dragged to arbitration hearings, courts or "workers' committees" – all of which would delay their planned departure for weeks and even months.

In spite of all this, thousands of foreigners still remained in Shanghai without passports, visas or any place to go. Among them were many members of the Jewish community. It was not much different in Tientsin, and in Harbin the situation was infinitely worse.

Deep in thought, I finally reached our apartment building, where I caught sight of my parents entering the elevator. What perfect synchronization! Following them into the vestibule, I could not help but wonder what the future had in store for each one of us in the family. And tonight I was not thinking of next year or even the one after that. For me the "real" future was to begin early the next day when, having spent six years in this beautiful small apartment that we all considered to be home, I would part from my parents and leave for Taiwan.

Yes, this was home as I knew it. All of this would now be gone forever. We must all leave home one day, but no one can convince me that it is ever easy. For me, it was one of the most difficult moments of my life.

Chapter 13

1947. FORMOSA (TAIWAN)

At the end of World War Two, the Nationalist Government of Chiang Kai-shek took over the island of Taiwan, better known as Formosa. Preoccupied with political and social problems, including an epidemic of corruption, General Chiang Kai-shek had little time to pay serious attention to the economic issues threatening the very existence of Taiwan. Only a year later would the Kuomintang (the Nationalist Party) Government begin to pay heed to the Taiwan Island, which would soon become its refuge and seat of power.

In 1947, Taiwan was still in a state of devastation and ruin. In *Modernizing China*, Anthony Kubek describes the bombing of agricultural and industrial facilities by the American forces and of extensive damages sustained. According to Kubek, rice production was cut in half, thus meeting only a quarter of Taiwan's minimum need, while sugar, the island's largest industry, had dropped to less than ten percent of its prewar level. Electric power production as well was substantially curtailed.[1] Conditions gradually improved, but the overall devastation that Kubek refers to was very much in evidence that autumn of 1947,

---

1. A. Kubek, *Modernizing China*. (Taiwan: Cave Books), p. 55.

when my plane landed at the airfield on the outskirts of Taipei, the capital city of the island of Formosa.

Virtually all that I knew about the island was that it had been used as a honeymoon retreat for the wealthy citizens and foreigners of the mainland. Prior to my departure I had read tourist brochures on Formosa and received some additional information about the place. I learned that Formosa was supposed to be a "romantic island of a million dreams" and that it was sparsely populated and picturesque, with palm trees and pines, mountains and lakes – a paradise on earth! From these brochures I discovered that Formosa means "beautiful" in Portuguese.

To my everlasting shame, I am inclined to appreciate people more than nature. Perhaps for this reason, upon my arrival, I was not impressed with what I saw. To my disappointment, I found Taipei to be a filthy city, lacking modern facilities, its buildings dilapidated, its streets poorly paved and its humidity level the highest in China.

Taiwan's population did not exceed five million during 1947. Although the Taiwanese population is of Chinese ancestry, fifty years of Japanese occupation, resulting in intermarriages and cultural integration, have created a unique breed neither purely Japanese nor completely Chinese. A minority of native Taiwanese zealously cling to their language, traditions and colorful dress. However, the language on the street and in business is usually Japanese, a linguistic phenomenon that can be attributed to fear of the occupant, force of habit, simple expedience or all of these factors combined.

Utilizing the scant knowledge of the Japanese language that I had acquired from teachers in Tokyo and "ladies of the night" in Yokohama, I negotiated my Warner Brothers film sales quite easily. No doubt, business transactions were facilitated by our company's exclusive contract with Errol Flynn, the indisputable favorite among all Hollywood stars on the Asian continent!

Several weeks before my departure for Taiwan, I visited the Abolnick family, friends who had always been helpful and generous in their assistance to our Betar youth movement. I also suspected that they covertly wished to promote my interest in their daughter. Mary was a lovely girl, and I was quite happy to invite her to an occasional movie or to meet with her in her parent's home. It was during one such visit that Mary introduced me to her friend, Lea Ginzburg, a bubbly young girl with a lovely face and an alluring figure. Both Lea and Mary were members of Betar, but young girls have a tendency to change quickly beyond recognition.

I had seen Lea once before and she had attracted my attention, although she was not more than sixteen at the time. One Sunday, I had attended a soccer match at the race course with friends. There, I noticed a group of Betar members seated on benches outside the goalposts. Among them stood out a radiant-looking girl in high heels, dressed in a faux fox fur coat. Her beautiful face, gently touched with a hint of makeup, was framed by shoulder-length curly brown hair. It was difficult not to notice her well-developed body and especially her long, perfectly sculpted legs. She looked all of eighteen or nineteen but it was obvious that she was younger, since no eighteen-year-old would be spending a Sunday afternoon with the fifteen-year-old kids around her. I did not think much about this brief encounter, but I proceeded to the YMCA for a chocolate cake and soda to be followed by a Betty Grable musical at the Grant Theatre next door.

Some two years later, I found myself gazing into the eyes of a beautiful woman. Meeting Lea at Mary's house, of course, had its disadvantages, for I was supposed to be courting her friend. Nevertheless, while I did not succeed in dating her prior to my departure, I did manage to extract a promise from her to meet me on New Year's Eve, when I returned for my winter vacation. Lea promised to write me, providing that I initiate the correspondence. Little did I know how important these letters would be and where this correspondence would lead. Amidst my eagerly awaited letters from parents and friends, I especially anticipated an envelope fragrant with Lea's perfume. Our correspondence soon progressed from "Dear Lea" to "Darling," and we both eagerly awaited our New Year rendezvous.

Meanwhile, I immersed myself in work and my sales records soared. My daily routine would take me to the offices of theater owners in Taipei, Keeloong and Kaohsiung, where I would negotiate contracts and sit in on screenings of our films for six to eight hours a day. The Taiwan theaters were all alike. They were converted garages or barns with hard seats or benches placed on hardened ground or roughly laid cement. In my second month there, I was selling films like hot cakes. In fact, films of major companies such as Warner Brothers, Metro-Goldwyn Mayer (MGM), Fox and Universal were not sold but rented for an agreed number of performances and it was up to one's negotiating skills to determine what percentage of the take went to the distributor and how much would stay with the theater. It was an exciting business, involving smooth public relations, and a thorough commercial know-how. In my case, work proved to be a prescription for loneliness and boredom.

Soon after my arrival in Formosa, I became involved in an intense culinary experience. The Movie Theater Owners' Association organized a welcoming dinner in my honor. A black-tie affair, held in a private banquet hall of a plush and famous Chinese restaurant, as is quite usual in the Far East, it was an all-male event. In Harbin, my experience with Chinese cuisine had been limited to occasional visits to a public diner for peasants where the menu usually consisted of a variety of boiled and fried dumplings, *jiaoza* (Chinese dumplings) and soup.

Shanghai boasted diversified Chinese eating establishments, and among the most popular restaurants for foreigners was the "Sun-Ya," located on Nanking Road in the International Settlement. What awaited me now in this palatial three-story building on the outskirts of Taipei, was truly out of a fairy tale.

Marble lions, a national symbol of wealth and good luck, flanked a huge marble staircase, leading to a colossal heavy oak wood door that measured approximately thirty feet in height. Inside, the restaurant was carpeted with heavy Tientsin rugs. The walls too were made from carved wooden panels as was the entire ceiling. The broad wall opposite the entrance consisted of wide French windows, hung with heavy gold braids with tied purple velvet curtains. The chairs and tables were lacquered in black and the seats were all cushioned with shiny golden silk from the Shantung Province. The mammoth hall was illuminated by fifty chandeliers covered with tiny pearls and blinding crystal leaves.

Soon I was seated at our table, and was introduced to the nine other guests in our group. Looking about, I noticed the appearance of three dozen white-liveried servants wearing white gloves who pushed in our chairs, opened our napkins and quickly disappeared back into the swinging kitchen doors. Within moments, the dinner, one dish at a time, was expertly served.

Never had I seen such an elegant presentation of food. Especially impressive was the arrangement on the plate of gaping fish and of bird nests surrounded with tiny trees that had been shaped out of different vegetables.

But the unforgettable dish of the evening was "warm monkey brains." Monkeys were brought, often screaming, to each table and placed on a shelf underneath. Here, they were tied with leather straps, with their heads protruding through a special opening in the middle of the table. Suddenly, I noticed that each table setting included a heavy silver utensil that looked like an axe on one side and a fork on the other. The host on my right took this utensil by the handle and with a swift motion of the silver axe cracked the monkey's scalp. His action was accompanied by an approving cheer from the guests, and each began to dip into the warm monkey brains.

Immediately following this ritual, everyone at the table picked a partner and drank a glassful of Chinese wine, "bottoms up." The Chinese traditionally do not drink in groups. They prefer to toast each and every one at the table, as a result of which the party grows louder and happier with each round of toasts. Embarrassing as it was for me to refuse to partake of the delicacy of the evening, I stood my ground, insisting that the consumption of monkey's brains is strictly against my religious dietary laws.

Evenings and weekends, whatever leisure I had would be spent in restaurants and theaters, or in my room, either reading or writing letters. Toward midnight I would try to fall asleep. Sleeping, however, had its own difficulty since the hotel was infested with rats. Noisy rats! They sounded like horses and were comparable in size. As I would be about to drop off to sleep, I could feel the rats jump on my bed from the adjacent wall or ceiling. Half asleep, I would kick them off through my blanket and hear them bounce against some piece of furniture in the room. And so it would go all through the night. When I mentioned this unpleasantness at the office, my local manager pointed out that new hotels soon would be built in Taiwan. One of them, the Mandarin Hotel, he said, would soon be the pride of Asia. Its future owner was none other than Madame Chiang Kai-shek!

Despite my busy schedule during the day, time moved quite slowly. I was cut off from my family and friends, from activity in the party and in Betar, and I was not up-to-date on the current struggle for the Jewish homeland. From newspapers and magazines I learned that the issue of the British Mandate now was in the hands of the United Nations, which had sent a team of diplomats to Palestine to meet with all the parties concerned.

During this time, the Arab States were openly threatening all-out war, the Yishuv in Palestine was mobilizing and world Jewry was uniting in an effort to offer the Jewish population in Palestine maximum financial and material assistance. While all this was going on, I was sitting in Taipei, selling Errol Flynn's one-man struggles against the Japanese military power! Of course, I felt lonely and isolated.

From my parents' letters I understood that they had settled in comfortably in Cuba and that together with three friends from China, they would soon be opening a chocolate factory. From friends in Shanghai I learned that, while the Jewish community was shrinking, Betar ranks were growing, since many Tientsin Betarim had decided to move to Shanghai. Rumors abounded that Marinsky and Muller were coming back to China.

Finally, toward the end of November 1947, I received a cable from Arie and Shmuel advising me to prepare to move back to Shanghai next month and to await their arrival. They would be carrying instructions from the high command.

My excitement was tempered with material concern. How would I live in Shanghai without a job and without money? I could rely on free room and board with my cousin, but how long could I impose on their hospitality? I was certainly not prepared to ask my parents to help me. The only solution I could think of at the time was either to convince Warner Brothers to transfer me to Shanghai, a very unlikely possibility, or to find another job that would not take too much of my time and yet provide enough money to live on. I decided to stay in Taiwan until the twenty-fourth of December, when my vacation began, and to hope for the best.

As the date of my departure drew nearer, I could hardly contain myself. I could neither concentrate on my work during the day nor sleep during the night. To avoid night combat with the hotel rats, I kept my room lights on throughout the night. While it did not alleviate my insomnia, it did allow me to spend my sleepless nights undisturbed.

The day of my scheduled flight, the sky was dark, the nearby mountains were thick with clouds and the flight ceiling was so low that planes were grounded for the rest of the day. These weather conditions prevailed for three days in a row. Finally, on December 27, 1947, I left Taiwan for Shanghai. Upon my arrival at the airport, I was met by a company representative and driven to the home of my cousin and her family.

♣ ♣ ♣

The events described in this chapter have an interesting postscript. Allow me to share only parenthetical glimpses of it here, because it is only fitting for the reader to know that after twenty-eight years, fate returned me and my family to Taiwan. In 1975, with the assistance of others, I organized a Jewish network of fifty-two families and was elected president of this group, serving in that capacity until I left the island for good.

In 1985, during a farewell banquet in our honor, the community presented me with a large silver shield, on which the following inscription was neatly carved:

LIFETIME HONORARY CHAIRMAN
OF THE JEWISH COMMUNITY

By a decision of the Taiwan Jewish community, meeting 15 January 1985, in appreciation of his inspired leadership and devotion, this title has been bestowed upon Y. S. Liberman, founder and first president of the community from 1975 to 1985. The title shall be awarded only once in a lifetime and will carry with it all of the privileges that accrue, including the right to chair board meetings whenever the awardee is present. Signed: TAIWAN JEWISH COMMUNITY. March, 1985.

We all collect a variety of accolades during our lifetime, some trivial, others of lasting value. I have had my share of both. Yet, from all of these tokens of peer recognition, I value none more than this heartwarming expression by a tiny Jewish community on the faraway island of Taiwan.

Now, in late 1947 my world in Taiwan was collapsing, and I realized that before my next visit, it perhaps would change beyond recognition. Back in Shanghai, my career in the film industry was coming to an end. I now faced the enormous question of what lay ahead.

Chapter 14

1948. THE IRGUN TZEVAI LEUMI

On the very first day of my arrival from Taiwan, I contacted Lea, my New Year's date, to make certain that she had not made other plans. I then proceeded to the Jewish Club to see my friends and to meet the new arrivals from Tientsin.

The next day I appeared at Jack Degal's office and informed him that I must prepare for my journey to Israel, and stated that I could only do so, were I to remain in Shanghai. Jack was kind and understanding, polite but firm. The conclusion of our friendly conversation was not an encouraging one: There was little I could do for Warner Brothers in Shanghai. I do not know what I would have done were it not for my dear friend Vova Rifkin, who enjoyed a profitable, modest business uptown. Vova offered me a part-time job as supervisor in his export-import business. He needed someone he could trust, and I was grateful for the job. New Year's Eve came and I anticipated with great excitement and some nervousness my first date with Lea Ginzburg. It was a wonderful date in one of Shanghai's well-known restaurants, "The Kavkaz," (The Caucasus), where we spent our evening dining, dancing and enjoying the special holiday program.

After our New Year's date, I realized that much more than perfume was drawing me closer to this beautiful young woman. In fact, I found it

* *

"Shoot for the moon. Even if you miss, you'll land among the stars." -Les Brown

"Shadowtint"

Fine Art Photography By: Heather

<u>http://www.shadowcatcherimagery.com/heather.htm</u>

-   maryeveswinner.jpg

difficult to stay away from her for even a day. Soon, I began to notice that my ever growing affection was turning into love, a feeling that I had never before experienced in such depth nor in such force of commitment. It soon became apparent that I could not think of life without her and, to my great good fortune, the feeling was mutual. Shortly thereafter we were engaged.

In January 1948, Arie Marinsky and Samby Muller returned from Palestine with orders sewn into their jacket shoulder pads: Judy Hasser was to assume the official position of *netziv* Betar, while I was to become the head of the Shanghai Branch. Muller, Marinsky, Tony Gabermann, Judy and I were to form the executive council of the Irgun in China.

There were two fundamental reasons for establishing an Irgun branch in China. The first had to do with the possibility that the British might not keep their commitment to leave Palestine as decreed by the United Nations. Should this happen, the Irgun planned a global attack on British targets. Singapore, Hong Kong and smaller, relatively unprotected port cities of China could be open to attack.

The second reason for establishing an Irgun branch in China was to train as many young men as possible and prepare them for combat in Israel, where an all-out Arab assault was expected immediately on the heels of British evacuation. We began recruiting our men carefully, faithfully following the prescribed code of conspiracy and self-preservation.

On an inconspicuous sidestreet of the former French Concession, Arie, Samby and I rented an apartment. In it we stored our modest arsenal of arms, we inducted new members, led courses on ideology and held meetings. We also took our meals in the new apartment, where our piles of unwashed dishes made entry into the kitchen virtually impossible. When that happened, a general cleaning day was called, and then the cycle would begin anew.

The other room was kept in perfect order so as not to impair our work in any way. Often our work kept us busy day and night. Prospective members were interviewed by us after nightfall with a screen separating the interviewer from the new member. He or she was brought in by Judy Hasser's car, blindfolded, and was totally unaware of the surroundings. Once a member was inducted and committed to secrecy, he or she was made aware of his or her whereabouts and assigned to a small group for initial training prior to an acceptance and oath-taking ceremony.

The Irgun training program was a difficult one. It had to be since the Irgun Tzevai Leumi was a national military organization – it was the Jewish underground. Training included mandatory all-night marches on the sandy beaches and the rugged mountainous terrain on the city outskirts, in addition to weapons study, target practice and sabotage instructions with live explosives. During our leisure we would sing songs, tell stories and enjoy the camaraderie of the group. An esprit de corps sprang up naturally.

Additional cover was presented by the Betar. All Irgun recruits either came from or joined the ranks of Betar, where more intense, nonconspiratorial training was included in its program. The Irgun recruits included Tientsin Betar, who had been brought in earlier, as well as those who had arrived only recently. They all knew that the first to go to the newly reborn Jewish State would be those from the Shanghai Betar, and they had come in order to be among this avant garde.

As the Irgun cadres grew and the training programs became a daily routine, we increased the supply of arms and ammunition in our little apartment where the three of us lived. All went well, until one morning Samby was demonstrating the blind assembly of a pistol and it suddenly went off, hitting the wall that divided our apartment from that of one of our neighbors. We could do little else except to hide all the weapons, dismiss the trainees from classes and sweat it out until someone came and knocked at our door to enquire who was shooting and why. Luckily, the bullet did not go clear through the wall, and no one pursued the incident any further.

We had another close call, when the adjacent building caught fire, and the fire brigade, together with police reinforcements, had to evacuate, not just the building, but the entire block. Leaving our personal possessions to the mercy of fate, we packed all our guns, pistols and hand-grenades into pillowcases and rushed out to the street. Although the damage was extensive, many eyes were focused on the three foreigners standing in their pajamas on the street, each holding two stuffed pillowcases.

Whether open or clandestine, our activities required large sums of money. Fortunately, we had many friends within the community. Among them was a young, successful and bright businessman, Izia Magit, who, with his wife, Ira, could always be counted on for both moral and financial support.[1] In fact, Izia became so interested in our activities that one day Arie Marinsky took him to our secret hideout where, without being seen, he observed our training procedures. Throughout these years, Izia proved to be a dependable friend and a devoted Zionist.

No sooner had we settled into our busy routine, than the Revisionist movement in Shanghai was informed by cable of the Irgun's decision to dispatch Mordechai Olmert to China to lead a financial campaign, "The Iron Fund," on behalf of the Jewish underground.[2]

Olmert's family, his mother, brother, a sister-in-law and a niece lived in Shanghai. He had many friends from school and Betar days in Harbin. Mordechai was greeted with enthusiasm by the entire Jewish community of Shanghai. He was welcomed as enthusiastically in Tientsin when he reached that city on the last leg of his campaign. Parlor meetings and large public events were organized to give him an opportunity to address every Jew within reach. Olmert was remembered for his brilliance as a former student at the Harbin School of Commerce. Neither an orator nor

---

1. Ira and Izia Magit left for Australia, where soon thereafter, Izia became a leading figure in his local Jewish community. For many years he not only served as president of the Jewish National Fund, but he also headed many other Jewish organizations as well. The Magits had two sons, one of whom died tragically in an accident in Europe, and a daughter.
2. Mordechai Olmert, who is revered as a founder of the Harbin Betar, became an early pioneer to Eretz Israel. See the Foreword to this book by Ehud Olmert.

a master of public relations, nevertheless, when duty called, he could excel in both areas. Olmert collected more than one hundred thousand dollars within a few weeks from the Jewish communities of Tientsin and Shanghai for the purchase of arms and ammunition in Europe, all of which was to be loaded on to the Irgun vessel the *Altalena* and transported to Palestine.[1] This sum represented the largest amount of money ever collected from China's Jewry. Many Jews sacrificed their savings. Women gave away their jewelry, and young men contributed their monthly earnings to this popular cause. Mordechai Olmert's visit was educational and uplifting. By the time that he left, there was no doubt in anyone's mind that the Jewish State was on the threshold of creation.

Shortly after Olmert's visit to China came that long, historic night, when together with the entire Jewish world we sat at our radio set listening to the UN vote in favor of the Jewish State. Now, in the eyes of the world at large, we, the eternal wanderers, were to possess a National Home, a state of our own, a haven of freedom and independence. On May 15, 1948, Ben-Gurion proclaimed to the world the existence of the State of Israel!

Two large celebrations marked the creation of the State of Israel. On Saturday evening, the Shanghai Jewish Club held open-house festivities with champagne, dancing, singing and speechmaking. The Club and its permanent orchestra, led by the Sherman Brothers, provided all entertainment gratis. The Jewish youth of Shanghai, however, after a few champagne toasts, drifted to the smaller building of Betar, where spontaneous celebrations broke out and lasted till the early hours of the morning. As I entered our little Betar Club that was packed to capacity, Bobby Bershadsky was playing the piano, a group around him was

---

1. "Altalena" also is the pen name of Vladimir [Ze'ev] Jabotinsky, under which he contributed articles during his years as a young journalist in Italy.

singing, "In Blood and Fire Judea Fell – In Blood and Fire Judea Will Arise," groups were dancing the *hora* and others were just standing around enjoying the atmosphere of complete happiness and extreme joy.

Soon the din died down, and I was greeted with shouts of "Speech! Speech!" Someone handed me the microphone. I looked around the room and saw some faces radiant with joy, others solemnly restrained and still others registering honest bewilderment. These were the faces of our many acquaintances who had left us to find solace in assimilation, Bundism or international Communism. They had all returned to Betar.

The look on their young faces moved me to say: "We can appreciate the sweetness of victory, having so long endured the bitterness of defeat." Indeed, the struggle within had been won. The days of cynical opposition to the idea of Jewish statehood were permanently behind us. The smug and often arrogant degradation of our Zionist ideals and efforts to achieve them were today buried with the victory of Zionism.

Our impromptu festivities lasted until the wee hours of the morning, when most of us had to rush home, shower, change into uniform and attend the official celebrations on the grounds of the Shanghai Jewish Club. The Jewish Club grounds were decorated with hundreds of Jewish national flags and with banners proclaiming the birth of the Jewish State. The stage was set for the festive parade and the show of colors.

On the open field at the entrance to the club stood some five hundred spectators. They awaited the first joint parade of Betar and Irgun units that was to begin under my command. Months of practice and training, education and indoctrination were clearly in evidence. Beautifully executed, the parade consisted of hundreds of well-disciplined healthy-looking young men and women, boys and girls, preceded by color-bearers with the flag of the State of Israel, followed closely by the banner of the Shanghai Betar. Our Shanghai Betarim marched to the stirring music of the Sherman Brothers band, as from the podium, *netziv* Hasser took the salute.

Leading the parade toward the open Club grounds, I noticed that there was hardly a dry eye in the audience. Here, at this very moment, men and women alike were witnessing an historic event and were visibly moved by its symbolism and by the spectacle of our dedicated youth. Some may have doubted the outcome, but all were aware of the moral struggle, sacrifice and need for endurance that lay ahead.

Chapter 15

1948. SHANGHAI'S LAST JEWISH WEDDING

A few days after the declaration of an independent Jewish State, I proposed to Lea. By then, I knew that she would accept my marriage proposal. We celebrated with a dinner and wine at "DD's" restaurant on Avenue Joffre and made the announcement of our engagement to relatives and friends the following day.

My parents did not know Lea. They had never met her or her parents, who had arrived from Tientsin several years before and at once had become a reluctant addition to the struggling, needy families who were too poor to belong to the established middle-class societies of Shanghai and too proud to request or accept assistance from Jewish philanthropic organizations.

They lived in one room, shared a bathroom and struggled to feed and clothe themselves from one day to the next. At the age of fifteen, Lea had to leave school and work as a legal secretary, becoming the main source of income for the entire family. According to the established standards of our society, the Ginzburgs were not considered an appropriate match for a son of the well-to-do, middle-class Liberman family. How wrong such standards can be!

My parents were not overjoyed with our news. And for a long while, I wondered whether they were upset with my choice of a mate or rather with the fact that I was getting married altogether. Whatever the case, they eventually met my future wife and came to love her dearly. My friends, on the other hand, were thrilled, as were our many acquaintances. Anyone who knew my bride congratulated me. How right they all proved to be![1]

With their blessings, my parents sent us six hundred dollars as a wedding gift. It was up to us to decide whether we would keep it for our impending journey to Israel or spend it on a wedding reception. After talking it over, we decided to have a big wedding and to share our joy and happiness with all of our many friends. Our decision may not have been a practical one, but neither of us has ever regretted it.

We were married on June 22, 1948. The synagogue, located on Route Tenant de la Tour, was full of guests and many curious young people. Only twice again, on Rosh Ha-shana and Yom Kippur, would this magnificent building play host to such a large assembly of Shanghai Jews. Soon after that, the synagogue would begin to be deserted. Within a year, it would be empty of Jews. Our wedding was to be the last public wedding in the Shanghai Jewish community.

As I entered the synagogue anteroom, I immediately saw my gorgeous young bride, who had just turned eighteen that week, seated in an armchair, surrounded by her female relatives and her bridesmaids. According to custom, I was escorted in, covered her face with a veil and left to await her slow walk to the *chuppah* (the Jewish wedding canopy).

I remember little else except for the fact that I did come to the wedding dressed in my Betar uniform, thus keeping my pledge given to Abram Milichiker in Harbin, on my Bar Mitzvah. I recall my bride circling around

---

1. In 1996, in the company of our two sons, our daughter, and their families, Lea and I celebrated our forty-eighth wedding anniversary.

me the traditional seven circles, then standing next to me as together we looked into the face of the venerable Rabbi Ashkenazi.

As we left the synagogue arm-in-arm, there were such crowds surrounding our rental car that it made us feel for the moment like real Hollywood celebrities. Finally, we managed to reach our car and were driven to the studio of Josepho-Shik to have wedding portraits taken. By that time all the guests had gathered in the Jewish Club and awaited our grand entrance.

We received congratulatory cables from all over the world – first from my parents in Cuba, from relatives and friends, from Revisionist Party and Betar heads, acquaintances in New York, Johannesburg, Paris, London, Melbourne and Tel Aviv. Like the speeches, the dancing was endless, highlighted by poignant new Israeli songs. Listening to the music and the toasts and dancing with my beautiful bride, I managed to look around me and to observe what was really happening. It seemed to me that we finally were at the threshold of a new era. This was not the Bamboo Curtain that was descending, nor was it the Iron Curtain, each of which has served the cause of tyranny. This was a curtain of time that was descending once and for all on the Jewish communities of China.

The curtain of history was coming down.

We spent our wedding night in the famous Cathay Hotel and left early the next morning for our honeymoon in Hongchow. Three days later, I received a cable from Shanghai advising me that Haganah forces had attacked the *Altalena* by the shores of Tel Aviv and requesting that I return to Shanghai at once. We left that very day.

Some dates leave acrid traces in one's memory and a smoldering grief, while others bloom into fragrant and sweet memories of family and love. The second is how I recall my wedding day – the first, how I remember the day of Jewish infamy, the day of the "sacred gun." Both are recollections of 22 June 1948.

The *Altalena* tragedy can be summarized in a few paragraphs:

With the knowledge of the Israeli government, this vessel of the Irgun was carrying arms and volunteers to Israel. It had been ordered to land in Kfar Vitkin, a Haganah stronghold. During the unloading of the ship and after most volunteers had been driven to their barracks, the Haganah commander demanded that all weapons on board be surrendered. This was contrary to an agreement that had been reached, stipulating that a part of the arms were to go to Irgun units fighting independently in the Jerusalem sector.

The Irgun command refused, and routed the *Altalena* back to sea, toward the shore of Tel Aviv. Commander Eliahu Lankin, Captain Fine and Menachem Begin were on board the *Altalena*. As the vessel approached the shores of Tel Aviv, Premier Ben-Gurion issued an order to fire on the vessel. Some members of the Irgun were killed, others wounded, the vessel, its arms and all ammunition were destroyed. The next day, ignoring severe and bitter criticism, Ben-Gurion declared: "Blessed be the gun that fired on the *Altalena*!"

For the Jews of China, the *Altalena* saga began to unfold almost a year before its fateful journey from Marseilles to Tel Aviv, carrying nine hundred trained Irgun volunteers and hundreds of thousands of dollars worth of arms and ammunition. It had begun with Olmert's visit to Shanghai and Tientsin, where every Jew worthy of the name contributed to the Irgun *Altalena* project. Another link between Chinese Jews and the *Altalena* was the ship's able commander, Eliahu Lankin, a former Harbin Betari. No wonder then that when a protest meeting was called by us in Shanghai, it was attended by almost three thousand members of the Jewish community. The meeting adopted a resolution condemning this act of fratricide.

After the protest meeting, Lea and I began to settle into our married life. We moved into a one-room apartment that was centrally located but noisy and infested with rats. Soon we began to prepare for our long-awaited journey to Israel. Our plan was to send out all the boys with Irgun training first. They were to be divided into two groups with Arie leading one and Shmuel, the other. Judy, Tony and others on the executive council would follow in the third group, which was to include Lea and me. At the end of the year, the remainder of the Betarim, together with other members of the Jewish communities here, in Hongkew and in Tientsin, would travel on boats specially chartered by the Jewish Agency.

Our activities intensified. The club was well attended and many people were still involved in charity work. Arrangements were made to assure free transport and appropriate accommodation for the destitute, the sick and the homeless. In Betar, we considered that despite all of our preparations, the sports and cultural programs had to continue without interruption. Our teams participated in competitions and meetings and lectures were organized regularly. In addition, social gatherings and camping filled our calendar.

One of our most successful public activities turned out to be the production of my three-act play, *Mehoratai*, which enjoyed a run of seven performances. The experienced Nissenbaums and I were upstaged by the extraordinary performances of Vovka Dichne, Bobby Bershadsky, Monia Pirutinsky and Sammy Poliak, all of whom would be among the first group of Irgun volunteers to leave Shanghai. Together with David Kopievker, Eliahu Levy, Yosef Jacobs, George Kanzepolsky, Shmuel Muller, Arie Marinsky, Aron Rothfield, Joe Burda and Boris Zilberg, they comprised the Irgun contingent that flew from China to Israel in two separate groups in early November 1948.

During these transitional days, we devoted time and effort to instilling in our youth the essence of Jabotinsky's ideology. Far from the centers of Zionist polemic and controversy, we could concentrate on the essence of Jabotinsky's thought. This ideology has been brilliantly summarized by Jabotinsky himself, as he composed the powerful verses of the Betar anthem, sung by tens of thousands of members of the movement around the world and – more significantly – by the Irgun soldiers who met their final hour at the hands of the British hangman.

This credo is based on three concepts:

1. *hadar*: Purity of body and of mind. Each Betari – a prince unto himself – an aristocrat of the spirit, a titan of the soul.

2. *Betar*: The indivisibility of past and future, between the people of Israel and the Land of Israel.

3. *tagar*: Struggle and sacrifice; devotion, courage and resolve.

Jabotinsky rejected all secondary goals. To him there was no room for any other "-ism" to detract from our people's sacred goal of rejuvenation. In his monism, he differed from the ideology of the Labor Movement, which would dominate official Zionism from the early days of the Zionist Congress, through the first twenty-nine years of the existence of the State of Israel.

Whereas Jabotinsky's political philosophy was often and bitterly challenged in Palestine and throughout the Jewish diaspora, in China it was enthusiastically applauded by a large segment of the Jewish population and especially by its youth.

Perhaps for this reason, Betarim and the Revisionists who arrived in Israel from China, after the creation of the Jewish State, had little difficulty in adjusting and being fully absorbed into its political, social and economic life. In my mind, this can be attributed to the fact that they were raised as patriots and admirers of the Jewish people – irrespective of individual political affiliation or of ideological belief. There was no hate in our hearts, merely pity for the futility of fraternal bickering and for the evil seeds that it sows even today.

As young Betarim in China, we never regretted being steeped in the philosophy of the Revisionist cause. It was important for our members to understand the sanctity of the goal of rejuvenation. Once this became obvious, Jabotinsky's ideological concepts would become clear. Especially now, when we were only days away from our final journey home bound, we felt that it was essential to spare no efforts in preparing our young people, and in exposing them to the perils of the divisive alternatives of Socialism, Communism and internationalism. In this, too, the Betar of China had brilliantly educated two generations of Jewish patriots.

Chapter 16

1948. THE FINAL MONTHS

In September of 1948, the Communists were steadily encroaching into south-east China. The Nationalists were in retreat and America was urging coalition and coexistence. Everyone could feel the change in the air. Although the foreign population was confident that General Chiang Kai-shek would survive, many émigrés and expatriates were preparing to leave. It became clear that whether under the Nationalists or the Communists, we foreigners had overstayed our welcome. The time had come to move on.

While many Chinese were aware of political realities, the average person was not. I am not speaking of the wealthy businessman, or of the government employee or of the intelligent high school student. They were an elite minority, who faithfully clung to the Kuomingtan regime and who were terrified at the prospects of a Mao Tze-tung takeover.

Rather, the average Chinese was poverty-stricken and underfed. Hungry peasants, street urchins and child beggars comprised the main population of China and, for them, any change could only be an improvement! For several generations, the majority of the population had gone uneducated and had only a vague concept of the basic philosophy of either Buddhism or Confucianism. Of Communism – they knew nothing and understood even less. But to these millions of deprived, poverty-stricken citizens of China, a full bowl of rice would speak louder than any social philosophy.

Food was the basic measure of well-being in China. Whereas in the rest of the world, people greet one other with the words, "How are you?" in China, they ask, "Have you eaten well?" Not until the Cultural Revolution of the late 1960s did the Chinese Communists teach the population of the mainland that a bowl of rice is no salvation when it comes poisoned with family separation and Party despotism!

While the foreign population was not aware of such complexities and the vast majority of Chinese did not care, the Kuomintang seemed to be cognizant of the hopelessness of its resistance. And so it came about that as its foreign guests of many generations were leaving China for new homes abroad, General Chiang Kai-shek's government was busy transporting billions of dollars of antique treasures from the mainland to Taiwan, where they planned to establish its new seat of power.

By now many of the friends with whom I spent so much time during the past eight years had emigrated. Lea and I, meanwhile, were surrounded by peers with whom we were destined to share our future. Among them were Leva Kiachko and Chaim Werrek, who, with their wives, have shared our lives as faithful and devoted friends.

Together, we would leave for Israel and build new lives. Others preceeded us to America, where they resumed their studies and sought new professional opportunities. While we have been dispersed around the globe from the United States, to Australia, to Israel, we have forged bonds that will keep us close to one another until our last days on earth.

In the eyes of the Jewish Agency and the government of Israel, the situation in China was considered to be volatile and dangerous for its

Jewish communities. Various organizations in Israel put our plight before the United Nations. As a result, the Jewish Agency, together with the United Nations Relief and Rehabilitation Association (UNRRA), began to make special arrangements to bring out the remaining Jews from China to Israel by means of chartered sea-going vessels and airplanes.

To facilitate these arrangements, the Jewish Agency requested that Moshe Yuval, the newly appointed Vice-Consul of Israel in New York, visit Shanghai and coordinate all efforts for a smooth evacuation of China's Jewry. Yuval arrived during the summer of 1948 and was met at the airport by a ten-member committee, myself included, representing the Jewish community of Shanghai. At the Cathay Hotel, the clerk asked Yuval for his signature and his profession. Calmly, in a matter-of-fact voice, Yuval replied, "I am the Vice-Consul of Israel."

Most likely, he did not notice the smiles of pride and happiness on our faces. Some of us could not control our tears. Just imagine that here in a Chinese hotel in Shanghai, we were hearing the words, "Vice-Consul of Israel!" At once, Israel became a state, and I ceased to be stateless. These four words said it all. We are no longer homeless! We have a Vice-Consul! We are equal among people! We have a Jewish state!

Together with Moshe, a committee, the Palamt, was formed to take charge of all preparations, interviews and financial arrangements for the various expeditions by sea and air. The Revisionists were strongly represented by Vulia Zubitsky, Judy Hasser and me. Dr. Bergman, a prominent Zionist from Poland, chaired the committee, which also included Abrasha Ifland, Boris Kopilevitch and Walter Citrin. We spent days and nights on preparations, arranging schedules and passenger lists for the first stage of this exodus.

Many members of our community had already left the city, and others were still in the process of packing up, liquidating their businesses or waiting for their visas. Several thousand had signed up for immigration to Israel.

At this time, my wife and I were happy to learn that she was pregnant. We knew not what awaited us – we had no money and I had no job – but we were both certain that the future would be bright and exciting. Our only desire was to be in Israel as soon as possible, so that our baby could be born there.

But Moshe Yuval had other ideas. By now we had become good friends and spent much time together. Moshe explained to me that the first ship was the most important one. It would serve as a test case for those that followed and it was important that its long voyage be a complete success. He also suggested that my wife, in her condition, would be better off on a boat than on an airplane. And so I became the commander in charge of the first voyage of the *Wooster Victory*. The ship was scheduled to depart on the twenty-fourth of December, 1948.

Time was now approaching to really get ready for the long voyage. My wife and I had but a few suitcases and one Chinese camphor chest. Among our belongings we carried the film of our wedding, a few suits and dresses, a Chinese brocade jacket for Lea and a lounge jacket for myself. The camphor chest and the Chinese brocade became the kind of mementos that all immigrants from China would treasure.

As November approached, the time for sad farewells was at hand. The time had come to say goodbye to my uncle Leva and his wife Sarah. Leva chose to remain in Shanghai because father left him in charge of the "Mars" restaurant. Within two years, they were both dead: My poor uncle died from liver cancer and Aunt Sarah ended her lonely life by her own hand. These are perhaps the last two graves in the Jewish cemetery in Shanghai. It was time to bid farewell to friends whom one might never see again, farewells to places, and people, to business associates, cooks, *amahs* and schoolmates.

The final list of passengers for the first voyage of the *Wooster Victory* was now complete. In addition to Tony Gaberman, I selected several veterans of Betar to assist me in the difficult tasks ahead. Many committees were organized before the *Wooster Victory* arrived to pick up its cargo: Among us were doctors, journalists, electricians and musicians as well as teachers, sports instructors, singers and actors.

On the list were close personal friends, as well as my cousin Bertha and her family. Among the prospective passengers were Riva and Leva Hanin who for many years had led the Betar movement in Shanghai, and who had done much in bringing it to life. Also on board were our dear friends, the Volovicks. David was a champion boxer in his weight category. Judy was a talented athlete and an excellent volleyball and ping-pong player.

During these final days of preparations, my mind often turned back to my younger days in Harbin. I had not been in touch with many of my friends there for more than two years. I knew that many of them would have joined us on our journey had circumstances allowed it. Instead, they were all trapped by Russian and Chinese Communism. Over and over I would query myself: Would it ever come to pass that they would find the stamina to endure, and the fortune to escape and join us all in Eretz Israel?[1]

Perhaps never before in the history of Jewish communities were Jews leaving a diaspora situation without a preceding or an accompanying tragedy. Here, it was happening in China. Without pogroms or threats, abuses or even signs of anti-Semitism, thousands of Jews from China were voluntarily closing down their centers, dismantling their social and rehabilitation institutions, their schools, hospitals, synagogues and organizations and emigrating to the land of their dreams, to the newborn State of Israel.

Jews could leave or stay, the choice was theirs. It was not a "choice by decree." Jews could take all their possessions and put them on board vessels that would take them to their selected homes, their future, their destiny. Indeed, here were Jews in the thousands, leaving homes which

---

1. By 1951, all of the Jews of Harbin had been successfully evacuated and most of them had reached Israel through Tientsin and Shanghai.

had been comfortable havens for three generations, leaving without a glance back, with no regrets, but also with no bitter memories and no sorrow. And where else were the young men and women of Betar or Maccabi able to liquidate the *galut* (the lands of Jewish dispersion) not by crawling under barbed wire fences or climbing over the barricades, but by marching onto the decks of awaiting planes and vessels, with their flags flying and their bands playing?

This indeed was a unique ending to a chapter of Jewish wanderings.

By now both Irgun groups had left on two different dates and, after passing through several nerve-wracking stopovers in Syria and Iraq, our boys had reached Israel and were immediately assigned to the Negev. There they participated honorably and bravely in the War of Independence. It was now December and the *Wooster Victory* was approaching Shanghai under orders to pick up the first eight hundred ninety-three immigrants who would board it, and to proceed across the oceans, around the Cape of Good Hope, to the shores of Haifa, in Eretz Israel. A journey of fifty-two days!

Others would soon follow. Whether destiny would take us to Israel or America, to Europe or to Australia, to Hong Kong or Japan, united by a special bond of nostalgia and pride in our common contribution to the welfare and growth of the wondrous, unique Jewish communities of China, we all would carry with us a sense of Chinese fraternity that warms the hearts of all of us from the Far East, from the days of our departure till this very day.

We were now ready to embark on our journey.

Chapter 17

FEBRUARY 1949. EXODUS

On the twenty-fourth of December 1948, my wife and I arrived at the pier early to settle in and to allow me to expedite the embarkation proceedings of all our passengers. Since Lea was in her sixth month of pregnancy, she was given a lower cot in the only four-bed cabin on the vessel. Others assigned to the same cabin were Helen Bistritskaya, an elderly lady who recently had lost her husband, another pregnant young woman, Difa, Dr. Katzenelson's young pregnant wife and my cousin Bertha. All others were assigned to men's and women's dormitories, set up with fifty to one hundred and fifty double-decked cots. The total roster of passengers numbered eight hundred ninety-three.

Before anyone else had come aboard, a Jewish drug addict, jailed by the Chinese authorities and given a short furlough, appeared before me on the deck of the *Wooster Victory*, begging for help. He told me exactly who he was, although I already knew what he had done, and what awaited him when he was rearrested. Since there was no one but the ship's crew on board at the time, the decision was mine to make. And I made it. No one ever learned that there was one extra passenger on board, who arrived in Israel, married there and died many years after, his death completely unconnected with his previous addiction.

By eight in the morning passengers began to trickle in from the city. Among the early arrivals were many members of Betar, whose job it was to assist in the embarkation of the elderly and to help passengers find their bunks, according to charts and diagrams that I had distributed in advance. With all the passengers came family and friends. By nine in the morning the pier was a wall-to-wall carpet of people milling around aimlessly with their children and friends and luggage. Hundreds of others from the Jewish community were also there just to witness this historic moment.

By noon, the first sound of the powerful gong resounded from the deck, and the ship's public address system carried the captain's voice to all corners on the pier: "All aboard!" However, it was not before late in the afternoon that the *Wooster Victory* slowly began to disengage itself from the *sampans* and the rowboats, and finally emerge from the Yangtze River. By evening, we were sailing toward the high waves of the dark blue South China Sea, on our way to the Indian Ocean.

My first order of the day was to activate the various committees that would assist us with life on board ship in every conceivable detail. My executive committee included Tony Gaberman, Yasha Shtofman, Alex Feldman and others. The very first assignments of these committees was to organize a synagogue, a school for children, Hebrew-language study groups, cultural programs on the main deck, sports events, a daily bulletin and an hour a day of radio news and commentary.

However, on the third day of our journey, it became evident that the Italian crew on board was both too small and too inexperienced to handle food and medical care. Thus it became essential to address the problems of the kitchen and ship's infirmary. We were fortunate to have many excellent housewives who soon upgraded the menu and redeemed the deficient culinary skills of the Italian sailors-turned-cooks. Thanks to them, despite the limited comestibles stored on board ship, the food served on the *Wooster Victory* became palatable.

Our medical problems were solved with even greater success. All doctors on board the ship, led by the young Katzenelson brothers, transformed the primitive ambulatory rooms into a first-class medical facility where all passengers received competent care.

Thus we entered into an organized routine of life as we faced the second week of our journey. The first days exposed some raw nerves among the usually calm and civil members of the community. Lavatory and washroom space was at a premium, especially among the women, and the claims on space in the women's toilets often led to raucous scenes and sometimes wrestling matches.

The Hongkew community members, a significant contingent on the *Wooster Victory*, participated in all aspects of our creative life on board, supplying doctors, journalists, teachers and entertainers for the comfort and pleasure of all the passengers. Only one incident marred our relationship, momentarily dampening relations between me and some of the passengers.

On one of the very first mornings of our journey, we noticed a large group of passengers from the German-speaking members of the Hongkew community arguing excitedly over an issue that had been brought to their attention. Evidently, someone in the group had spread a rumor that the JOINT had given ten dollars in pocket money to every refugee on his or her way to a new home.[1] This information was true, but evidently it applied only to those going on commercial vessels to Europe or to the United States. It clearly and definitely did not apply to anyone going to Israel, where food and transportation were being provided free of charge to everyone. (In the case of wealthy immigrants-to-be, the Palamt in Shanghai collected funds to assist the Jewish Agency in bearing the enormous expenses involved in this venture.)

During this encounter, those spreading the news of the handout were asked, "Where is the money?" Some replied, without hesitation, that the money had been given to me as a representative of the Palamt for distribution among them once they got on board the ship. Once learning

1. The JOINT [The American Jewish Joint Distribution Committee] was created in 1914 to assist Jewish refugees.

of these false statements, I immediately joined the gathering and explained that no monies had been received on their behalf for distribution among the passengers en route to Israel. All but a handful left the meeting with embarrassed apologies and the episode was closed. Only a few of the organizers continued to provoke the other passengers, but they were unsuccessful in their efforts. Within a few days, complete calm and a mutual desire for cooperation returned to the decks of the *Wooster Victory*.

A busy schedule prepared and activated by various committees added spice and anticipation to an otherwise monotonous journey under conditions far from luxurious. But not all the excitement was premeditated and planned.

Early one morning I was approached by Alex Feldman and Tony Gaberman. They were both extremely upset as they related the tragedy they had just witnessed: An elderly woman had jumped overboard! Within moments, I consulted the ship's captain and orders were given for the vessel to turn back and begin the three-hour circling of the area that is prescribed by international naval ordinance.

While this was going on, the woman's husband was found. He was a man in his seventies who spoke only German and insisted on addressing his wife over the ship's public address system. This frustrating experience only added to the overall sense of tragedy, as it became obvious that the woman had suffered severe depression, while her poor husband just could not believe that she was not hiding somewhere on the ship. To prevent any possible repetition of such unfortunate occurrences, I instructed the Betarim to organize small patrols that would circle the decks twenty-four hours a day.

Several joyous events lit up our journey. One couple decided to be married at sea, and I was given the honor of performing the ceremony. In this, as in many other instances, I sought and received advice from my wise and able friend, Yasha Shtofman. Together, we managed to prepare for the ceremony, which I conducted to everyone's satisfaction. As a gift to the newlyweds, I "negotiated" with the captain that he offer the bridal pair the use of his cabin for their wedding night.

A second happy episode of our journey came about when, in the middle of the night, I was awakened and informed that a passenger was experiencing contractions. Her husband was worried that the ship might not be sufficiently equipped to handle this type of emergency. After alerting our medical staff, immediate preparations were made in the ship's hospital room for a delivery and, within an hour, the *Wooster Victory* had a new passenger! The newborn baby was a boy and our doctors suggested that we not wait the three weeks until our arrival in South Africa, but that we have the *Brit Milah* (circumcision) performed right there on the ship. The next week, therefore, provided another "first" on our long journey. The ceremony was performed to perfection and the entire ship, both passengers and crew, celebrated the happy occasion. Another birth took place on board shortly after this one; we now had two new passengers, a boy and a girl.

Thus we continued on our route, slowly rounding the Cape of Good Hope, on the way to our first stop, Cape Town, South Africa. We well knew that none of us would be allowed to disembark on our stopovers. Through constant telegraphic contact with the Jewish Federation and the Revisionist Party of South Africa, we learned that a great interest had been aroused in our journey and imminent arrival. We therefore expected that representatives of these organizations would visit us on board ship.

By sunrise, some passengers already saw the contours of Cape Town on the horizon. By nine in the morning we were docking at one of its piers. Hundreds of people were waving to us from shore, as the captain came out to show me personally the cable he had received from the South African authorities: "No passengers allowed to disembark, with the exception of Ya'acov Liberman – commander of passengers on the *Wooster Victory*. Please issue Liberman identifying document." By the time I read the cable, authorities were boarding the ship, followed by a delegation of the Jewish Federation and our friend and correspondent, Harry Hurwitz, General Secretary of the Revisionist Party in South Africa and Rhodesia.

I recognized Harry from pictures and felt I knew him from the letters we had exchanged so often. It is no exaggeration to say that I considered him a very dear friend before ever having met him. After years of friendship that followed, I can proudly say that I was not mistaken.

Once the formalities had been completed, I requested that Tony, Alex and Yasha take care of the guests, while I prepared to leave the vessel with Harry as my escort. It was through his efforts that I received permission to leave the *Wooster Victory*.

My wife Lea, in her seventh month of pregnancy, was unable to accompany me but she was happy that I would have the opportunity to see Cape Town. She thanked Harry for the flowers he brought her and joined others on the deck to see us walk down the narrow wooden steps that led to the *terra firma* of the pier.

Harry was not only a superb speaker and writer, who edited the *Jewish Herald* in South Africa, but was an excellent guide as well. We toured the synagogue, the Betar Club of Cape Town and the office of the Revisionist Party. I was also shown a Jewish sports club and the offices of the Federation. We returned to the pier by four o'clock in the afternoon and the sight that greeted my eyes was unbelievable!

Thousands of Jews, with truckloads of food and clothing, filled the pier from one end to the other. Women took off their jewelry and threw it to the passengers. They also offered shoes, hats, chocolates and whatever else they could lay their hands on.

Immediately upon reboarding the vessel, it was decided to give all the food to the kitchen for use by the passengers, and to store all clothing in packages, for presentation to the WIZO (Women's International Zionist Organization) which would distribute them to the needy under their care and supervision in Israel.

It was also decided that somehow I must thank all of the good Jews of Cape Town for their wonderful outpouring of fraternal affection. It was an easy decision – but how to implement it? How to address thousands of people from a deck of a ship crowded with hundreds of passengers?

The Italian captain came to our rescue. He ordered that the narrow wooden disembarkation ladder be placed in a slanting position between the two decks of the vessel. I was to climb these slanted stairs and stop midway, between the two decks – clearly visible from below.

My good friend and veteran volleyball partner, Mark Kaptzan, was in charge of the public address system arrangements. Within minutes I had a working microphone in my hands, and the rest was quite easy.

As I thanked the vast crowd below, I told them what must have been on all our minds during this entire, unbelievable day: "Today, we have seen in practice and in life wherein lies the eternal spirit and the indestructible strength of our people. Here we are coming together from two different corners of the world – yet united in love, care and brotherhood, from the moment this vessel landed at the pier of Cape Town."

What happened next was like a scene from a beautiful movie: As the sun began setting on the horizon, the *Wooster Victory* slowly pulled away from the pier. Suddenly, from far away, then closer and closer, came the sound of "Hatikva," the Jewish anthem, as the throng below and the passengers on deck joined in this "Song of Hope" while the boat slowly moved out to sea, on its way to the State of Israel.

It was not easy to settle back into the routine of life aboard the *Wooster Victory*. However, we were constantly encouraged by the news of victories by the Israeli Armed Forces against the armies of the neighboring Arab states. During one such broadcast transmitted over the *Wooster Victory* public address system, we learned that the State of Israel had been finally recognized by the Republic of France!

By coincidence, we were now rounding the African continent, sailing through the north Atlantic and nearing the Straits of Gibralter and the Mediterranean Sea. Soon we reached Dakar, where we were scheduled for a brief stopover of three to four hours in the evening. Hearing of our proximity, and in direct reaction to the news of French recognition of Israel, the French governor of Dakar sent us a telegram indicating his willingness to come aboard and meet the passengers on the ship.

Our cultural committee was assigned the job of preparing an appropriate program for the dignitaries. As the governor and his party came aboard they were welcomed by an honor guard from the ranks of Betar, carrying an Israeli flag, while our band, led by Boris and Leva Sherman of Shanghai, greeted the visitors with "La Marseillaise" followed by "Hatikva." After a successful show by our singers and dancers, starring Mira Kaptzan, who became a successful performer in Israel, the governor thanked us for a beautiful reception and wished us and the State of Israel success in overcoming its "birth pangs of independence."

Finally, we were now on our way to Haifa with but one more stop. There would be a smooth transfer from the *Wooster Victory* to Israel's own vessel, the *Negbah*. It took place in Genoa and lasted a few hours.

Our four days aboard the *Negbah* were shared with hundreds of additional new immigrants, picked up from all over Europe. Their health was poor, their economic situation difficult; they were shabbily dressed, yet their spirits were high and they were filled with hope and excitement. Together we crossed the Mediterranean, eastbound to Haifa.

Throughout the journey, Lea managed well. She assisted passengers in need, attended to her parents and spent time on the deck, where I had secured a chaise lounge for her comfort. Now that we were on our last segment from Genoa to Haifa and, given the presence of Jewish Agency personnel aboard ship, my job as commander of the transport had almost come to an end.

I spent the final evening in my wife's company and together we reminisced on our wondrous fifty-two days aboard ship. It was a lovely night on the Mediterranean, as our boat slowly approached the shores of Israel. Although quite heavy with child, Lea was up on deck with me, long into the night hours of February 13th. We were scheduled to dock at Haifa at 9:15 on the following morning.

As we stood by the railing on the *Negbah*, I drew my wife close to me and gave her a long emotional kiss. It was a kiss of love, but also of gratitude for her patience and tolerance, constant care and total selflessness. Lea playfully rumpled my hair and said: "I don't know what awaits us – but I hope we will have a room to ourselves when we arrive in the Holy Land!" "Darling," I replied, "I shall make this my first priority."

Finally, the long-awaited moment was at hand. From the early hours of the morning on 14 February 1949, passengers began to occupy the best places along the decks of the *Negbah*. The band was ready to strike up the notes of the national anthem and the Betarim formed neat rows on the open deck below the captain's quarters.

All of us gazed at the scenery before us, trying to etch into eternal memory this first glimpse of Haifa. And there it was – Haifa, spread out on the mountains of Carmel, its picturesque buildings dotting the view from shore as far inland as the eye could see. At the pier stood friends and relatives who had arrived a few weeks earlier by plane, and others who had pioneered our path almost two decades ago.

The circle could now be closed – the story of our Jewish communities in China was about to come to an end. And as I peered out at the city of Haifa and the coastline of Israel to its left and to its right, I realized – at last! After fifty-two days ... NO! ... after two thousand years – we returned to our home, to the free and independent State of Israel!

In February 1949 Yana and Lea Liberman settled in Nahlat Jabotinsky. Here, among new Israeli friends, Lea awaited the birth of their first child, and the former track star put his physical stamina to a new purpose and became a day laborer in the nearby orange groves of Benyamina. A month later, in the middle of the night, a twelve-ton truck transported Lea from Benyamina to a Hadera hospital where she gave birth to a son, Naphtali (Tovik).

How to provide for his young family? How to assimilate into the new Israeli society? Each settler would venture his own solution. Liberman left the orange groves for the city, to join a taxi enterprise in Ramat-Gan, near Tel Aviv. A calling? Certainly not, and he was soon invited to assist the Israeli Betar leadership in reinvigorating its youth movement, that during the 1940s had been overshadowed by the Irgun underground. Yana (Ya'acov) soon became a popular leader, friend and activist. A year later, in 1950, he was brought into the National Headquarters of Betar and dispatched to Paris to seek out former Betarim and Revisionist members, to promote their group affiliation and to collect funds for the Israeli organization. His success paved the way for future assignments on behalf of the youth movement, as well as of Menachem Begin's Herut Party. Travel he did! During the 1950s, Yana addressed large audiences in

Finland, Sweden, Belgium, Italy, France, England, Australia and South Africa. At this time, the Libermans were blessed with a daughter – Rina. In 1956 Liberman became Betar emissary to the United States, where he encouraged emigration to Israel, collected funds and popularized the Israeli Organization and the Revisionist Party. His lifelong impassioned service seemed to be acknowledged when in 1957 Yana Liberman was elected *netziv* of the Betar Youth Movement in Israel and appointed to the National Executive Committee of the Herut movement.

A commitment to serve carried him further into the leadership of the Organization Department of the Herut Party and, in 1960 as its appointed head, he became directly responsible for all of the party branches and ran the party's 1962 election campaign. Exceeding the election results of the past thirteen years, the election campaigning under Liberman's direction brought seventeen members into the Knesset, the Israeli Parliament. But in 1962, when Herut decided to join the Histadrut, the Israeli Labor Organization, Liberman, together with other prominent party leaders, adamantly opposed this decision. Should he join a smaller national political party, as did some of his colleagues? Or should he retreat into obscurity? Yana opted for the latter.

In 1962 when the future of Israeli politics seemed so uncertain, a new opportunity beckoned – in Tokyo. Yana's father, who headed a newly established Jewish club there, brought to his attention an opening in a Jewish-owned company. Although reluctant to leave Israel, after intense inner deliberation, once again, Liberman struck out for the unknown. After a few months he changed jobs, and in 1963 he joined the Shriro International Trading Company, where he was soon advanced to a new post as manager of its export department. In the 1960s Yana decided to continue his university training at Sophia University, Tokyo. Completing his bachelor's degree in economics in 1965, he then went on to earn a master's degree in political science in 1968.

The Libermans remained in Tokyo for ten years. Despite the responsibilities of business and study, Liberman became an active leader of the Tokyo Jewish community as well. For many years he was in charge of its cultural events and in 1970 was nominated to the post of community vice-president. During this period, the Liberman family expanded to include Leor, their third child, a Down's Syndrome boy. The recipient of combined Liberman efforts, Leor grew up a happy, productive human being. In the Liberman tradition, Leor became multilingual, fluent in English, Russian, Hebrew and Chinese.

The Libermans returned to Israel in 1972, where for the next three years Yana engaged in independent importing and exporting. In 1975, when a challenging business opportunity presented itself – once again in the Far East – and Yana was proposed as managing director of the Eisenberg company in Taiwan, the Liberman family moved to Taiwan which became home from 1975 to 1985. As numerous Jewish families made their way to Taiwan in these years to establish or to represent foreign trade offices, Yana recognized the urgency of the need for organized Jewish communal life. In 1976, in company with several others, he helped establish new institutional structures. He and his associates rented a club, formed a synagogue, set up a dairy kitchen, organized a Sunday school and inaugurated a weekly cultural program. Money came in abundance from Jewish companies and grateful tourists. Not surprisingly, Yana was elected president of the Taipei Jewish community, a post that he held for ten years.

Indefatigable and devoted to Jewish causes, nonetheless, in 1986 Yana decided that his work in Taipei could progress well enough without him, and he decided to retire. The Liberman family moved to Hawaii, in order to be close to their son, Tovik, who had long settled there. Pulling up stakes for the last time, Yana and Lea moved to San Diego, California, where they reside today. The author of *From One Jew to Another*, a collection of articles on Israeli politics, and several plays, as well, Yana Liberman is preparing to embark on a lecture tour before getting down to work on his next book. The subject? Yana promises to reveal it in due time.

– Ruth Rischin

aliyah. (Hebrew). "Ascent." Name for the waves of immigration from the lands of the Jewish Diaspora to Palestine, after 1948, to the State of Israel. The first aliyah took place in 1882.

Betar. Jabotinsky's Youth Movement bearing the name of a pioneer hero – Joseph Trumpeldor. Memeber of betar is known as a betari (pl. betarim). Originating in Latvia in 1923, Betar became a national Jewish youth movement, dedicated to the building of a secure and independent Jewish State in Eretz Israel.

bimah. (Hebrew). Platform. The dais or raised platform in a synagogue where the lectern is placed.

booza. (Russian, buza). A beverage concocted from a fermented yeast base.

bubliki. (Russian, diminutive). Bagels.

chuppah. (Hebrew). Canopy. The portable canopy under which a Jewish wedding ceremony is conducted.

Eretz Israel. (Hebrew). The Land of Israel.

galut. (Hebrew). Exile. The Jewish diaspora.

GPU. (Russian. Gosudarstvennoe Politicheskoe Upravlenie. Acronym for the Soviet State Political Administration). Replaced the Extraordinary Commission (the Cheka) in February 1922.

Haganah. (Hebrew). Literally defense. Adopted as the name of the clandestine self-defense organization that in 1920 succeeded Ha-shomer.

halutz. (Hebrew, plural, **halutzim**). Pioneer.

Hapoel. (Hebrew). Worker. Israeli Workers' sports organization, founded in 1924.

Ha-shomer-ha-tzair. (Hebrew). The Young Watchman. A Jewish youth movement founded in Galicia in 1913, whose members emigrated with the Third Aliyah (1919-1921).

Havlaga. (Hebrew). Non-resistance.

Herut. (Hebrew). Freedom. Political party in Israel, associated with the federation of the same name outside of Israel. Founded in 1948 by Menachem Begin.

Hevra Kadisha. (Hebrew). Jewish burial society.

HIAS. Acronym for Hebrew Immigrant Aid Society, created in New York in 1909.

Igud Yotzei Sin. (Hebrew). The Organization of Expatriates from China in Israel.

Irgun Tzevai Leumi. (Hebrew). National Military Organization, founded in 1937 by members of Betar and Revisionists, headed by Jabotinsky.

JOINT. Abbreviation for the American Jewish Joint Distribution Committee, created in 1914.

Kai-fung-fû. A small city in central China and the seat of the only known historic Chinese Jewish community. Ruined by flood in 1652, the city rebuilt its synagogue. Eventually the community disintegrated, but isolated Jews remained there well into the twentieth century.

kefir. (Russian). A beverage made from fermented goat's milk.

Kuomintang. The Chinese Nationalist Party, founded by Sun Yat-sen in 1912.

Manchukow. Country of the Manchus. The Japanese installed a puppet regime in Manchuria 1938-1945.

Mapai. (Hebrew). Acronym for Miphleget Poale Eretz Israel, the Israel Workers' Party.

Nahlat Jabotinsky. The first permanent settlement of Betarim in Eretz Israel.

netziv, **netzivut**. (Hebrew). Federal leader. National executive council.

Palamt. Local office of the Jewish Agency in China.

Plugot Avoda. Working brigades of Betarim in Palestine.

Yishuv. (Hebrew). Used collectively to refer to the Jewish communities of Israel.

ABOUT THE AUTHOR

Yaacov Liberman was born in Harbin, China in 1923. One of the three Chinese cities to which Jews from Russia fled in the wake of the Bolshevik Revolution, Harbin housed an extensive community of Jewish life. There were synagogues, Jewish schools, community centers, youth movements, newspapers, theater and even kosher restaurants.

At the age of nine, Liberman went to live with his aunt and uncle to study at the English School in Shanghai. With approximately 10,000 Jews, Shanghai boasted an even larger Jewish community than Harbin. In Shanghai, the young Liberman first became acquainted with the Betar youth movement, an organization he would remain involved with through his adult years. The Betar movement consisted of Jewish Zionists who were followers of Ze'ev Jabotinsky, the leader of the Zionist Revisionist movement prior to World War II. Jabotinsky and his followers insisted on the full rights of the Jewish people to their homeland and were prepared to fight for the implementation of their civil and national rights.

Liberman graduated from the Pyeng Yang Foreign School in Korea, and holds both a B.A. and M.A. from Sophia University in Tokyo. Between 1941 and 1948, he held various positions in the Betar Movement in China, prior to leaving for Israel in 1949. During the late 50s and 60s Liberman was the head of Israeli Betar and the Chairman of Herut's Organizational Department. In 1962, he moved to Japan to work for *Shriro International Trading Company*. While in Japan, Liberman joined the Board of Directors of the Jewish Community and remained active in Jewish life there. Briefly returning to Israel in 1973, Liberman once again headed east, this time to Taiwan, to become the Managing Director of the *Eisenberg Company*, and served as the First President of the Taiwan Jewish Community.

Yaacov Liberman retired to the United States to be near his children, Tovik, Rina and Leor. He lives with his wife, Lea, in San Diego and frequently lectures about Israel and China in local Jewish communities, synagogues and universities.

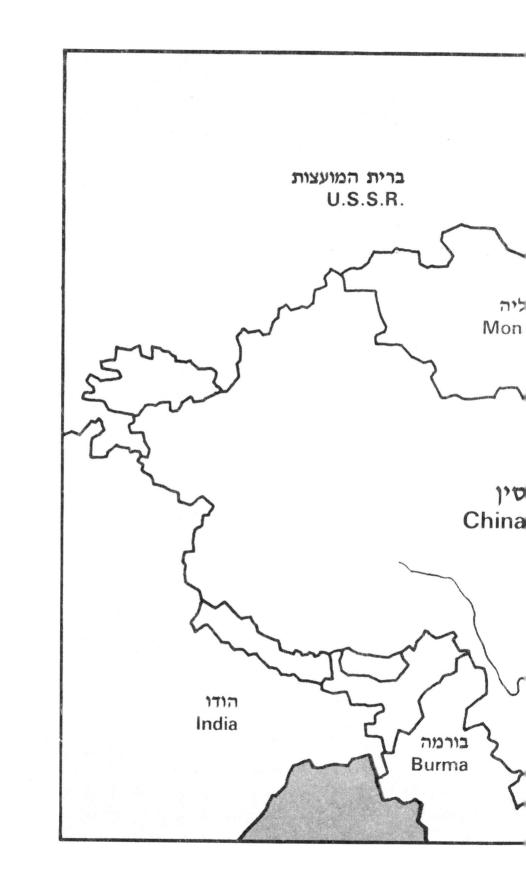